MATH
Connections®

A Secondary Mathematics Core Curriculum

2a

William P. Berlinghoff
Clifford Sloyer
Robert W. Hayden

IT'S ABOUT TIME®

Published in 2003 by
It's About Time, Inc.
84 Business Park Drive
Armonk, NY 10504
Phone (914)273-2233
Fax (914)273-2227
www.ITS-ABOUT-TIME.com
www.mathconnections.com

President
Laurie Kreindler

Design
John Nordland

Studio Manager
Jon Voss

Production Manager
Joan Lee

Cover Illustration
Robert Conge

Illustrations
Dennis Falcon

Photos
© 1997 PhotoDisc Inc., ©1998 Digital Stock, Inc.

MATH *Connections*®: *A Secondary Mathematics Core Curriculum* was developed under the National Science Foundation Grant
No. ESI-9255251 awarded to the Connecticut Business and Industry Association.

ISBN 1-891629-14-X
ISBN 1-891629-76-X (Year 2, 2 Book Set)
3 4 5 6 7 Q 07 06 05 04 03

This project was supported, in part,
by the

National Science Foundation
Opinions expressed are those of the authors
and not necessarily those of the Foundation.

Welcome to **MATH** *Connections*®!

This book was written for you. It is designed to provide you with mathematical experiences that will excite your curiosity, stimulate your imagination, and challenge your skills. It bridges mathematics with the real world of people, business and everyday life. It isn't finished until you take an active part in the interesting problems and projects that invite you to explore important mathematical ideas. You'll want to discuss these ideas with other students, your teacher and your family. You might find that not all your ideas work, but try again, perhaps a different approach will work—that is all part of learning. And the learning is up to you!

<u>In the Margins</u> **The Learning Outcomes** are in the margins of the first page of each section. These will alert you to the major topic. The **Thinking Tip** in the margins will help you in gathering your ideas and in solving problems. **About Words** will show you how some words we use in mathematics relate to words you already know and use every day. **About Symbols** will explain particular notations and their use in mathematics.

<u>In the Text</u> **A Word to Know** and **A Phrase to Know** appear in the text and signal particularly important definitions. Similarly, **A Fact to Know** signals an important mathematical result.

<u>In the Profiles</u> you will meet people in various careers and professions who use mathematics in their everyday work.

<u>In the Appendices</u> at the back of your book you'll find some more sections to assist with learning and problem solving.

- Appendix A: Using a TI-82 (TI-83) Graphing Calculator
- Appendix B: Using a Spreadsheet
- Appendix C: Programming the TI-82 (TI-83)
- Appendix D: Linear Programming With Excel
- Glossary
- Index

From time to time you'll see these graphic icons that call you to action.

Do this now
Identifies questions for you to answer.

Discuss this
Identifies questions for you to discuss as a class or in groups.

Write this
Usually requires you to gather information or reflect on a particular topic.

How MATH Connections® takes you to the real world.

MATH *Connections* begins with you!
Each **MATH** *Connections* chapter introduces a concept by asking you to think about what you already know. You bring a lot of your life experiences into the classroom and with **MATH** *Connections* those experiences are strengths.

Provides a solid foundation in mathematics.
Building on your knowledge, **MATH** *Connections* connects your experiences with comprehensive mathematics. You'll learn algebra, geometry, statistics, probability, trigonometry, discrete mathematics plus dynamic programming, linear programming and optimization techniques.

Relates the mathematics to real situations.
As you learn the mathematics, you will apply it to real situations from hundreds of professions and careers ranging from architecture to micro-surgery to managing a grocery store. Whether it is at home, in games, in sports or at work... **MATH** *Connections* connects mathematics to the real world of science, literature, art; and the things you do every day.

Think math. Do math. Talk math. Write math.

Ultimately, math is a language that can help you in every aspect of your life. And with **MATH** *Connections* you really make mathematics your own by exploring, looking for patterns and reasoning things out. Whether you are working on your own, in small groups or as a class to solve problems, with **MATH** *Connections*, you will achieve real understanding of mathematics.

Classroom tested for excellence.

MATH *Connections* works! **MATH** *Connections* was field-tested by more than 5,000 students like yourself, in more than 100 high school classrooms. During the 4-year field test, it was continuously refined by its developers and high school teachers. And year after year it has proven to make the learning of mathematics more effective and more enjoyable. Plus, bottom line, **MATH** *Connections* students score higher on state and national tests.

Prepares you for your future.

Whether you plan to pursue a career in the sciences, the fine arts, or sports.... **MATH** *Connections* prepares you for the real world and your future.

Algebra, geometry, probability, trigonometry, statistics, discrete mathematics, dynamic and linear programming, optimization...

MATH Connections ties these all together.
Just like bridge cables that sustain and connect the span of a bridge, MATH Connections supports and relates to what you do in school, at home, in games, in sports, in college and at work to make you stronger in math and stronger in life.

Director: June G. Ellis

ADVISORY COUNCIL

MATH *Connections®* TEAM

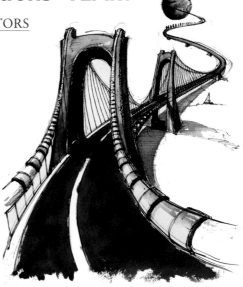

PRINCIPAL INVESTIGATORS

June G. Ellis, Director

Robert A. Rosenbaum
Wesleyan University

Robert J. Decker
University of Hartford

SENIOR WRITERS

William P. Berlinghoff
Colby College, Maine

Clifford Sloyer
University of Delaware

Robert W. Hayden
Plymouth State College,
New Hampshire

THE STAFF

Robert Gregorski
Associate Director

Lorna Rojan
Program Manager

Carolyn Mitchell
Administrative Assistant

THE CONTRIBUTORS

Don Hastings (retired)
Stratford Public Schools

Kathleen Bavelas
Manchester Community-
Technical College

George Parker
E. O. Smith High School,
Storrs

Linda Raffles
Glastonbury High School

Joanna Shrader Panning
Middletown High School

Frank Corbo
Staples High School, Westport

Thomas Alena
Talcott Mountain Science Center,
Avon

William Casey
Bulkeley High School, Hartford

Sharon Heyman
Bulkeley High School, Hartford

Helen Knudson
Choate Rosemary Hall, Wallingford

Mary Jo Lane (retired)
Granby Memorial High School

Lori White Moroso
Beth Chana Academy for Girls,
Orange

John Pellino
Talcott Mountain Science Center,
Avon

Pedro Vasquez, Jr.
Multicultural Magnet School,
Bridgeport

Thomas Willmitch
Talcott Mountain Science Center,
Avon

Leslie Paoletti
Greenwich Public Schools

Robert Fallon (retired)
Bristol Eastern High School

FIELD-TEST SITES

Hill Career Magnet High School, *New Haven*:
John Crotty
Martin Hartog, SCSU
Harry Payne II
Angel Tangney

Cheshire High School:
Andrew Abate
Pauline Alim
Marcia Arneson
Diane Bergan
Christopher Fletcher
John Kosloski
Christina Lepi
Michael Lougee
Ann Marie Mahanna
Carol Marino
Nancy Massey
Denise Miller
John Redford
Cynthia Sarlo

Coginchaug Regional High School, *Durham*:
Theresa Balletto
Anne Coffey
John DeMeo
Jake Fowler
Ben Kupcho
Stephen Lecky
Philip Martel

Crosby High School, *Waterbury*:
Janice Farrelly
Rosalie Griffin

Danbury High School:
Adrienne Coppola
Lois Schwaller

Dodd Middle School, *Cheshire*:
William Grimm
Lara Kelly
Gay Sonn
Alexander Yawin

Manchester High School:
Pamela Brooks
Carl Bujaucius
Marilyn Cavanna
Paul DesRosiers
Mariamma Devassy-Schwob
Frank Kinel
Larry Olsen
Julie Thompson
Matthew Walsh

Montville High School:
Lynn Grills
Janice Hardink
Diane Hupfer
Ronald Moore
Mark Popeleski
Henry Kopij
Walter Sherwin
Shari Zagarenski

Oxford Hills Comprehensive High School, *South Paris, ME*:
Mary Bickford
Peter Bickford
Allen Gerry
Errol Libby
Bryan Morgan
Lisa Whitman

Parish Hill Regional High School:
Peter Andersen
Gary Hoyt
Vincent Sirignano
Deborah Whipple

Southington High School:
Eleanor Aleksinas
Susan Chandler
Helen Crowley
Nancy Garry
John Klopp
Elaine Mulhall
Stephen Victor
Bernadette Waite

Stonington High School:
Joyce Birtcher
Jill Hamel
Glenn Reid

TECHNOLOGY SUPPORT

Texas Instruments:
Graphing Calculators and
View Screens

Presto Press
Desktop Publishing

Key Curriculum Press:
Geometer's Sketchpad

PROFILES

Barbara Zahm
David Bornstein
Alex Straus
Mimi Valiulis

Table of Contents

Welcome to **MATH** *Connections*!

MATH *Connections*® Team

Chapter 1 The Building Blocks of Geometry:
Making and Measuring Polygons

    Profile: John Hoffman, Aerial Mapping Specialist . . . 2
1.1 Measuring Lengths. 3
    Problem Set 13
1.2 Paths, Polygons, and Perimeter 15
    Problem Set 21
1.3 Symmetry 24
    Problem Set 29
1.4 Regular Polygons. 32
    Problem Set 40
1.5 Areas of Right-Angled Figures 43
    Problem Set 50
1.6 Area and Algebra. 55
    Problem Set 64
1.7 Triangles and Triangulation 66
    Problem Set 77
1.8 The Pythagorean Theorem 80
    Problem Set 87
1.9 It Varies With the Square 91
    Problem Set 95
1.10 Volume 99
    Problem Set 103

Chapter 2 Similarity and Scaling: Growing and Shrinking
Carefully

    Profile: Brad Bower, Special Effects Director 106
2.1 The Same Shape. 107
    Problem Set 116
2.2 Similar Triangles and Rectangles. 121
    Problem Set 128

2.3 How to Measure Angles 133
     Problem Set 143
2.4 Finding Angle Size Efficiently 147
     Problem Set 152
2.5 Parallel Lines and the Angle Sum of a Triangle . . . 157
     Problem Set 162
2.6 Parallelograms and Congruent Triangles 167
     Problem Set 174
2.7 Other Tests for Congruent Triangles 178
     Problem Set 187
2.8 Other Polygons 190
     Problem Set 197
2.9 Stretching and Shrinking Angles and Areas 200
     Problem Set 207
2.10 Stretching and Shrinking Volumes 211
     Problem Set 215

Chapter 3 Introduction to Trigonometry: Tangles With Angles

     Profile: Farah Brown, M.D., Radiologist 218
3.1 The Sine of an Acute Angle 219
     Problem Set 226
3.2 The Cosine of an Acute Angle 232
     Problem Set 239
3.3 The Tangent of an Acute Angle 243
     Problem Set 250
3.4 What do these SIN^{-1}, COS^{-1}, and TAN^{-1} Keys Do? . 254
     Problem Set 261
3.5 The Law of Sines—The Law of Cosines 263
     Problem Set 269
3.6 Sine and Cosine Curves: Going Around in Circles . 271
     Problem Set 279

Appendix A: Using a TI-82 (TI-83) Graphing Calculator A-1
Appendix B: Using a Spreadsheet B-1
Appendix C: Programming the TI-82 (TI-83) C-1
Appendix D: Linear Programming With Excel D-1
Glossary G-1
Index I-1

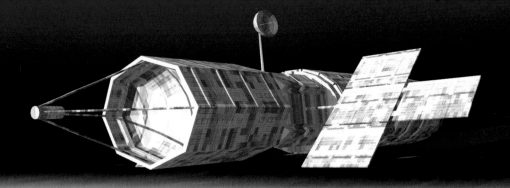

John Hoffman
Mapping the Surface of the Earth

John Hoffman's firm, Aerial Images, takes photos of Earth from outer space. Cameras mounted on satellites send back digitized pictures. These shots are used to make maps or just to see what's happening anywhere on Earth. "The new digital image technologies along with aerial photography are rapidly changing the way maps of the Earth's surface are made," he exclaims.

John became an expert in this field while in the military. He studied to be a pilot and later he learned aerial photography. He explains that while using aerial images to make maps was at first a big step forward, "You can't get high enough to get a broad picture of Earth. So you end up with a perspective problem. The outer edges of the image lean and you have diverging scales from the center to its edges. To solve this curvature problem we take many overlapping images. Then we piece them together using basic geometric theorems. Without geometry, we can't do our work.

"Satellite photography has revolutionized the whole field," John continues. "We've changed the altitude, getting the camera way up. Now the delta — the change in the angle from the center of the image to the outer — becomes much smaller.

"Future technologies will be amazing," John exults. "They'll give us much greater control over many large-scale planetary issues. Using this system, we can now even count trees. So if you're concerned about the deforestation of the rain forest in Brazil, we can actually inventory those trees."

The Building Blocks of Geometry: Making and Measuring Polygons

CHAPTER 1

1.1 Measuring Lengths

You can think of geometry as the visual side of mathematics. It deals with shape, form, and size. We begin this book by looking carefully at some of the surprisingly simple, fundamental ideas on which all of geometry rests. *Really* understanding these few simple ideas is the key to this powerful part of mathematics.

Earlier in **MATH** *Connections* you used geometry to visualize some of the other things you were doing. For example, you learned to use coordinate geometry to create graphs of functions and equations. You also used tree diagrams to visualize counting processes. One role of geometry is to provide pictures that help us to understand some other part of mathematics. A picture often gives a quick, intuitive grasp of a situation, which then can be made more precise by a symbolic expression or an exact computation. The connection between geometric figures and algebra or arithmetic is measurement. When we measure a geometric shape, we get numbers. We can do arithmetic with the numbers, or plug them into an algebraic equation. For this reason, we will start with measurement.

About Words

The word *geometry* comes from Greek roots that mean earth measurement. One of the earliest uses of geometry was to measure the boundaries of farmland.

Probably the most basic thing we can measure is length. Our units for area and volume measurements are based on length units. In addition, many measuring devices express their results as length along a scale rather than in terms of the thing measured. For example, in a traditional thermometer we do not see the heat directly. Instead, we see how far the column of mercury has risen. The speedometers of some cars are read on a similar scale turned sideways. We judge speed by how *far* the indicator has moved clockwise, not by how fast it moves. Studying how length is measured will help us to understand other kinds of measurements, so this is where we begin.

 What other things in your everyday life are measured or sized in terms of length? Can you think of half a dozen? A dozen? More?

The tenth grade mathematics class at Euclid School has been studying China. Two of the students found a pen pal in Beijing! The class reads their letters. The students are curious to know where Beijing is, how far away it is, and how long it would take to get there. They know that there are planes to China leaving from Philadelphia, and they know where Philadelphia is. They decide to make plans for an imaginary trip to Beijing. They are looking at maps to see how to get there. They also want to know how far they would have to travel and how long it would take. Look at a flat map of the world (in an atlas or on a wall chart) and help them out by answering these questions.

1. **What route would the class fly? Do you think they would fly over Denver? Hudson Bay? California? Japan? Siberia?**

2. **About how far would they travel? To figure this out from the map, you need a scale for judging distances. It is approximately 25,000 miles around the Earth at the equator. Measure the width of your map and figure out the scale of the map at the equator. Then measure how far it is from Philadelphia to Beijing on the map. If the scale at the equator works for this route, how far is it from Philadelphia to Beijing?**

Unfortunately, the world is not flat like a map. The students decide that they also want to look at their trip on a globe. That's a good idea for us, too.

1. Use a flexible ruler or cloth tape to measure on a globe the route you chose from Philadelphia to Beijing. Be sure that the tape follows the route accurately! (Check some places along the way to make sure.) Then measure around the globe at the equator. The Earth is about 25,000 miles around. Find the scale for your globe and use it to find the length of your path.

2. How great is the east-west distance around the world at the latitude of Philadelphia?

3. Use your answer to part 2 and the measurements you made on your flat map to recalculate the distance from Philadelphia to Beijing. Compare this result with your result for part 1.

The Earth is a three dimensional object, and we live on or near its surface. A flat map is an attempt to represent this surface. Because the Earth is not flat, any flat map is an approximation. There are different ways of making flat maps. Each has its advantages and disadvantages. The classic flat map of the world is called a **Mercator map.**

The Mercator map was designed for planning long trips for ships on the ocean. It represents directions very well. If *A* is northwest of *B* on a Mercator map, then sailing northwest from *A* will eventually get you to *B*. However, the farther you move away from the equator, the more a Mercator map distorts size. Other types of flat maps of the world preserve size, but they distort other things, such as shape or direction. It is not possible to make a flat map of the world that preserves both size and direction at the same time. (The fact that this cannot be done was actually proved by Leonhard Euler, an 18th century Swiss mathematician.)

About Words

The *Mercator map* was devised by Gerhardus Mercator, a Flemish mapmaker who lived from 1512 to 1594. He named North and South America and was the first person to call a collection of maps an atlas.

1. How big is Greenland compared with South America on a Mercator map? Now compare them on the globe. How accurate is the map, compared to the globe?

2. Besides distorting distance, a flat map can mislead us about the shortest route from one place to another. To find the shortest route from Philadelphia to Beijing on a globe, put one end of a string at Philadelphia, pull the string taut, then mark the point where the string reaches Beijing. Measure that length and then calculate the distance between Philadelphia and Beijing by that route. How does this distance compare with the east-west distance (along the 40th parallel) that you found before?

3. Would the class fly over Denver if they took the route you found in part 2? Over Hudson Bay? California? Japan? Siberia?

The flat map and the globe are **models** of the surface of our planet. Each one represents some features of our world that are considered important for a particular purpose and leaves out many others that are not. Neither model is perfect. The globe is a better model for charting paths of long air flights. The flat map is more useful if you just want to find your way around a small region, like Minneapolis. It's also a lot easier to fold up and put in your pocket!

Maps and globes are models made of paper, metal, or plastic. We can also make models with mathematics. When a mathematical object such as an equation or a function is used to describe a situation outside of mathematics, that object is a *mathematical model*. For example, if a record club sells CDs at $10.99 each and charges $3 per order for shipping, then the total amount billed, b (in dollars), is a function of the number n of CDs ordered. That is, the function

$$b(n) = 3 + 10.99n$$

is a mathematical model of the billing process. You saw many similar mathematical models of real situations earlier in **MATH** *Connections*.

George Box, a well-known statistician, once said, "All models are wrong; some models are useful."[1] What do you think he meant by this?

For many years, the traditional subject of *plane geometry* was a mathematical model of how flat maps work. Plane geometry began with the surveying of land in ancient Egypt. This mathematical model does not describe the entire surface of the earth accurately, because that surface is not flat. However, it is accurate enough for surveying fields or for taking short trips. This book begins with a long, close look at the plane geometry model and its power to describe many things well.

One reason why plane geometry is such a powerful tool is that it is built on a small number of very simple, basic ideas. But be careful! Their simplicity can be deceiving. You must think hard about these basic ideas until you really understand why they are important. Otherwise, like a house of cards with one or two bottom cards just a little out of place, your understanding of geometry may fall apart without warning.

Measurement is one of those basic ideas. Like the ancient Egyptians, this is where we begin our study of geometry. Measurement is one of two main ways of relating numbers to the world around us. The other way is by counting. You have had lots of practice with counting things—pennies, dollars, candy bars, cars, tickets, pages, people, and so on. Any time we want to know *how many* of some object, we count. The objects have to be separate, distinct things; they are said to be *discrete*. The branch of mathematics that deals with processes related to counting such things is called **discrete mathematics**. The counting principles and probability laws that you studied before are part of discrete mathematics. The rest of this section, like most of this book, is *not* about discrete mathematics.

About Words

A Spanish word for *flat* is *plano*.

---

[1]Box, George, *"Robustness in the Strategy of Scientific Model Building,"* in Lanner and Wilkerson, eds., *Robustness in Statistics* (New York: Academic Press, 1979), pp. 201–236.

The other main way in which we connect numbers to things is by measuring properties of a single object, such as its weight, length, or temperature. Any time we want to know *how much* of something, we measure. These measurements are not restricted to the counting numbers; they may take on any values, including negative values, fractions, and others. The branch of mathematics that deals with this kind of situation is called *continuous mathematics*. The most famous branch of continuous mathematics is calculus, but the part of geometry that deals with measuring lengths, areas, and volumes is continuous mathematics, too.

Which of the following questions refer to counting, and which refer to measuring? (You don't have to answer the questions.)

1. What is the population of your state?

2. What is the average annual rainfall in your state?

3. What is the record high temperature for your state?

4. How many people in your class are left-handed?

5. How many people in your class are over six feet tall?

6. What quantity of hot dogs was sold at yesterday's ball game?

7. What quantity of popcorn was sold at yesterday's ball game?

Measuring continuous quantities starts with choosing a unit. The key word here is "choosing." Any measurement system is based on a small number of independent units of measure, sometimes called **base units**. These base units are *chosen* for their *convenience*. All other units of measure within the system are then defined in terms of the base units. For instance, the base unit of length measure in the metric system is the *meter*; in the English system, it is the *foot*.

Many older units of length, such as the *foot,* were based on parts of the body of a "typical" person. Others that were used include:

- the *span:* the distance from the tip of the thumb to the tip of the little finger with the fingers spread out;

- the *palm:* the width of the palm of a hand or of the four fingers held close together;

- the *digit:* the width of the first finger.

Here are some lesser known units of length based originally on objects from everyday life.

cable   chain   fathom   furlong   hand

Write a sentence or two about each, describing
- the object on which it is based,

- how it compares with inches, feet, or miles, and

- the occupation, activity, or situation in which it is used.

Look up the ones you don't know.

The problem with units of length such as *span, palm, digit,* and *foot* is obvious: the sizes of hands and feet vary from person to person. Having a unit of measure that is different for each person would be like each person speaking a different language. Nobody would know what anyone else was talking about! One way around this problem is to pick some special person, such as a king, to define a unit. In England, King Henry I (1068–1135) declared a yard to be the distance from the tip of his nose to the tip of his right thumb with his arm outstretched. That became the basis for the English system of measurement, the system still used today in the United States.

How long would a "yard" be if *you* were the monarch on which it was based? Collect data from each member of your class on the distance from the tip of the nose to the tip of the right thumb with the arm outstretched. Make a boxplot of all the data, and find the mean and median. Is either one close to the standard 36 inch yard?

In order for any system of measurement to work well, the base unit must be constant; it cannot change from time to time or from place to place. To make sure this happens, person-based units of length have been replaced with units defined by metal bars kept in scientific laboratories. These bars stay the same size year after year. In the United States, the National Bureau of Standards oversees these official units of measure (and many others).

Once a unit of length is chosen, we measure something by applying the unit over and over, counting how many units it takes to make up the whole. Unlike your feet, rulers usually are marked in a variety of units and subdivisions. For example, a ruler may be marked in centimeters and millimeters on one side, and inches on the other. The inches may be divided into tenths, or eighths, or sixteenths. In a sense, these subdivisions are just a way of choosing smaller, related units when they are needed for more exact measurement. We can measure the lengths of many different things, but most of them have the same mathematical model: the measurement of a line segment.

 Display 1.1 shows four line segments. Measure each segment with a ruler, using these three different base units of length: inches, centimeters, millimeters. In each case, which base length did you think was easiest to use? Why?

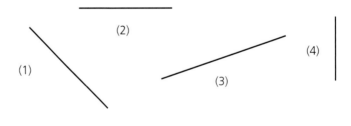

Display 1.1

In geometry, we distinguish between a *line,* which goes on forever in both directions, and a **line segment,** a piece of a line which does *not* go on forever in either direction. A segment consists of two endpoints and all the points on that straight line that are between those endpoints. It is common to label interesting points with capital letters, and we usually label the end points of a line segment. Display 1.2 shows a line segment with its endpoints labeled *A* and *B.* We can refer to this segment simply as *AB.* (Notice that point *C* is not part of the line segment because it is not on the line through *A* and *B.*)

Display 1.2

Whenever you measure a length, you can think of it as the length of a line segment. For example, if you measure the width of your classroom, you have to pick some (imaginary) line along the floor or wall on which you can make your measurement. (Note: In measuring length, we assume that all the lines and line segments are straight. As you saw earlier in this section, straightness is not always as obvious or as simple as it seems. This assumption simplifies our work, but we have to be careful not to apply the results to situations where "straightness" doesn't hold.)

One way to work with basic measurements is to use a compass. If you have a segment to measure and a base unit of length, set the distance between the two points to match the unit. Then use the compass to mark off copies of the base length on the segment. Display 1.3 illustrates this method with a compass of the type drafters use. First the compass is set to match the unit. Then we put the point at *A* and use the pen to mark off one unit, at *B*. We repeat the process, starting at *B*, and keep on going until we run out of segment. This shows that it is somewhat more than four units from *A* to *C*.

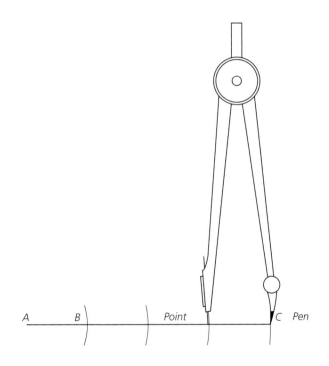

A   *B*   Point   *C*   Pen

Display 1.3

Trace or copy the longer of the line segments in Display 1.4. Then measure it with a compass, using the shorter segment, the wobbit, as your unit length.

The Wobbit, a Unit of Length

Display 1.4

Problem Set: 1.1

1. Find what looks like the shortest route from Miami, Florida to Oslo, Norway, on a flat map and also on a globe. Which of these routes passes closest to Nova Scotia? Which route is shorter?

2. In which ways is a globe *not* an accurate model of the Earth? Make a list. Which things on your list are also inaccuracies of flat maps?

3. Two campers get up in the morning and find that a bear has raided the food supply at their camp. They set out after the bear. They walk one mile south, then one mile east, then one mile north. At this point they find themselves right back at camp, where the bear is having lunch! What color is the bear?

4. (a) Measure the width and the height of a page from your notebook in wobbits. (Use a compass set to one wobbit.)
   (b) In centimeters, how long is a wobbit?
   (c) In wobbits, how long is a foot? (Measure a ruler using a compass set to one wobbit.)
   (d) In centimeters, how long is a foot? (Answer this by any method you choose.)
   (e) Which is longer, a 15 centimeter stick or a 15 inch stick?
   (f) If a stick is 10 wobbits long, is it more or less than 10 inches long? Is it more or less than 10 centimeters long?

5. Time is a little harder to define and measure than length. You can't see a second.

    (a) List as many different units of time as you can. Relate each unit in your list to another one in your list. Example: 14 days = 1 fortnight.

    (b) Units of time are usually based on some repeated event, such as the motions of the Earth or Moon. A globe is usually built so that it can turn like the Earth.

       (i) How long does it take the Earth to rotate once on its axis?

       (ii) How long does it take the Earth to go around the Sun?

    (c) On Mars, the day length is very similar to that on Earth. It takes Mars 24.6 hours to rotate once on its axis. However, it takes Mars 687 days to go around the Sun. Calculate your age, to the nearest year, if you lived on Mars. Would you have more or fewer birthday parties on Mars than on Earth? Explain.

6. Sometimes people misuse the words *discrete* and *discreet*. When one of the authors told his mother he was teaching discrete mathematics, she thought that was very funny. Why was she laughing? A dictionary might help you.

7. Who was Euclid? Read about him in an encyclopedia or history book. Write a paragraph summarizing what you find out. Please be sure to write it in your own words. Using someone else's writing as if it were your own is *plagiarism*, a form of stealing.

1.2 Paths, Polygons, and Perimeter

Suppose you want to get to the principal's office. Chances are you cannot go there in a straight line because there are walls and furniture in the way. A single line segment is not a good model of your route. But you could probably chart a route made up of several line segments, as in Display 1.5.

Display 1.5

Display 1.5 shows a path that starts in a classroom at *A*, goes out into the hallway at *B*, down that hallway to *C*, where it turns left and goes to the entrance to the principal's office at *D*, and finally into that office at *E*. This is an example of a **polygonal path**, a sequence of line segments in which each is connected to the next by having an endpoint in common. The first segment (for example, *AB* in Display 1.5) has an endpoint (*B*) in common with the second segment (*BC*); the second segment has an endpoint (*C*) in common with the third segment (*CD*); and so on.

Some more examples of polygonal paths appear in Display 1.6. Notice that some segments may cross others, and that the last segment may connect to the first.

Do you think *all* the paths in Display 1.6 should be called *polygonal*? Why or why not?

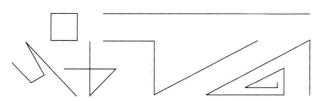

Display 1.6

Learning Outcomes

After studying this section, you will be able to:

Describe situations that can be modeled by polygonal paths;

Distinguish polygons from other planar shapes;

Use the standard names for polygons with 3 to 10 sides;

Write and use algebraic formulas for finding the perimeters of some polygons.

About Words

A *polygonal* path is a path with many knees. In ancient Greek, the prefix *poly-* means many, and the root *-gon* comes from the word for knee (or corner).

To find the length of a polygonal path, just measure each segment and add up the lengths. Polygonal paths are often used to model such things as driving distances between cities, railroad or airline routes, and many other time or distance relationships between things. For example, on the map of Display 1.7, the mileages and driving times between the cities are represented by polygonal paths. In such cases, the actual length of a segment on the map or diagram may not be directly related to the "length" it represents. In Display 1.7, the length in miles that a segment represents is the whole number (above it). Its length in driving time is the number below it, with hours and minutes separated by a colon. (The length of the segment between Des Moines, Iowa, and Hannibal, Missouri, is 271 miles, or 5 hours and 8 minutes.)

These questions refer to Display 1.7.

1. Find the shortest polygonal path between Kansas City and Texarkana. Calculate its length in distance and in time. What is unusual about two of the segments on this path?

2. If you want to go from Kansas City to Texarkana, but want to avoid Ft. Smith (for personal reasons), is it shorter to go by way of Springfield, Missouri, and Little Rock, Arkansas, or by way of Fort Scott, Tulsa and Atoka, Oklahoma? Is the shorter route in miles also the shorter route in time? Justify your answers.

3. Using the map as is, measure (in millimeters) the segments that make up the two polygonal paths of part 2. Which is the shorter path? How does this answer compare with your answers to part 2?

You can think of a polygonal path as a trip with some turns along the way. Often, when we travel, we want to make a round trip, to come back to where we started. If the polygonal path describes a round trip that doesn't visit any place twice along the way, then it is a *polygon*. In other words, a **polygon** is a polygonal path that starts and ends at the same place and doesn't cross over itself anywhere in between. In Display 1.7, for instance, the polygonal path that describes the trip from Lincoln to Sioux City to Dubuque to Des Moines to Omaha to Lincoln is a polygon.

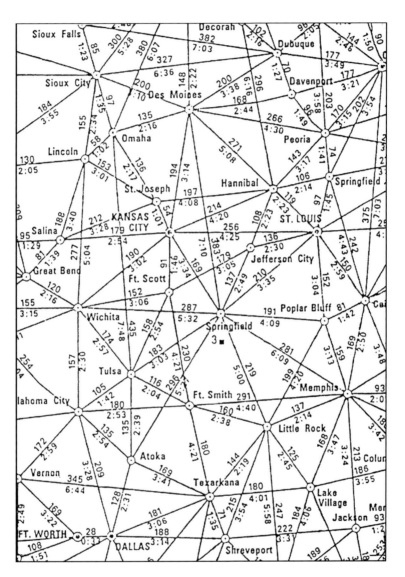

Display 1.7

Which of the figures in Display 1.8 are polygons? Justify your answers.

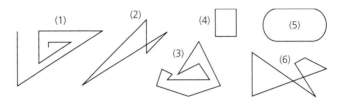

Display 1.8

The segments that make up a polygon are usually called its *sides*. It is hard to tell from a picture of a polygon which is the beginning side (segment) and which is the ending one. The good news is that it doesn't usually matter.

Mathematicians and scientists (and other people, too) like to *classify* things. That is, they like to separate things into groups whose members share some common property. This often makes it easier to deal with a whole collection of things all at once. Polygons are classified in a variety of ways. One way is to classify them by the number of sides they have. Display 1.9 lists the standard names of polygons of three to ten sides.

No. of Sides	Name of Figure	Root of Name
3	triangle	Greek: *tria* = three
4	quadrilateral	Latin: *quattuor* = four
5	pentagon	Greek: *pente* = five
6	hexagon	Greek: *hex* = six
7	heptagon	Greek: *hepta* = seven
8	octagon	Greek: *okto* = eight
9	nonagon	Latin: *nonus* = nine
10	decagon	Greek: *deka* = ten

Display 1.9

The table in Display 1.9 explains only the first part of each word. As for the second part.
* tri*angle*: three *corners*
* quadri*lateral*: four *sides* (In football, a *lateral* is a "sideways" pass.)
* penta*gon*: five *corners* (literally, five *knees*)

a

Label each of the polygons in Display 1.10 with one of the names in the table of Display 1.9.

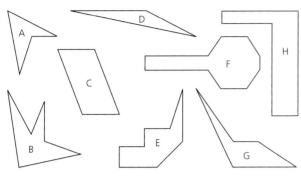

Display 1.10

The distance around a polygon—its length as a polygonal path—is called its **perimeter**. The perimeter of a polygon is the sum of its sides.

In some cases, this tedious addition process can be replaced by multiplication. For instance, if all the sides of a polygon are the same length, its perimeter is just the product of the length of any one side times the number of sides. Such polygons are called *equilateral*. In symbols, the perimeter, *P*, of an equilateral polygon with *n* sides, each of length *s,* is

$$P = n \cdot s$$

1. An equilateral decagon has a side 7 cm long. How long is its perimeter?

b

2. What is a simpler name for an equilateral quadrilateral? Write a formula using multiplication to find the perimeter of such a figure. Be sure to state the meaning of any letter you use.

3. Rectangles are quadrilaterals that have two pairs of equal sides. Write an efficient formula for finding the perimeter of such a figure. (Be sure to state the meanings of the letters.) Use your formula to find the perimeter of a 12 foot by 17 foot rectangle.

4. Some hexagons have three pairs of equal opposite sides. Write a formula for finding the perimeter of such a figure. (State the meanings of any letters you use.)

About Words

The Greek prefix *peri-* means around. A *periscope* is a tool for looking around. The *perimeter* of a figure is the measurement around it.

1.2 Paths, Polygons, and Perimeter

5. The "footprint" (the shape of the base) of an historic brick house in Farmington, Maine, is an equilateral octagon. Each side is 25 bricks long. A standard brick is 8 inches long. In feet, what is the perimeter of the footprint of this house?

Here are some customs that make writing and speaking about polygonal paths more efficient.

- The endpoints of the segments in a polygonal path are called its **vertices**. (A single one is called a **vertex**.) If you are walking along a polygonal path, a vertex is a point where you change direction. We usually label vertices with capital letters—A, B, C, etc.—in order along the path. (See Display 1.11.)

- With the possible exception of the endpoints of the path, a vertex is also a place where the endpoints of two segments are joined together. Any time two segments have an endpoint in common, they form an **angle**. The angle is named by the three endpoints of the segments, with the letter of the common endpoint in the middle. For instance, in Display 1.11, the angle at B can be called either ∠ABC (angle ABC) or ∠CBA (angle CBA).

1. Sketch a copy of the path in Display 1.11 and finish labeling its vertices in order.

2. List all the angles along this path, using the three-letter notation just described.

3. Which of the following are not angles of this path? Justify your answers.

| ∠DCB | ∠BDC | ∠DEF | ∠DFE | ∠GFE |

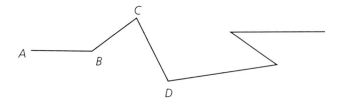

Display 1.11

Problem Set: 1.2

1. This problem refers to the driving map of Display 1.7. You are planning a trip from your home in St. Louis to see the Dallas Cowboys play a home football game.

   (a) Find the shortest route in miles from St. Louis to Dallas. (List the cities at the vertices of your path.) How long is it?

   (b) Find the shortest route in hours and minutes from St. Louis to Dallas. Does your answer agree with part (a)? How long is it?

   (c) On your way home from Dallas, you want to visit a friend in Wichita, Kansas. Plan the most efficient way to make this return trip. (List the cities at the vertices of your path.) How long is it in miles and in driving time?

   (d) Your round trip is represented on the map by a polygon. What type of polygon is it? (See the list of Display 1.9.) Is the real driving route a polygon? Why or why not?

   (e) According to the map, what should be your average driving speed (in mph) for the trip down to Dallas? For the return trip to St. Louis? For the round trip? Round your answers to one decimal place. Be prepared to justify your answers.

   (f) On which half of the trip do you think there are more Interstate highways? Why? (See part (e).)

2. One of the polygon types listed in Display 1.9 has the same name as a famous building.

   (a) Which one is it?
   (b) Who works in the famous building?
   (c) Where is the famous building located?
   (d) How did it get its name?

3. Label each polygon in Display 1.12 with an appropriate name from the list in Display 1.9.

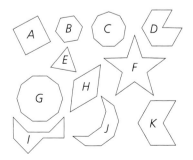

Display 1.12

4. Four of the names in Display 1.9 are related to the names of months.

    (a) Which polygons go with which months?
    (b) Do the names make sense in terms of the numerical meanings of the root words? Explain.

5. Amanda Leport, an architect, is making designs for windows above doorways. She is considering two different designs, shown as polygons (1) and (2) in Display 1.13. In both designs, the base segment must be 34 inches, which is the width of the doorway.

    (a) In design (1), she is experimenting with the length of the short sides, all of which are equal in length. If each short side is 12 inches, what is the perimeter of the window?
    (b) Write a formula for the perimeter in inches of design (1) if each short side is s inches.
    (c) For design (2), she tries to get a sense of balance by choosing the perimeter first and then calculating the lengths of the short sides, all of which are equal in length. If the perimeter is to be $2\frac{1}{2}$ times the length of the base, what is the length of each short side?

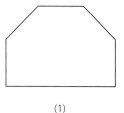

(1)

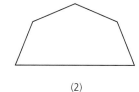

(2)

Display 1.13

(d) The result of part (c) doesn't look quite right. In order to try different perimeters, she writes a formula for the length s of each short side of design (2) as a function of its perimeter, P. What is the formula? Try it out by finding the side length for a perimeter of 90 inches.

6. Trace or sketch each polygon in Display 1.14 and label its vertices, starting wherever you like. Then make a list of all the vertices, sides, and angles. Do you think that everyone will label the figures in the same way? Do you think that everyone will get the same list of parts? Check with some of your classmates to see if your answers agree.

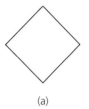
(a)

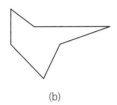
(b)

(c)

Display 1.14

1.3 Symmetry

1.3 Symmetry

Symmetry is a fundamental idea of nature, art, and science. There are many kinds of symmetry. The kind you are going to study in this section is symmetry about a line. The idea is that if you take the part of the figure that lies on one side of the line and fold it over to the other side, you want it to match the other half of the figure exactly. We might also call this "inkblot symmetry." Think about putting a drop of ink or finger paint on a piece of paper and folding the paper along a line through the drop. If you squish the folded paper down, and then open it, you will get a blot that is symmetric about the line of the fold, as in Display 1.15.

Display 1.15

The line of the fold is called the **line of symmetry** or **axis of symmetry**. This line divides the figure in half, so that the half on one side of the axis is a "mirror image" of the half on the other side. Sometimes you can find an axis of symmetry of a figure by tracing it onto a piece of paper. Then use trial and error to see if you can find a way to fold it so the two halves line up. If you succeed, the crease in the paper where you folded it will be the axis of symmetry.

For each of the four drawings in Display 1.16:

1. Find all axes of symmetry of its outline (its shape as if it were just a shadow).

2. Find all axes of symmetry of the drawing itself. For any drawing that is *almost* symmetric, say what keeps it from being exactly symmetric.

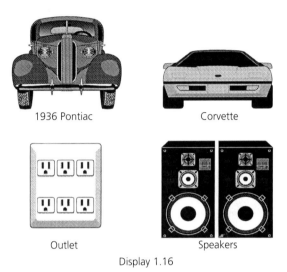

1936 Pontiac   Corvette

Outlet   Speakers

Display 1.16

Display 1.17 shows two boxplots.

1. Is either one symmetric about the horizontal line through its whiskers? Are they both?

2. Is either one symmetric about the vertical line through its median? Are they both?

3. What (if anything) can you say about the distribution of data if its boxplot is symmetric about its median line?

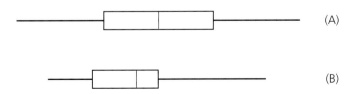

(A)

(B)

Display 1.17

Many geometric figures have axes of symmetry. Display 1.18 shows three copies of a triangle, $\triangle ABC$, with its three axes of symmetry marked.

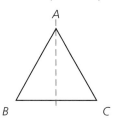
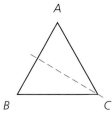
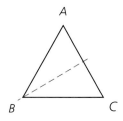

Display 1.18

Trace the first copy of $\triangle ABC$ onto a piece of paper. Fold it along its line of symmetry through vertex *A*. What do you notice about sides *AB* and *AC*?

When you can put a copy of one segment on top of another so that the two match exactly, we say the two segments are **congruent**. In particular, the endpoints of the two segments must match up, so the two segments must have the same length. In fact, two segments are congruent *whenever* their lengths are equal.

These questions refer to Display 1.18.

1. What does the axis of symmetry through vertex *C* tell you about the sides?

2. What does the axis of symmetry through vertex *B* tell you about the sides?

3. What special property of $\triangle ABC$ follows from your answers to questions 1 and 2?

Display 1.18 also illustrates some other important ideas.

Look again at your copy of $\triangle ABC$ that you folded along the line of symmetry through *A*. Label the point where the fold intersects *BC* as *M*. What can you say about the lengths of *MB* and *MC*? Why?

The **midpoint** of a segment is a point of the segment that is the same distance from each end. You can find it by measuring or by folding, as you just did. (Point *M* is the midpoint of *BC*.)

You can also find the midpoint of a line segment with an unmarked straightedge and a compass. This is a particularly accurate method. A procedure for creating a geometric object with straightedge and compass is called a **geometric construction**. Work through the following steps to see how this midpoint construction works.

- Take out a piece of paper. Draw a line segment on it, somewhere near the middle, and label its endpoints *A* and *B*. Its exact length is not important, but make it a convenient size to work with. Somewhere between 2 and 4 inches will work pretty well.

- Set your compass to a distance that is longer than half the length of *AB*. Setting it to the full length of *AB* will work, but is not necessary. Use that setting to draw two arcs, one centered at each endpoint. Be sure to keep the same compass setting for both arcs. Draw enough of each arc so that they intersect above and below *AB*, as in Display 1.19(a).

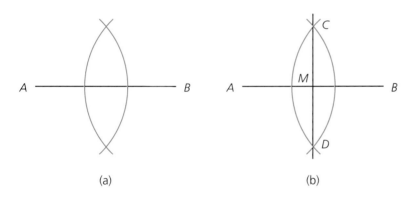

(a)   (b)

Display 1.19

- Label the two points where the arcs intersect *C* and *D*. Draw line *CD*. Line *CD* intersects *AB* at its midpoint, *M*. Your completed constructions should look like Display 1.19(b). Check– Does *AM* = *MB*? It should.

On your diagram, choose a point *P* somewhere along *CD*. Draw *AP* and *BP*. Now fold your diagram along *CD*.

1. What do you observe about segments *MA* and *MB*?

2. What do you observe about ∠*AMC* and ∠*AMD*?

3. What do you observe about segments *PA* and *PB*? Explain why your observation would be true, no matter where along *CD* you chose *P*.

4. Rephrase your answer to part 3 as a statement about all points of the line *CD*.

About Words

The prefix *bi-* means two. The rest of *bisector* comes from the same root as *section*. A section is a piece of something. To *bisect* means to cut into two equal pieces.

The folding exercise you just did illustrates that the line *CD* is an axis of symmetry for the segment *AB*—in fact, for the entire diagram in Display 1.19(b). It is called the **perpendicular bisector** of *AB*. This means that *CD* intersects *AB* at right angles and cuts it into two equal parts.

When two intersecting lines form matching angles next to each other, the angles are called **right angles**. Lines that form right angles are said to be **perpendicular**. Part 2 asks you to notice that ∠*AMC* and ∠*AMD* are right angles; they coincide when the diagram is folded along *CD*. Your answer to part 4 is an important property of perpendicular bisectors. (What was it?)

A perpendicular bisector can be used to construct the shortest path from a point to a line, usually called "dropping a perpendicular" from a point to a line. To see where this name comes from, look at Display 1.20(a). Think of line *L* as floor level. From point *P* above it, you want the shortest path to *L*. Imagine holding a weighted string at *P* (like a surveyor's plumb line) so that the bottom of it just touches the floor. That's the perpendicular path from *P* to *L*, but is it the shortest? Yes! Just think of swinging the weighted string back and forth like a pendulum, as in Display 1.20(b). The string touches the floor *only* at the perpendicular ("straight down"); any other path from *P* to *L* would have to use more string. That is, the perpendicular distance is the shortest distance from *P* to *L*.

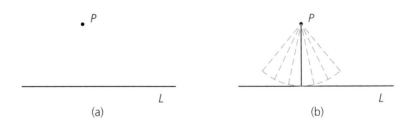

(a)   (b)

Display 1.20

The geometric construction of a perpendicular from a point to a line is an easy extension of the perpendicular bisector process. Look at Display 1.20(a) again. If P were the same distance away from two points, say A and B, on L, then the line of symmetry that matches segments PA and PB would have to be the perpendicular bisector of AB. Can you justify this statement? We'll ask you again in the problem set. So the problem is solved if we can find two points on L that are the same distance away from P.

1. **Draw a copy of Display 1.20(a). Then use a compass to locate two points on L that are the same distance away from P. Label them A and B.**

2. **Now finish constructing the perpendicular from P to L.**

Problem Set: 1.3

1. The figure in Display 1.21 is called a **pentagram**. It was a special symbol of the Pythagoreans in ancient Greece. Its outline is the familiar five pointed star that appears on the flag of the United States.

   (a) Draw a careful copy of this figure as a polygonal path without lifting your pencil from the paper. How many line segments are in your path?
   (b) Is the pentagram a polygon? If so, how many sides does it have? If not, why not?
   (c) Is the outline of the pentagram a polygon? If so, how many sides does it have? If not, why not?
   (d) How many axes of symmetry does the pentagram have? Draw them all on your copy of this figure.
   (e) How is a pentagram related to a pentagon?

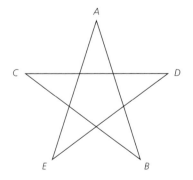

A pentagram
Display 1.21

2. The figure in Display 1.22 is called a **hexagram**. It is a traditional symbol of Judaism, called "the Star of David." A form of this figure appears on the flag of the Republic of Israel.

   (a) Is this figure a polygonal path with six sides? Is it a polygonal path at all? (That is, can it be drawn completely without lifting your pencil from the paper?)

   (b) Is the hexagram a polygon? If so, how many sides does it have? If not, why not?

   (c) Is the outline of the hexagram a polygon? If so, how many sides does it have? If not, why not?

   (d) Describe all axes of symmetry for this figure.

   (e) How is a hexagram related to a hexagon?

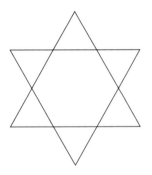

A hexagram

Display 1.22

3. Symmetry is important in decorative designs. Find all axes of symmetry for the designs in Display 1.23.

Display 1.23

4. Many letters of the alphabet are symmetric, although the details depend on the particular font. Display 1.24 shows the letters of a popular sans-serif font. Find all axes of symmetry for each letter.

ABCDEFGHI
JKLMNOPQR
STUVWXYZ

Display 1.24

5. The set of symbols in Display 1.25 is actually a typesetting font called "Zapf Dingbats" (a registered trademark of International Typeface Corporation). For each symbol, say *how many axes* of symmetry it has.

Display 1.25

6. (a) Justify the claim that *any* axis of symmetry of *any* triangle must pass through a vertex of that triangle.

   (b) Is it possible for a triangle to have two axes of symmetry, but not three? Justify your answer.

7. Justify this statement:

   If a point P not on a line L is the same distance away from two points on L, say A and B, then the line of symmetry that matches segments PA and PB must be the perpendicular bisector of AB.

1.4 Regular Polygons

Learning Outcomes

After studying this section, you will be able to:

Identify congruent angles;

Classify quadrilaterals as squares, rectangles, parallelograms, and rhombi;

Identify regular polygons;

Show by example that the converse of a true statement need not be true.

In this section, we will apply the idea of symmetry to polygons. In particular, we shall study a special kind of polygon called a *regular polygon*. We could define a **regular polygon** as a polygon with as much symmetry as possible. This definition comes close to explaining the reasons why these polygons are important in the first place. However, it is a little hard to apply. How do we know when we have as much symmetry as possible? For that reason, you will also see how to describe regular polygons in terms of their sides and angles.

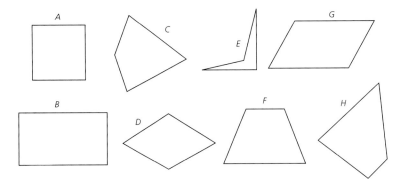

Some quadrilaterals

Display 1.26

 Some quadrilaterals appear in Display 1.26.

1. Why are these figures called *quadrilaterals*?

2. How many axes of symmetry does each quadrilateral have?

3. Choose the quadrilateral you think has the *most* symmetry. How are the sides of your chosen quadrilateral related? Which of the other quadrilaterals also have this property?

4. How are the angles of your chosen quadrilateral related? Which of the other quadrilaterals also have this property?

Symmetry isn't just nice to look at —it's practical. Once you have made a design for one side of an automobile grille or a bicycle helmet, it's easy to do the other side if you have symmetry. A symmetric load on a big truck is less likely to cause the truck to tip over on a sharp corner. If you want to fence in a polygonal area, a regular polygon will give you the largest enclosed area for the least amount of fencing. We begin our study of polygons with lots of symmetry by reviewing what we know about symmetries of the fewest-sided polygons of all—triangles.

In the previous section, we looked at the symmetries of an equilateral triangle. See Display 1.18 to refresh your memory, if you want. We found that a triangle with three axes of symmetry has all its sides congruent. Of course, if the sides match up when the triangle is flipped over, then so do the angles formed by those sides. Thus, a triangle with three axes of symmetry must have all its *angles* congruent, too.

We need to be a little careful about what we mean by angles being congruent. A polygonal path is made up of segments and angles that are interrelated. If you take away the segments, the angles disappear too! An angle is not so much an object, like a segment, as a relationship between two objects. An angle is the way in which two segments come together. When we talk about congruent angles, we are saying that certain segments come together in the same way. In other words, two angles are congruent if one can be placed on the other so that their corners match up, regardless of the lengths of the segments that form them. Here is another way to think about it: If you start with any angle, you can cut the sides off shorter and they will still come together in the same angle. You can do this over and over. No matter how short the sides may get, the angle remains unchanged.

1.4 Regular Polygons

a

1. In Display 1.27, all but one of the *angles* are congruent. Which angle is *not* congruent to the others?

2. In Display 1.27, three of the *polygonal paths* are congruent to each other. None of the others are congruent. Which are the three congruent paths?

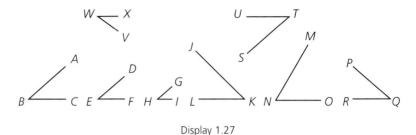

Display 1.27

You have seen that a triangle with all of its sides congruent also has all of its angles congruent, and vice versa. A triangle with all of its angles congruent has all of its sides congruent. Four-sided polygons are not so simple. A quadrilateral with all its sides congruent (and therefore all the same length) is called a **rhombus**. If you have more than one, they are called **rhombi**.

b

Find all the axes of symmetry of the rhombus in Display 1.28. Are any of the angles congruent to one another? Are *all* the angles congruent to one another?

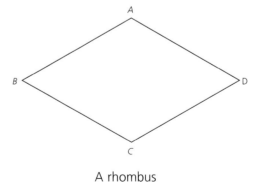

A rhombus

Display 1.28

How can you use axes of symmetry to show that the diagonals of a rhombus are perpendicular bisectors of each other? Do it, if you can. *Hint:* To illustrate your answer, draw or trace a rhombus, and then fold it along its axes of symmetry.

The corners of the rhombus in Display 1.28 came in two flavors. ∠ABC is congruent to ∠ADC but not to the other two angles. Those other two angles, ∠BCD and ∠DAB, are congruent. This makes a rhombus a somewhat special kind of quadrilateral. A quadrilateral may have no angles that are congruent, or it may have just two, or it may have more.

These questions refer to Display 1.26, which appears at the beginning of this section.

a

1. Find all the quadrilaterals in that display that have no congruent angles.

2. Find all the quadrilaterals in that display that have exactly one pair of congruent angles.

3. Find all the quadrilaterals in that display that have two pairs of congruent angles but not all four angles congruent.

4. Find all the quadrilaterals in that display that have all four angles congruent.

5. Can a quadrilateral have three congruent angles, but not four? If so, explain how to make one. If not, explain why not.

Unlike the rhombus in Display 1.28, *all* the angles of a square or a rectangle are congruent. They are right angles. In fact, a **rectangle** is *defined* as a quadrilateral with four right angles.

Find all the axes of symmetry of the rectangle in Display 1.29. How are the sides of a rectangle related?

b

A rectangle

Display 1.29

A square has four axes of symmetry. The square shown in Display 1.30 is symmetric about a vertical line, a horizontal line, and lines through opposite vertices.

1. Is every square a rectangle? Why or why not?

2. Is every square a rhombus? Why or why not?

3. Use your answers to questions 1 and 2 to define a square.

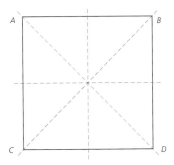

The axes of symmetry of a square

Display 1.30

Rectangles, rhombi, and squares all are special cases of *parallelograms*. A **parallelogram** is a quadrilateral in which both pairs of opposite sides are congruent, as in Display 1.31. This is a perfectly good definition, even though it doesn't say anything about "parallel." But it doesn't explain the name.

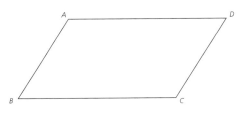

A parallelogram

Display 1.31

Another way to define a parallelogram is as a quadrilateral with both pairs of opposite sides parallel. To see if opposite sides are parallel, you can drop perpendiculars from both ends of one side to the line determined by the other side.

(Do you remember how to drop a perpendicular from a point to a line?) If those perpendicular segments are the same length, then the sides are parallel. This definition is equivalent to the one we stated first. That is, any figure that satisfies either definition also satisfies the other one. We prefer the first one right now because it fits in better with our discussion of rectangles, rhombi, and squares.

> **Find all axes of symmetry for the parallelogram in Display 1.31. Find all congruent angles.**

Let's organize what we know about types of quadrilaterals. We have seen that a rhombus has all of its sides congruent, a rectangle has all of its angles congruent, a square has all of its sides *and* all of its angles congruent, and a parallelogram has opposite sides congruent. A diagram showing how these types are related appears in Display 1.32.

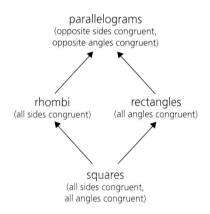

Types of quadrilaterals

Display 1.32

As you read from top to bottom, Display 1.32 goes from the more general type of quadrilateral to the more specialized. In particular,

- All rhombi are parallelograms.

- All rectangles are parallelograms.

- All squares are rhombi.

- All squares are parallelograms.

- All squares are rectangles.

Besides knowing what these statements say, you should also know what they do *not* say! Sometimes it is easy to confuse a statement of the form

"All [something] are [something else]."

with its *converse,*

"All [something else] are [something]."

When you're talking about everyday things you know well, it's easy to keep the subject and the predicate straight. For instance, you wouldn't confuse:

"All parakeets are birds"

with

"All birds are parakeets."

The first statement is true, and the second one is false. But when you're studying less familiar things, such as polygons, the distinction between a statement and its converse may not be so obvious.

A statement like: "All parakeets are birds" is called a **universal statement**. It's a *guarantee* that anything of the first kind is also of the second kind. You can prove the statement is false just by finding a single example where the guarantee fails–in the case of: "All birds are parakeets" just find one bird that's not a parakeet—maybe a robin, a crow, a chicken, or a goldfinch. An example that proves a universal statement false is called a **counterexample**.

Here again are five true universal statements about quadrilaterals.

1. All rhombi are parallelograms.

2. All rectangles are parallelograms.

3. All squares are rhombi.

4. All squares are parallelograms.

5. All squares are rectangles.

Write the converse of each statement. Then decide if the converse is true or false. If you think it's false, find or draw a counterexample. If you think it's true, explain why.

We'll start you off. The converse of the first statement is "All parallelograms are rhombi." Do you think that's true? Can you find a counterexample?

We have seen that the various kinds of quadrilaterals may have various amounts of symmetry, measured by counting axes of symmetry. The square has the most (4) of any quadrilateral we considered, and it is an example of a regular polygon. We know that an equilateral triangle is also a regular polygon, but we still do not know how to recognize regular polygons in general. The following questions should help you to figure that out.

The figure in Display 1.33 is a *regular* pentagon.

1. How many sides does this figure have? Are they all the same length?

2. The picture shows one axis of symmetry. Find as many more as you can.

3. These axes of symmetry are more like those of an equilateral triangle than like those of any quadrilateral. Explain this statement.

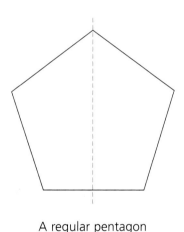

A regular pentagon

Display 1.33

1. Use all the regular polygons you have encountered in the text to make a two column table. One column of the table should show how many sides the regular polygon has. The other column should show how many axes of symmetry it has.

2. Using this table, can you make a guess as to the relationship between these two numbers? Is your guess true for the two regular polygons in Display 1.34? Explain.

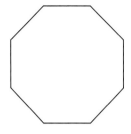

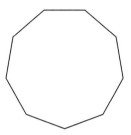

A regular octagon   A regular nonagon

Display 1.34

Problem Set: 1.4

1. (a) When is a square a rhombus?
   (b) When is a square a rectangle?
   (c) When is a square a parallelogram?
   (d) When is a rectangle a rhombus?
   (e) When is a rhombus a rectangle?
   (f) When is a rectangle a parallelogram?

2. (a) Draw a rhombus that has four axes of symmetry.
   (b) Draw a rectangle that has four axes of symmetry.

3. A square has four axes of symmetry, while a rhombus has only two. A rectangle also has two axes of symmetry. Describe how the axes of symmetry for a rectangle differ from those for a rhombus.

4. (a) Is there a quadrilateral with exactly *one* axis of symmetry? If so, draw one. If not, explain why not.
   (b) Is there a quadrilateral with exactly *three* axes of symmetry? If so, draw one. If not, explain why not.

5. A rhombus has an axis of symmetry through each pair of opposite vertices. Write an explanation of why a quadrilateral with two such axes of symmetry *must* be equilateral.

6. This problem refers to the figure in Display 1.35.

   (a) How many sides does this figure have?
       Are they all the same length?
   (b) What would you call this figure?
   (c) The picture shows one axis of symmetry.
       Find as many more as you can.
   (d) Do you think that this figure is a regular polygon?
       Explain.

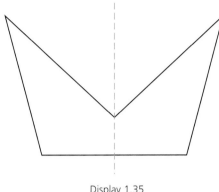

Display 1.35

7. Fred says that all equilateral polygons are regular polygons.

   (a) Can you give a counterexample to Fred's claim?
       That is, can you find an equilateral polygon that has
       less symmetry than another polygon with the same
       number of sides?
   (b) What is the converse of Fred's claim? Is it true?
       Give an explanation or a counterexample.

8. Freda says that all equi*angular* polygons are
   regular polygons.

   (a) Can you give a counterexample to Freda's claim?
       That is, can you find an equiangular polygon that has
       less symmetry than another polygon with the same
       number of sides?
   (b) What is the converse of Freda's claim? Is it true?
       Give an explanation or a counterexample.

9. (a) How are the angles of a regular polygon related?

   (b) How are the sides of a regular polygon related?

10. Find an example of an "All *A* are *B*" type of sentence in the text, or make one up.

    (a) Find the converse of your chosen statement.

    (b) Find the converse of the converse.

    (c) Do you notice anything? Explain.

11. Find all axes of symmetry for the 11 polygons in Display 1.36 and determine which are regular.

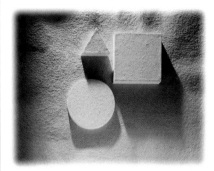

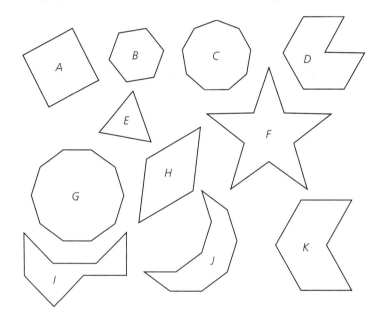

Display 1.36

12. The converse of "If a triangle has all its sides congruent, it also has all its angles congruent" is "If a triangle has all its angles congruent, it also has all its sides congruent."

    (a) Is the original statement true? Explain or give a counterexample.

    (b) Is the converse true? Explain or give a counterexample.

    (c) What are the analogous statements for a quadrilateral?

    (d) Is either of these analogous statements true? Are they both true? Explain or give counterexamples.

1.5 Areas of Right-Angled Figures

In previous sections you learned about the perimeter of a polygon. Another important property of figures and surfaces is *area*. If you think of perimeter as a measure of the boundary of a piece of land, you can think of area as a measure of how much land lies within the perimeter. You need to know the area of a lawn or garden if you want to buy fertilizer for it. If you want to paint or paper the walls of a room, their area tells you how much paint or paper to buy. If you want to cover a floor with tile or carpet or linoleum, you need to know its area.

Describe some other situations in which you need to know (or find) the area of a polygonal region.

Euclid School has a Photography Club. The school is going to let the club members make a darkroom in an unused storage space. They need to cover the floor with tile to protect it from possible spills of darkroom chemicals. One of the custodians gave them a sample square tile of the kind they need. He says he will try to get the club members enough tile to cover the floor if they will let him know how many tiles they need. Display 1.37 is a picture, drawn to scale, of the tile the custodian gave the students and of the floor they want to cover.

Tile   Floor

Display 1.37

 Sometimes "simple" and "easy" are not the same thing.

1. What's the simplest way to figure out how many tiles are needed? Can you think of a way that would make sense to a typical six year old child?

2. What's the easiest way to figure out how many tiles are needed? How would you do it if you were in that club?

3. How many tiles are needed? Explain why you will get the same answer the simplest way and the easiest way.

4. Can you think of any reason to know the simplest way if you know an easier way?

The floor-tiling example you just did is an area problem. In that case, the tile was the unit of area measure. The most common units of area are 1 by 1 squares based on some unit of length measure. This creates an important link between measuring length and measuring area. We might choose a unit of area that is one inch or one centimeter or one wobbit on a side. Then we would call the area unit a **square inch**, a **square centimeter**, or a **square wobbit**. See Display 1.38. (A few units of area, such as the acre, do not have such a simple relationship to a length unit.)

Area measurement is easiest for a rectangle. In that case, a simple formula lets you find the number of square units you need without counting tiles. Just measure the length and width, and then multiply.

The square inch   The square centimeter   The square wobbit

Units of area

Display 1.38

Another room is available as a possible darkroom for the Euclid School Photography Club. It measures 8 feet by 6 feet.

1. Find the area of this room. What unit of measure are you using?

2. Is the area of this room more, less, or the same as the area of the original room? (Why can't you answer this question?)

3. We forgot to tell you that the size of the custodian's sample tile is 1 foot by 1 foot. Now, which room has more area?

4. Find the perimeter of this room. Is it more, less, or the same as the perimeter of the original room? What unit of measure are you using?

5. Write a formula for finding the area of a rectangle. Be sure to say what each variable means and how the units of measure are related.

6. Write a formula for finding the perimeter of a rectangle. Be sure to say what each variable means and how the units of measure are related.

You can find the area of a rectangle by counting squares or by using a formula. Each approach has advantages and disadvantages. The formula is easy to use (if you remember it), but it works only for rectangles. Counting is very simple and works for any shape. However, most shapes cannot be covered exactly with a whole number of unit squares. (See Display 1.39 for some examples.) In such cases, we need to estimate fractions of a unit.

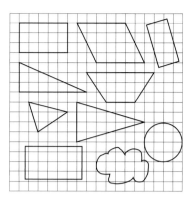

Display 1.39

1. Some of the figures in Display 1.39 are covered by whole unit squares and parts of unit squares. How might this affect the way you find the area of a shape? Explain.

2. Estimate the area of each of the ten shapes in Display 1.39. Rate each of your estimates as "exact," "pretty close," or "pretty rough."

Here's a way to estimate the area of *any* shape and to get an idea of the accuracy of the estimate. We'll use the circle in Display 1.39 as an illustration.

1. There are four small squares completely inside the circle. Is 4 square units a good estimate of the area inside the circle? We'll call this an *inner estimate*. Is it too low or too high?

2. You can get another estimate of the area of the circle by counting all the small squares that are wholly *or partly* inside the circle. How many of these are there? Is this a good estimate of the area inside the circle? We'll call this an *outer estimate*. Is it too low or too high?

3. Make inner and outer estimates for the area of the cloud shape in Display 1.39. Save your answers for use in problem 6 at the end of this section.

Thinking Tip

Try to improve estimates. Any time you make an estimate, try to find some way to make a *better* one.

Once we have these two estimates (inner and outer), we know the true area must be somewhere between them. If the estimates are close to one another, we know we have a fairly accurate idea of the area. If the two estimates are far apart, we know we only have a rough idea of the area.

Find inner and outer estimates for the three rectangles in Display 1.39. Describe any differences in accuracy among the estimates for these three rectangles. Can you suggest a way to combine the two estimates for a single figure to get a new and more accurate estimate? If you can, apply it to these rectangles.

For rectangles, of course, the area formula gives you an exact result *provided that* you know the lengths of the sides exactly. In Display 1.39, the grid tells you the exact length and width of one of the rectangles but not of the other two. The accuracy of their areas calculated by any formula depends on how accurately you measure the sides of these rectangles.

We can also find the area of triangles with a formula. The formula for triangles is based on the area formula for rectangles. That's because every rectangle can be divided into two triangles by connecting opposite vertices (see Display 1.40) *and* any triangle can be related to one or two rectangles in this way.

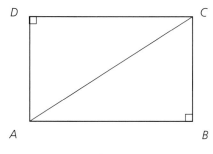

Display 1.40

To see how this works, notice first that each of the triangles in Display 1.40 includes a right angle that is also a corner of the rectangle. (In a diagram, a right angle often is identified by putting a little square inside it.) A triangle that has a right angle as one of its three angles is called a **right triangle.** We realize that this probably is not a great surprise to you; it is stated here to make sure that all the terms we use are clearly defined.

Is it possible to make a triangle that has two right angles? If it is, draw one. If not, explain why it cannot be done.

This relationship between right triangles and rectangles leads to a simple area formula for right triangles. When we break a rectangle into two right triangles, as in Display 1.40, the triangles are related in a special way: they are *congruent.* So far, we have only defined congruence for segments and for angles. Now we extend this idea to planar figures of all kinds.

Two figures are **congruent** if you can place (a copy of) one on top of the other in such a way that they match up exactly. They are alike except for their positions in the plane. For polygons, this means that all their sides and all their angles must be congruent. It also means that they must have equal areas!

These questions refer to Display 1.40.

1. Are you convinced that △ ABC and △ CDA are congruent? How would you check?

2. How are the areas of △ ABC and △ CDA related to each other? To the area of the entire rectangle?

3. Explain how to find the area of one of the triangles if you know the area of the entire rectangle.

4. Do you know the area of the entire rectangle? How could you find it?

5. Find the area of the rectangle and the area of each triangle.

But what if you have only one right triangle? How do you find its area?

Explain how Display 1.41 shows you a way to find the area of any right triangle. That is, supply the words that go with this picture.

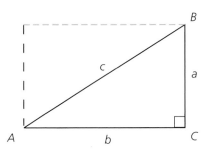

Display 1.41

The longest side of a right triangle is called the **hypotenuse**. It is also the side opposite the right angle. The other two sides are called the **legs** of the right triangle. Display 1.41 illustrates some customs that many people use when they label a right triangle:

- The vertices are labeled with capital letters, A, B, and C, with C at the vertex of the right angle.

- The sides are labeled with lowercase letters that represent the lengths of the sides. The lowercase letter used for a side usually corresponds to the capital letter used for the opposite vertex.

This isn't the only way to label a right triangle, but it's very common. Knowing this custom will make it easier for you to deal with other mathematics books and with standardized tests.

Using this notation, we can write a formula for the area of *any* right triangle. The lengths of the legs are a and b, so the area of the triangle must be half the area of the rectangle with side lengths a and b. That is, the area A of the right triangle is

$$A = \frac{ab}{2}$$

The edges of a right triangular sail measure 7.2 ft., 9.6 ft., and 12 ft. What is the area of the sail? *Hint:* **Draw a sketch and think about rectangles.**

Thinking Tip

When you learn a formula or put one in your notes, be sure to include the information you need in order to use it correctly:

- What do all the variables stand for?
- To what does the formula apply? For example, this area formula applies to *right* triangles.

We now have area formulas for rectangles and right triangles. In Section 1.7 you will see how to generalize these ideas to get a formula for the area of *any* triangle. Formulas can be a handy shortcut for finding the areas of some common geometric figures. But there are so many different figures in the world that we cannot memorize a formula for every one. For those many, many other figures, you still need the simple underlying principle from which we started.

Area is based on tiling a region with a unit square.

Find the areas of regions *A* through *I* of Display 1.42 by counting how many times you can fit the given unit into each region. (Is it useful to learn a formula for each different shape?)

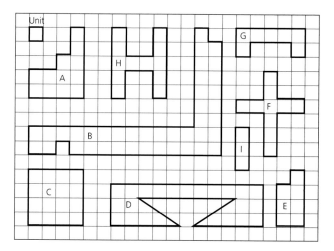

Display 1.42

Problem Set: 1.5

1. This problem refers to Display 1.43. Answer these questions about triangles 1–6.

    (a) Which triangles are congruent to triangle 0?

    (b) Of the triangles congruent to triangle 0, which are "flipped over"?

    (c) Of the triangles that are *not* congruent to triangle 0, which are congruent to one another?

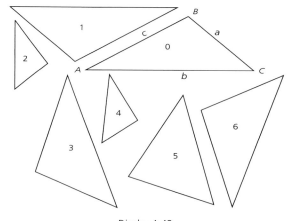

Display 1.43

2. (a) There are ten centimeters in a decimeter. How many square centimeters are in a square decimeter? (*Hint*: Draw a diagram.)

   (b) There are 100 centimeters in a meter. How many square centimeters are in a square meter?

   (c) How many millimeters are in a centimeter? How many square millimeters are in a square centimeter?

   (d) How many millimeters are in a meter? How many square millimeters are in a square meter?

3. (a) There are three feet in a yard. How many square feet are in a square yard? (Make a scale drawing.)

   (b) How many inches are in a foot? How many square inches are in a square foot?

   (c) There are 1760 yards in a mile. How many square yards are in a square mile?

   (d) To find out how many square feet are in a square mile, should you multiply your answer to part (c) by 3, by 6, by 9, or by 12?

   (e) Check your answer to part (d) by answering these questions: How many feet are in a mile? How many square feet are in a square mile? What do you get when you divide this number of square feet by your answer to part (c)? Why should this answer be the same as your answer to part (d)?

4. (a) It takes one can of prepared frosting to cover the top of an 8 inch square cake. (An 8 inch square cake is 8 inches on each side.) Mr. Cardullo is making a 16 inch square cake for his daughter's birthday party. How many cans of frosting will he need to cover the top?

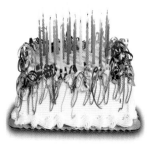

   (b) Makeda wants wall-to-wall carpeting for her living room floor, which is rectangular and measures 14 feet by 18 feet. The carpeting she wants is sold by the square yard. How many square yards will she need?

5. Here are the measurements of the walls and windows of a room.

   Wall 1. 14 ft. by 11 ft., one door

   Wall 2. 10 ft. by 11 ft., one window

   Wall 3. 10 ft. by 11 ft., one window

   Wall 4. 14 ft. by 11 ft., no windows

   The windows are 4 ft. by 2.5 ft. and the door is 8 ft. by 2.5 ft.

   (a) Find the total wall area.
   (b) Paint comes in cans that cover 300 square feet each. How many cans of paint will be needed?

6. We found that covering a shape with squares in order to find its area may not give accurate results. One way to overcome this problem is to use smaller squares. This problem asks you to try that approach on the cloud shape from Display 1.39. An enlargement of that shape is shown in Display 1.44. The square at the lower left represents the original unit; the new units (the small squares of the grid) are one third as long on each side.

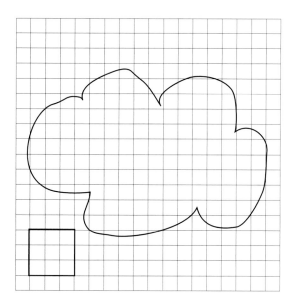

Display 1.44

   (a) Make two estimates of the area of this figure

by counting smaller squares that are

(i) completely inside the cloud;

(ii) completely or partly inside the cloud.

(b) Convert your estimates to the original units.

(c) Compare your new estimates to the ones you did before. Which gives greater accuracy?

(d) If this is still not accurate enough, what can you do?

7. Display 1.45 is another picture of our old friend, the rhombus. Your teacher will give you a copy of this figure to use for this problem.

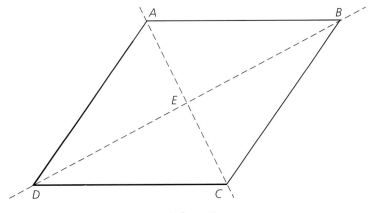

Display 1.45

(a) Find four triangles in the figure that are all congruent to one another. How do you know that they are all congruent?

(b) Justify the claim that these four triangles are right triangles.

(c) Next to each of these four triangles, draw another congruent copy with the same hypotenuse, as in Display 1.40. When you are done, you should have a big rectangle. Give a formula for the area of this rectangle in terms of the length of the diagonals *AC* and *BD*.

(d) Use your result from part (c) to write a formula for the area of a rhombus in terms of the lengths of its diagonals.

(e) Can you give a formula for the area of a rhombus in terms of just the length of its sides? If so, do it. If not, explain why.

8. (a) Graph the equation $y = 5$ on an xy coordinate plane.

   (b) Determine the missing coordinates for the points $(2, ?)$ and $(10, ?)$ on the line of part (a). Label these points M and N, respectively.

   (c) Now locate the points $(10, 0)$ and $(2, 0)$ on your graph. Label these points O and P, respectively.

   (d) Find the area of rectangle $MNOP$.

9. (a) Graph the equation $y = \frac{2}{3}x$ on an xy-coordinate plane.

   (b) Determine the missing coordinates for the points $(6, ?)$ and $(9, ?)$ on the line of part (a). Label these points R and S, respectively.

   (c) Now locate the points $(9, 0)$ and $(6, 0)$ on your graph. Label these points T and U, respectively.

   (d) Find the area of the polygon $RSTU$.

1.6 Area and Algebra

In your past studies you have seen how drawing a picture or a diagram can help you to understand an idea better. We can use pictures to connect the geometric idea of area to some of the laws of algebra that you studied earlier in **MATH** *Connections*. In particular, the areas of rectangles can be used to show how the Distributive Law works.

First we need to review what is meant by "an algebraic law." In this section, we shall consider only laws that are expressed as equations. Of course, not every equation deserves to be called a law of algebra. See if you can figure out what we mean by a law from the following questions and examples.

These questions are about equations in one variable.

1. What does it mean to "solve" an equation? Can an equation in one variable have more than one solution?

2. Solve the equation $x - 2 = 0$. How many solutions are there? Describe them all.

3. Solve the equation $x^2 = 9$. How many solutions are there? Describe them all.

4. Solve the equation $2x = x + x$. How many solutions are there? Describe them all.

5. Solve the equation $\frac{x}{x} = 1$. How many solutions are there? Describe them all.

6. Two of these four equations are different from the other two in some essential way. Which are alike and which are different? In your own words, what's the key difference?

How did you do? Did you see a difference that separates the four equations above into two different kinds? Here's the idea we want you to see. Some equations are true for some numbers and false for others, but other equations are true for *all* numbers for which the equation makes any sense at all.

For instance, putting any number into

$$x - 2 = 0$$

gives us a statement that's clearly either true or false, but we get a false statement for every substitution except $x = 2$. On the other hand,

$$2x = x + x$$

not only makes sense for every number, it is true for all of them. The equation

$$\frac{x}{x} = 1$$

doesn't make sense for $x = 0$ because division by 0 doesn't make sense. However, for every other number, it makes sense *and* it's true.

We call the set of all numbers for which an equation makes sense (is either true or false) its **domain**. (This is like the domain of a function.) An equation that is true for *all* numbers in its domain is called an **identity**. Thus, the equations

$$2x = x + x \text{ and } \frac{x}{x} = 1$$

are identities, but the other two (in questions 2 and 3) $x - 2 = 0$ and $x^2 = 9$ are not.

 Which of the following are identities? For those that are not, see if you can find *any* values for x that make the equation true.

1. $x + 4 = 0$
2. $x + 0 = x$
3. $3x - 7 = 2$
4. $x^2 - x^2 = 0$
5. $x^2 + x^2 = 0$
6. $x^2 - x = 0$
7. $(x^2 + 7) - (x^2 + 3) = 4$
8. $x^2 - 4 = 0$
9. $x^2 + 4 = 0$
10. $2x + 4 - 2(x + 1) = 2$

We can apply this same distinction to equations involving two or more variables. The equation

$$x \cdot (y - 4) = 0$$

is not an identity. It is true if $x = 2$ and $y = 4$, but it is not true for $x = 2$ and $y = 3$. (In fact, there are infinitely many numbers for which it is true and also infinitely many numbers for which it is false. Do you see why?) On the other hand, the equation

$$xy - xy = 0$$

is an identity because the equation is always true, no matter what numbers are substituted for x and y.

We can continue to find identities and solutions to equations for any number of variables. Practical problems in industry may involve thousands of variables. However, if you understand the pattern for a few variables, you can handle any number. This is the power of patterns.

Which of the following equations are identities? Do any of the identities have names? If so, what are they? Find at least one solution and one nonsolution for each equation that is not an identity.

1. $(x - 1) y = 0$

2. $x + y = y + x$

3. $(xy - 1) + (xy + 1) = 2xy$

4. $(x - 4)^2 + (y + 3)^2 = 0$

5. $x + yz = xy + z$

6. $(x \cdot y) \cdot z = x \cdot (y \cdot z)$

In algebra, a **law** is an identity that people consider important. Most identities are not important enough to be called laws of algebra. For example,

$$10^{-1} \cdot 34.96^0 x = 0.1x$$

is an identity, but not one worth memorizing. On the other hand, the various forms of the Distributive Law come up and are used all the time. It is worth knowing such laws.

Now that you have a better idea of what algebraic laws are, we can investigate an example that shows a useful connection between the area of a rectangle and the Distributive Law.

$$x \cdot z + y \cdot z = (x + y) \cdot z$$

Several years ago, Ms. Bocciarelli inherited a small piece of land in a popular vacation area. She has been saving to build a little summer cottage on this land. Yesterday she received a letter from her neighbors. They have a small cottage on the property next to hers. Now they are going to retire and build a house on their property. They were going to tear down their old summer cottage, but they thought Ms. Bocciarelli might like to buy it. They have offered to sell her the cottage and a small part of their land that the cottage sits on.

Display 1.46 is a map of these two pieces of land.

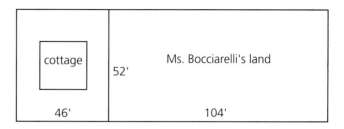

Display 1.46

Ms. Bocciarelli's original property is a 104' by 52' rectangle. The land her neighbors have offered to sell her is an adjoining rectangle measuring 46' by 52'. She wants to buy the cottage, but the sale has to be approved by the local zoning board. They want to know the total area of the land involved.

a

1. **Find the area of Ms. Bocciarelli's original piece of land, in square feet.**

2. **Find the total area of the land Ms. Bocciarelli will own after she buys the neighbors' cottage lot. Express your answer in square feet.**

How did you calculate the total area of the combined lot? There are two ways to do it.

- You could think of her land as made up of two separate lots, one 104' by 52', the other 46' by 52'. You could find the area of each lot separately and add them up.

- You could add the two horizontal lengths to get the total length of one side of the combined lot, 104' + 46' = 150'. Then you could multiply that by the width, 52', to get the total area.

Which did you do?

b

Use your calculator to do the following two computations. Be sure to key them in exactly as shown.

104 * 52 + 46 * 52   (104 + 46) * 52

How do the two results compare? What happens if you leave out the parentheses?

In measuring areas, it is easy to see that we should get the same result for either $104 \cdot 52 + 46 \cdot 52$ or $(104 + 46) \cdot 52$. In fact, we should get the same result both ways regardless of the particular sizes of the lots. We could replace 104, 52, and 46 with any other positive numbers. This general statement is the Distributive Law,

$$x \cdot z + y \cdot z = (x + y) \cdot z$$

In terms of Ms. Bocciarelli's property, the Distributive Law says we can find the area of the lot two ways.

• The $x \cdot z + y \cdot z$ way amounts to finding the area of each piece of the lot and adding those areas.

• The $(x + y) \cdot z$ way amounts to finding the dimensions of the new lot first, and then finding its area.

A practical difference between these two methods is that the first requires two multiplications while the second requires only one. This makes the second method easier if you have to do the calculation without a calculator. You might think that we don't have to worry about that with today's technology, but the fact is that the use of computers has led to *more* concern about the speed of an algorithm. Generally, multiplications take so much longer than additions on a computer that computer scientists just count the number of multiplications needed and ignore the number of additions. If we can use the Distributive Law to cut the number of multiplications in a long calculation in half, that would be a big timesaver.

The map of Ms. Bocciarelli's property is a geometric illustration of a form of the Distributive Law. You don't need the cottage or the story, of course. The figure itself is a geometric interpretation that can strengthen your understanding of the law and show how it applies to geometry. The following questions will help you review and extend these ideas.

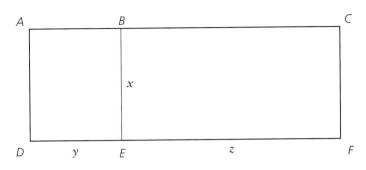

Display 1.47

 These questions refer to the rectangles in Display 1.47. In that diagram, *x* is the length of *BE*, *y* is the length of *DE*, and *z* is the length of *EF*. State your answers in terms of *x*, *y*, and *z*.

1. How long are the segments *AB*, *AD*, *BC*, and *AC*?

2. What are the dimensions of the large rectangle, *ACFD*? What is its area?

3. What are the dimensions of the small rectangle, *ABED*? What is its area?

4. What are the dimensions of the rectangle, *BCFE*? What is its area?

5. Use your answers to questions 2, 3, and 4 to explain how Display 1.47 illustrates the Distributive Law. Be sure to state the law in algebraic form as part of your explanation.

6. Does this diagram illustrate the Distributive Law for all numbers of its domain, or only for some numbers? Explain your answer.

When Ms. Bocciarelli took her plan to the zoning board, they told her that she could not have a cottage on her land unless she owned at least $\frac{1}{5}$ of an acre. Her plan does not give her a big enough piece of land.

1. An acre is 43,560 square feet. How many square feet of land does Ms. Bocciarelli need all together?

2. She wants to see if she can buy from her neighbors a strip of land that is long enough to satisfy the zoning board. To figure out how much she needs, she draws the diagram shown in Display 1.48.

Express the total area of the big rectangle as a function of y. What is the unit of measure here?

3. Use your answers to parts 1 and 2 to find out how long a strip of land Ms. Bocciarelli would need to buy from her neighbors. Round your answer *up* to the nearest foot. Why up?

4. Did you use the Distributive Law? If so, how?

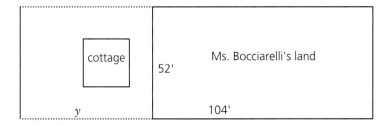

Display 1.48

The neighbors don't want to sell that much land to Ms. Bocciarelli because it would put the boundary too close to the house they plan to build. She decides to forget about the cottage. She can get a break on her taxes and insurance if her property is $\frac{1}{10}$ of an acre or less, so now she is thinking of selling the neighbors a strip off the 52 ft. edge of her property to reduce the area to $\frac{1}{10}$ of an acre. That will be enough to camp on once in a while.

How much land must Ms. Bocciarelli sell?

1. Suppose she sells a strip w feet wide. Express the area of the remaining piece of land as a function of w.

2. Use algebra, including the Distributive Law, to solve Ms. Bocciarelli's latest problem. Point out where you use the Distributive Law.

In this latest problem, you used a form of the Distributive Law that relates multiplication to subtraction. There are quite a few forms of the Distributive Law, but not as many as there seem to be. Most of them are just variations of one another. The important thing about *any* form of the Distributive Law is that it relates *two* operations. The first one we used in this section relates multiplication to addition.

Here's another example of how areas of rectangles can help you understand algebraic expressions. Do you believe that

$$(x + 3)^2 = x^2 + 6x + 9$$

is an identity? Maybe, maybe not. One way to convince yourself is to work out the algebra, step by step, until the two sides of the equation are identical. But first let's look at a picture that should make the answer clear.

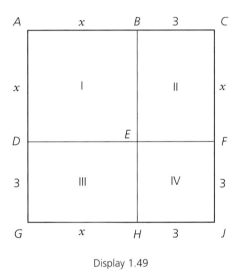

Display 1.49

 This refers to Display 1.49, in which all the angles are right angles.

1. Write an algebraic expression to represent each of the following objects:

   (a) the lengths of *AC* and *AG*

   (b) the area of square *ACJG*

   (c) the area of square *ABED* (region I)

   (d) the area of rectangle *BCFE* (region II)

   (e) the area of rectangle *DEHG* (region III)

   (f) the area of square *EFJH* (region IV)

2. Relate your answers for the previous part to the equation
$$(x + 3)^2 = x^2 + 6x + 9$$

   Is this equation an identity? Why or why not?

It may not be obvious to you that this example is related to the Distributive Law, but it is. In fact, you might think of Display 1.49 as a picture of how the Distributive Law works in this case.

You know that $(x + 3)^2$ is shorthand for $(x + 3) \cdot (x + 3)$, right? Now think of the first copy of $(x + 3)$ as a single thing, t. Then, by the Distributive Law, we have

$$(x + 3)^2 = t \cdot (x + 3) = t \cdot x + t \cdot 3$$

Now, put back $(x + 3)$ for t. You get

$$(x + 3)^2 = (x + 3) \cdot x + (x + 3) \cdot 3$$

Use the Distributive Law again on each piece of this sum.

$$(x + 3)^2 = x \cdot x + 3 \cdot x + x \cdot 3 + 3 \cdot 3$$

Finally, tidy up the right side of this equation, using the fact that addition and multiplication are commutative.

$$(x + 3)^2 = x^2 + 3x + 3x + 9$$

Of course, $3x + 3x = 6x$, so there you have it!

$$(x + 3)^2 = x^2 + 6x + 9$$

This example also teaches us something about when distributivity does *not* work. Exponentiation is *not* distributive over addition. That is, you CANNOT rewrite $(x + 3)^2$ as $x^2 + 3^2$ and expect to get the same thing. Display 1.49 should convince you of that. $(x + 3)^2$ is the entire area of the large square, but $x^2 + 3^2$ is just the area of regions I and IV, two smaller squares. The two rectangular pieces of the regions II and III have been left out.

Can you generalize the two approaches you just saw to products that are not perfect squares? Try it. Consider the expression $(x + 2) \cdot (x + 5)$.

1. Draw a diagram like Display 1.49 that illustrates what you should get when you convert this expression to the form $\_\_x^2 + \_\_x + \_\_$.

   Hint: You'll need to start with a rectangle.

2. Use the Distributive Law to multiply out this expression. Does your result agree with what you got in part 1? It should.

1.6 Area and Algebra

1. Which of the following equations are identities? Do any of the identities have names? If so, what are they? Find at least one solution and one nonsolution for each equation that is not an identity.

   (a) $2y + 8 = 0$

   (b) $y(y + 3) = 3y + y^2$

   (c) $9 - y^2 = 5$

   (d) $(y^2 - y) - (y^2 - 9) = 8$

   (e) $(y^2 - 1) - (y^2 - 9) = 8$

   (f) $4(y + 5) = 2y + 2(y + 10)$

2. For each part, find the areas of rectangular regions I, II, III, and IV. Then use these areas to express the area of the large square algebraically in two different ways.

(a)

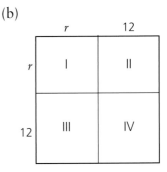

(b)

(c)

(d)

3. For each part, make a diagram that will help you write an equivalent form of the given expression. Then use the Distributive Law to show algebraically that the two forms are equivalent.

   (a) $(y + 10)^2$

   (b) $(k + r)^2$

   (c) $(2z + 4)^2$

   (d) $(x + 7)(x + 5)$

4. Draw a diagram to explain to a friend why $(x + y)^2 \neq x^2 + y^2$. What is the difference between the two sides of this expression? Describe that difference both geometrically and algebraically.

5. Mrs. Alvarez has a long, rectangular room, 12 ft. by 30 ft., that serves as a living room and a dining area. She wants to put wall-to-wall carpeting in the dining area at one end of the room. How big can she make the dining area and still leave 210 sq. ft. of living room space uncarpeted? Draw a diagram to illustrate your work. Be sure to define any variables you use.

6. Display 1.50 is an illustration of $(x + 3y + 5)^2$. It is subdivided into nine rectangular regions. Expressions for three of these areas have been filled in.

   (a) Copy this diagram and fill in expressions for the rest of the areas.

   (b) Use your answers for part (a) to rewrite $(x + 3y + 5)^2$ in a form that doesn't need parentheses. Write your new expression with as few separate terms as possible.

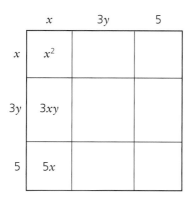

	x	$3y$	5
x	x^2		
$3y$	$3xy$		
5	$5x$		

Display 1.50

1.7 Triangles and Triangulation

Learning Outcomes

After studying this section, you will be able to:

Construct a triangle from the lengths of its sides;

Construct all three altitudes of a triangle;

Find the area of any triangle by breaking it down into right triangles;

Explain and use a formula for finding the area of any triangle;

Find the area of any polygon by dividing it into triangular regions.

The first thing you will learn in this section is how to use a compass and a straightedge to make accurate drawings of various triangles. There are many reasons why this is a valuable skill. If you want to discuss a geometric figure in general terms, a rough sketch may be good enough. If you want to determine axes of symmetry or try to figure out if a certain angle is a right angle, you will need an accurate drawing. If you want to solve a real world problem by making a scale drawing and measuring its parts, you need a *very* accurate drawing!

There are many uses for accurate drawings outside of school, as well. Buildings and mechanical parts are usually made from accurate scale drawings. Many paintings and graphic designs start out with careful line drawings to which color or paint are added later. There is even an algorithm for using accurate scale drawings to find the area of an irregular region.

As a first example, we'll construct a triangle whose three sides are 3, 4, and 5 wobbits long. Do you remember the wobbit? We use wobbits, instead of inches or centimeters, because we want to discourage you from measuring lengths with a ruler. Measuring involves too much "eyeball" approximating to be as reliable as the construction process we use.

―――――――― **The wobbit, a unit of length**

Display 1.51

Take out a compass and a straightedge (a ruler will do, if you promise to ignore the markings) and work along with the text. Your goal is to draw a triangle, $\triangle ABC$, with side lengths of 3, 4, and 5 wobbits.

1. Start by drawing a line segment more than 5 wobbits long. (Estimate.) Choose one end as a vertex of the triangle and label it A. Then use your compass to mark off five wobbits along the line, starting from A. Use the official wobbit in Display 1.51 to set your compass. Label the fifth wobbit point B. At this stage, your drawing should look like

Display 1.52, but larger. (The text displays are much smaller than the actual triangle you are constructing.)

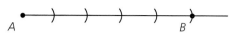

Display 1.52

2. Now use the marked line to set your compass at 3 wobbits. Put the point of the compass at *A* and mark off an arc of points that are 3 wobbits from *A*, as in Display 1.53.

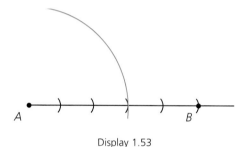

Display 1.53

3. Next, set your compass for 4 wobbits, put the point at *B*, and draw an arc of points 4 wobbits from *B*, as in Display 1.54. This arc should cross your arc centered at *A*. (If it doesn't, back up a step or two and extend the two arcs until they cross.) Label that crossing point C. (Actually, if you extend the arcs far enough, they'll cross at *two* points, one above the line *AB* and one below it. Either one will do for what we want.)

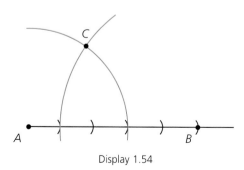

Display 1.54

4. Notice that C is exactly 3 wobbits away from *A* (because it is on the arc centered at *A*), and it is exactly 4 wobbits away from *B*. (Why?) Use your straightedge to draw segments *AC* and *BC*, and you're done! △ *ABC* has side lengths of 3, 4, and 5 wobbits.

Use the procedure just described to construct triangles with the following side lengths:

1. 4 wobbits, 2 wobbits, and 3 wobbits

2. 2 wobbits, 5 wobbits, and 4 wobbits

3. 4 wobbits, 3 wobbits, and 5 wobbits

4. 5 wobbits, 3 wobbits, and 3 wobbits

Are any of these triangles the same as the triangle of Display 1.54? If so, in what way are they the same? Explain.

Suppose you are given *a triangle* and need to construct a new triangle congruent to the old one. This might happen in an artistic or engineering drawing if you want to repeat the same triangle in several places. You can construct the new triangle without using a ruler to measure the sides. Just use the given triangle to set your compass.

Construct a triangle congruent to the one in Display 1.55. Write down your steps in order. When you're finished, check with some of your classmates to see if you all have the same triangle. Did you all start your construction with the same side? Did you all use the same sequence of steps?

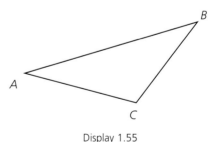

Display 1.55

Now you know how to construct a triangle from the lengths of three sides, either by copying another triangle or by measuring off the sides in terms of a unit length. But an important question remains unanswered. Is it ever possible to construct two *different* triangles from the same three side lengths?

Is it? Before you rush to answer the question, it needs some sharpening.

1. Think of a meaning for *different* which allows you to answer Yes. Then give an example of two triangles with the same three side lengths that are different according to your meaning of the word.

2. What if *different* means not *congruent*? Are there two triangles with the same three side lengths that will not match, no matter how one is placed on top of the other? If so, give an example. If you don't think that's possible, justify your opinion with a persuasive argument.

Triangles occupy a special place in the world of polygons. They are the only polygons whose size and shape are completely determined by the lengths of their sides. You already figured that out, didn't you? Moreover, any polygonal region can be broken into triangular regions, as you will see later in this section. This means that, if we can find the area inside *any triangle*, we will also know how to find the area inside *any polygon*.

In Section 1.5 you learned how to find the area of a right triangle. Now we combine that skill with constructing a perpendicular from a point to a line (from Section 1.3) to find the area of *any* triangle. The key to the process is a line segment called an *altitude*.

About Words

The *altitude* of a plane in flight is its vertical distance above sea level.

Words to Know: An **altitude** of a triangle is a line segment that is drawn from one vertex to the line of the opposite side and which meets that line at right angles. If the altitude lies within the triangle, then the opposite side is called the **base** for this altitude.

Display 1.56 illustrates an altitude and base for a typical triangle. It also shows you why we are interested in this line: It divides this triangle into two right triangles, which we already know how to handle.

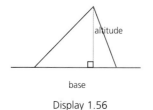

Display 1.56

1.7 Triangles and Triangulation

Do you think that altitude and base are good names for these line segments? Can you think of other names that you would like better? Defend your answers.

A triangle actually has three altitudes, one for each vertex. Sometimes an altitude actually lies outside the triangle. Display 1.57 shows the three altitudes for △ *RST*, two of them outside the triangle.

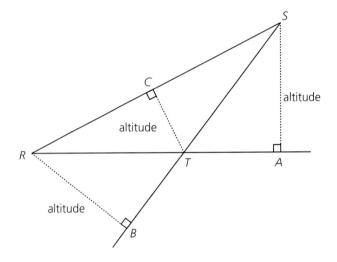

Display 1.57

It is not possible for all three altitudes to lie outside the triangle. If you use the longest side as the base, the altitude will always be inside. This means, for any triangle, there is always at least one altitude that divides it into two right triangles, as in Display 1.56. We use this altitude for the diagram that leads to the general formula for the area of a triangle.

Since you already know how to do all the pieces of this process, we'll let you put them together. The following questions guide you step by step.

1. On a blank sheet of paper, use a compass and a ruler to construct a triangle, $\triangle ABC$, with side lengths as follows: $AB = 7.5$ cm, $AC = 10$ cm, and $BC = 5$ cm. Put side AC at the bottom (horizontally), so that vertex B is above it. Put the drawing in the middle of your paper, with lots of room all around it.

2. Draw the altitude from vertex B, using the construction method for dropping a perpendicular from a point to a line. (See Section 1.3 if you need to refresh your memory.) Label as D the point at which the altitude meets the base.

3. For reference, mark each segment of your figure with a lowercase letter to stand for its length, as shown in Display 1.58.

4. Measure your figure as accurately as you can to find the lengths of d, e, and h. (You should already know the lengths of a, b, and c. What are they?) Notice that $d + e$ should equal b. Does it? If not, check your measurements.

5. Express the areas of $\triangle ABD$ and $\triangle BCD$ in terms of the letters of your diagram. Explain why your answers make sense. Then calculate these two areas from your measurements.

6. Calculate the area of $\triangle ABC$ from your numerical answers to part 5.

7. Use the Distributive Law to show how your algebraic answers to part 5 say that the area of $\triangle ABC$ is $\frac{1}{2}bh$.

Keep this diagram. You will need to use it again soon.

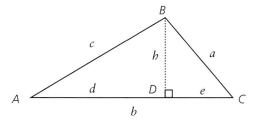

(Note: This is a labeling guide only, not drawn to exact scale.)

Display 1.58

People following the same directions can come up with very different results from measuring and approximating, even when they are careful. In such cases, the tools of data analysis can help make the results more reliable.

1. Gather the answers for the area of $\triangle ABC$ from everyone in the class. Make a stem-and-leaf plot and a boxplot of these data.

2. Find the mean and standard deviation of these data.

3. In this case, do you think the mean or the median is a better measure of the actual area of a triangle with side lengths of 5 cm, 10 cm, and 7.5 cm? *Hint:* Ask yourself: Are there any outliers in this data set? If so, how do they affect the mean and the median?

A Fact to Know: The area of a triangle can be found by calculating $\frac{1}{2}bh$, where h is the length of any altitude and b is the length of the base for that altitude.

Now that you have worked this formula out for yourself, you should be able to explain how it comes from finding the areas of right triangles and rectangles. That will help you to remember what the formula says and to know how to use it.

There's just one problem here: Our development of this formula depended on having an altitude *inside* the triangle. But the statement of this formula says that h can be "the length of any altitude." What if the altitude is outside the triangle? Does the formula still work?

Take out the paper with your construction of $\triangle ABC$ on it.

1. Construct the altitude from vertex C by extending side *AB* and dropping a perpendicular to it. See Display 1.57 for help in visualizing this.

   (a) What is the base for this altitude?

   (b) Measure this altitude and its base carefully. Then calculate the area of the triangle, applying the formula to these two lengths.

(c) Does your result agree with your previous answer for this area? If not, do you think it is close enough to be within measurement error?

2. Now construct the altitude from vertex *A*, measure it and its base, and use the area formula again. Does your result agree with your previous answers? Explain any differences.

In the previous example you saw that the area formula for triangles works even if the altitude you choose is outside the triangle. Problem 8 at the end of this section guides you through an algebraic proof of the fact that this always works. Now it's time to consider polygons with more sides.

Let's review what we have done so far with area. We found that rectangles are easy to deal with. Then we found that we could handle any *right* triangle by relating it to a rectangle. Finally, we found we could handle *any* triangle by relating it to a right triangle (and thus to a rectangle). Now we will see how to find the area of *any* polygon by breaking it up into triangles. Display 1.59 shows the example we will work with.

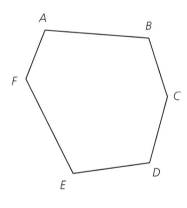

Display 1.59

How many sides does the polygon in Display 1.59 have? What would you call it? Is it regular?

We can use an algorithm—a step-by-step procedure—to divide the polygon in Display 1.59 into triangles.

Here's how the algorithm works. Your teacher will give you a larger copy of Display 1.59. Use it to follow the steps listed below. As you do each step, copy and complete the corresponding item in the Results column.

a

Steps	Results
1. Pick a starting vertex.	1. I chose vertex ____ as my starting vertex.
2. Pick a direction to walk around the polygon.	2. I chose to begin walking toward vertex ____ .
3. Walk around the polygon to the second vertex past the starting vertex.	3. I stopped at vertex ____ .
4. Draw the diagonal from that vertex to the starting vertex.	4. I drew the diagonal ____ .

Display 1.60 shows how one of the authors worked through these steps. If you made different choices, your diagram may look different. (That's OK.)

Results
1. I chose vertex *F* as my starting vertex.
2. I chose to begin walking toward vertex *A*.
3. I stopped at vertex *B*.
4. I drew the diagonal *BF*.

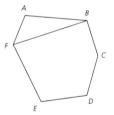

Display 1.60

We started with the hexagon *ABCDEF*. Now we have broken it into a *FAB*ulous triangle (we know how to find its area) and the polygon *FBCDE*.

How many sides does *FBCDE* have? What is this kind of polygon called? Is it regular? What letters name the corresponding polygon in your diagram? How many sides does it have?

b

Now we ignore the triangle we cut off (for the time being) and focus on the remaining polygon. We cut off another triangle by applying the same algorithm as before.

Apply the steps listed to your remaining pentagon. As you do each step, copy and complete the corresponding item in the Results column.

Steps	Results
1. Pick a starting vertex.	1. I chose vertex _____ as my starting vertex.
2. Pick a direction to walk around the polygon.	2. I chose to begin walking toward vertex _____ .
3. Walk around the polygon to the second vertex past the starting vertex.	3. I stopped at vertex _____ .
4. Draw the diagonal from that vertex to the starting vertex.	4. I drew the diagonal _____ .

Display 1.61 shows how one of the authors worked through these steps.

Now we have two triangles and a quadrilateral, *BCDE*. (Your quadrilateral may have a different name.)

Results
1. I chose vertex _E_ as my starting vertex.
2. I chose to begin walking toward vertex _F_.
3. I stopped at vertex _B_.
4. I drew the diagonal _BE_.

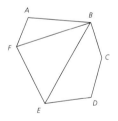

Display 1.61

What do you think we should do next? How many choices do we have for a starting point? After we choose a starting point, how many choices do we have for a direction to go in? How many choices in all? Are there really that many ways to divide this quadrilateral into triangles? Explain.

Display 1.62 shows one way of dividing the quadrilateral *BCDE*.

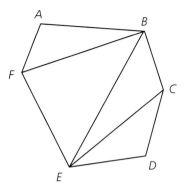

Display 1.62

The process of dividing a polygon into nonoverlapping triangles is called **triangulation**. The algorithm we have been using is a triangulation algorithm. Its purpose is to divide a polygon into triangles. Each time it is applied, one triangle is "sliced off" the remaining polygon. (You will see a slightly different triangulation algorithm in a later chapter.)

One important feature of an algorithm is some way to tell when you are done. For this algorithm, you are done when the remaining polygon is itself a triangle. We are done.

1. How many times did we need to apply this algorithm to our hexagon?

2. How many times would you need to apply this algorithm to a pentagon? To an octagon? To a decagon?

3. How many times would you need to apply this algorithm to an *n*-gon? Explain.

4. What would happen if you applied the algorithm to a triangle?

Now you can find the area of any polygon. All you have to do is triangulate the polygon, find the area of each triangle, and add.

1. Use your diagram to find the area of each triangle in your triangulation of the hexagon. Add up these areas to find the area of the hexagon.

2. Compare your answer with those of your classmates. Do you see a pattern? Is it what you expected? If so, explain why you expected this pattern. If not, explain how things are not as you expected.

Problem Set: 1.7

Note that in these problems, *construct* means *use a compass and a straightedge to draw.*

1. Construct a triangle with side lengths 4, 5, and 6 wobbits. Is it a right triangle? If so, which angle is the right angle?

2. (a) Construct a triangle with side lengths 12, 5, and 13 cm. Is it a right triangle? If so, which angle is the right angle?

   (b) Construct a triangle with side lengths 8, 5, and 13 cm. Does anything troublesome happen? How can you spot a problem like this in the future?

   (c) Construct a triangle with sides of lengths 7, 5, and 13 cm. Does anything troublesome happen? How can you spot a problem like this in the future?

3. Construct two congruent copies of the triangle in Display 1.63 in such a way that they share the same segment as their longest side and together form a parallelogram.

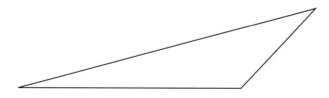

Display 1.63

4. Two radar stations are 130 miles apart. They both spot a UFO directly above a line connecting them. According to the radar, the UFO is 120 miles from one station and 50 miles from the other.

   (a) Why don't these last two distances add up to 130 miles?

   (b) Make an accurate scale drawing of the situation.

   (c) About how high is the UFO flying?

5. In this section we divided a hexagon into triangles in stages. At each stage, we had a new polygon to divide. For example, after the first stage, we had the pentagon *FBCDE* to work with. *FBCDE* eventually was divided into three triangles. Complete the table in Display 1.64. Make sketches to help you visualize some cases, if you want. Can you see a pattern to put into the last line of the table? Can you justify it?

Name	No. of Sides	No. of Triangles
quadrilateral	4	
pentagon	5	3
hexagon	6	
octagon		
decagon		
n-gon	n	

Display 1.64

6. Construct an equilateral triangle with sides 2 inches long.

   (a) Construct three altitudes, one connecting each vertex to the opposite side. Do you notice anything interesting?
   (b) Measure the lengths of the altitudes. Do you get three different answers?
   (c) Use an altitude and its base to find the area of the triangle.

7. Construct a triangle with sides 8, 10, and 12 cm long.

   (a) Construct three altitudes, one connecting each vertex to the opposite side. Do you notice anything interesting?
   (b) Measure the lengths of the altitudes. Do you get three different answers?
   (c) Use each altitude and its base to find the area. Do you get three different answers?

8. To prove algebraically that the area formula for triangles works even if the altitude you choose is outside the triangle, consider the situation shown in Display 1.65. Angle *C* of $\triangle ABC$ is greater than a right angle, and the altitude from *B* meets the extension of side *AC* at *D*. The length of *AC* is *b*, the length of the extension *CD* is *e*, and the length of the altitude is *h*.

(a) In terms of these variables, how long is *AD*?

(b) Express the area of △ *ABC* as the difference of the areas of two right triangles, both of which contain the right angle at *D*.

(c) Express the area equation of part (b) algebraically, and then work out the algebra to complete the proof. Justify each step you take. When you get to your last step, explain how you know you're finished.

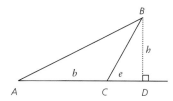

Display 1.65

9. A spider named Charlie is decorating the tracks of the Burlington Northern Railroad. Charlie ambles along one track and every 30 inches spins a spider web connecting the current location to two fixed points, *A* and *B*, on the other track. So far this morning Charlie has done this at ten locations, as shown in Display 1.66. The tracks are 56 inches apart.

(a) Does Charlie's pattern have any symmetry?

(b) Charlie made ten triangles. Each triangle has *A* and *B* as two of its vertices. The other ten vertices are labeled 1–10. Do any of these triangles appear to be right triangles?

(c) What is the approximate distance between *A* and *B*?

(d) Find the area of each of the ten triangles. (*Hint:* This part requires more thinking than calculation.)

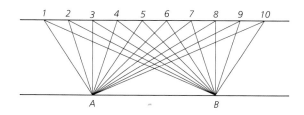

Display 1.66

1.8 The Pythagorean Theorem

Learning Outcomes

After studying this section, you will be able to:

State the Pythagorean Theorem and its converse;

Explain how the Pythagorean Theorem is a statement about areas;

Use the Pythagorean Theorem to find lengths and areas;

Use the converse of the Pythagorean Theorem to construct right angles.

As you have seen, right triangles are very important building blocks in geometry. In this section you will study the most important fact about right triangles. In fact, it is probably one of the half dozen most important statements in all of mathematics. It's called the *Pythagorean Theorem*.

The theorem got its name from a community called the Pythagoreans, who lived in southern Italy during the 6th century, B.C. They were followers of Pythagoras, a teacher, scholar, and religious leader. Because they believed that everything could be explained by numbers, they were pioneers in applying mathematical ideas to the real world. For instance, they developed a mathematical theory of musical harmony, and they knew that the Earth was a sphere nearly 2000 years before Columbus sailed from Spain.

We really know very little about Pythagoras himself. Many legends about him have come down to us, but after 2500 years it is hard to tell fact from myth. One of the legends about Pythagoras says that he discovered the theorem named after him while contemplating a floor tile pattern like the one in Display 1.67.

This was a familiar pattern, but Pythagoras looked at it in a new way. Many discoveries are made this way. He noticed a relationship among three squares built on the sides of a right triangle. To show you how Pythagoras looked at this floor pattern, in Display 1.68 we have shaded the squares he concentrated on.

1. Find the areas of the three squares. Use one square tile as your area unit. Each small triangle is one quarter of a unit.

2. Pythagoras might have noticed *two* special relationships among these areas. What are they?

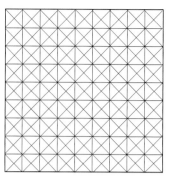

one tile

Display 1.67

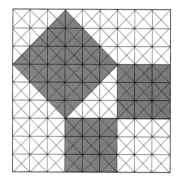

one tile

Display 1.68

The triangle in Display 1.68 is rather special. It is an *isosceles right* triangle. This means that it has two sides of the same length that form a right angle between them.

Do you think that the relationships Pythagoras noticed still hold if the right triangle is not isosceles? If it is isosceles, but not a right triangle? If it is neither isosceles, nor right? How can you find out?

Use whatever tools you want (ruler, compass, protractor) to draw and measure the following figures as precisely as you can.

1. Draw a right triangle that is not isosceles. Make the sides whatever length you want. Then draw a square on each side of your triangle. Measure the lengths of the sides carefully and compute the areas of the squares. Which of the two area relationships of Display 1.68 still holds? Do they both hold? Compare your results with those of your classmates.

2. Repeat part 1 for an isosceles triangle that is not a right triangle.

3. Repeat part 1 for a triangle that is neither isosceles nor right.

4. What do you think the Pythagorean Theorem says?

This is what Pythagoras observed.

The **Pythagorean Theorem** (geometric version).
The square on the hypotenuse of a right triangle is equal to the sum of the squares on its legs.

Notice that we say "the square(s) *on*," rather than "the square(s) *of*." Pythagoras would have said "on" because he was thinking of the actual squares and their areas. To Pythagoras, a square was a geometric figure, not a number. And when he said "equal," he meant it that the two smaller squares could actually be cut up and put together to form the big square. He didn't think or write in the language of algebra. In fact, algebraic notation would not be invented for another 2000 years!

Nowadays we often think of the Pythagorean Theorem algebraically. This makes it more useful for many things that Pythagoras never even dreamed about. Using the fact that a square of the side length s has area s^2, we can restate the theorem like this.

The **Pythagorean Theorem** (algebraic version).
If $\triangle ABC$ is a right triangle with hypotenuse of length c and legs of lengths a and b, then

$$a^2 + b^2 = c^2$$

In the algebraic version, $\angle C$ is the right angle of $\triangle ABC$. It's the angle opposite the hypotenuse.

1. What if you change the triangle by making $\angle C$ bigger than a right angle? How should the algebraic statement change? Does it help if you visualize the geometric form of the theorem?

2. What if you make $\angle C$ smaller than a right angle? How should the algebraic statement change?

The Pythagorean Theorem is a statement about *all* right triangles. It says that *every* right triangle has this special relationship between the squares of its sides. What about its converse? Roughly speaking, its converse says that any triangle with this special relationship between the squares of its sides must be a right triangle.

The converse of the Pythagorean Theorem

If $\triangle ABC$ has sides of lengths a, b, and c such that

$$a^2 + b^2 = c^2$$

then the angle opposite the side of length c must be a right angle.

As you have seen, a true statement can have a false converse. However, in this case, the converse is true, too. Moreover, it is a very convenient tool for identifying right triangles.

Use the converse of the Pythagorean Theorem to determine which of the triangles with the following side lengths are right triangles. For the ones that are not, say whether the angle opposite the longest side must be greater than or less than a right angle. Explain.

1. 3 cm, 10 cm, 11 cm

2. 5 cm, 12 cm, 13 cm

3. $\frac{3}{10}$ m, $\frac{2}{5}$ m, $\frac{1}{2}$ m

4. 0.5 m, 2.1 m, 2.5 m

5. 0.9 km, 2.6 km, 2.7 km

6. 0.7 km, 2.4 km, 2.5 km

The converse of the Pythagorean Theorem was used by surveyors in ancient Egypt. They measured by using ropes with knots at regular intervals. They knew that if they marked off a 3–4–5 triangle, it would contain a right angle. The ancient Chinese knew that the theorem itself is true for isosceles right triangles. The contributions of the Greeks was to prove that it holds for any right triangles. The Pythagorean Theorem is a statement about areas. But many applications are more concerned with the lengths of the sides than the areas of the squares on them, as in the following example.

Joel, a ham radio operator, wants to put up a 42 foot antenna pole. If the antenna leans to one side or another, it might fall over in a high wind. For that reason, he wants to build it at right angles to the ground. He plans to use support wires to hold the antenna upright. The antenna, the ground, and each support wire form a right triangle. We consider only one wire at a time; they all can be handled in the same way. A mathematical model of this situation is a right triangle, $\triangle ABC$ in Display 1.69.

Each support wire will be attached to the antenna 40 feet above the ground, right near the top. To know how much wire to buy, Joel needs to know the length of each support. He decides to anchor one wire to the ground 30 feet from the base of the antenna. Then he uses the formula from the Pythagorean Theorem.

$$a^2 + b^2 = c^2$$

In this case, $a = 40$ ft. and $b = 30$ ft., so

$$40^2 + 30^2 = c^2$$

This tells him that $c^2 = 2500$.

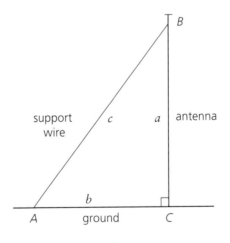

Display 1.69

1. How long is this support wire? What is its unit of measure?

2. Joel doesn't have enough room to put one of the support wires 30 feet from the base. He has to anchor it 22 feet from the base. How long is this support wire? Round your answer to one decimal place.

If you know the length of *any* two sides of a right triangle, the Pythagorean Theorem tells you the length of the third side. In the previous example, it was used to find the length of the hypotenuse from the lengths of the other two sides. In this next example, the hypotenuse and one other side are known.

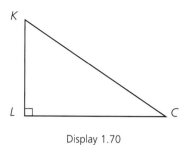

Display 1.70

Charlie Brown finally has his kite off the ground in the school parking lot. He has 100 feet of string stretched out to the kite, and he wants to know how high off the ground it is. Lucy measures the distance from where Charlie is standing to a point, *L*, at which she is directly under the kite. This is 75 feet.

1. Is Display 1.70 a good mathematical model for this situation? What do the letters represent? What simplifying assumptions are we making when we use this model?

2. How high is Charlie's kite, according to the model in Display 1.70? Round your answer to the nearest foot.

3. How might you modify your answer to part 2 in order to account for the assumptions of this model?

Sometimes, but not often, *all three* side lengths in an application of the Pythagorean Theorem are whole numbers. The two most common examples, which you have seen already, are

$$3, 4, 5 \text{ and } 5, 12, 13$$

There are many others, but they are not always easy to find. Curiosity about such numbers has led people to search for more examples and to investigate what special properties such triples of numbers might have. They even gave these numbers a special name: Three positive whole numbers *a*, *b*, and *c* such that $a^2 + b^2 = c^2$ are called a **Pythagorean triple**. If the sides of a triangle form a Pythagorean triple, then we know (from the converse of the Pythagorean Theorem) that the triangle must contain a right angle opposite its longest side. This is a handy shortcut in some situations.

1. Which of the following are Pythagorean triples? Justify each answer.

   (a) 15, 36, 39   (d) 8, 12, 16

   (b) 7, 9, 11   (e) 20, 30, 40

   (c) 7, 24, 25   (f) 30, 40, 50

2. Check that all of the following are Pythagorean triples.

   3, 4, 5   6, 8, 10   9, 12, 15   12, 16, 20

   In your own words, what's the pattern here?

3. We can state the pattern of part 2 algebraically, like this: If n is a natural number, then $3n$, $4n$, $5n$ is a Pythagorean triple. Prove it. *Hint:* Use the Distributive Law and a little algebra.

   We end this section with one more important use of the Pythagorean Theorem. In a rectangular coordinate system, it is the key to finding the distance between two points by using their coordinates. Display 1.71 shows a typical example of this. The line segment between the points (2, 1) and (6, 4) is the hypotenuse of a right triangle with its legs parallel to the coordinate axes. Its length is the *distance*, d, between the two points. The right angle vertex is (6, 1).

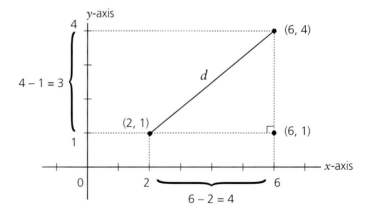

The distance between (2,1) and (6,4)

Display 1.71

   Notice that the right angle vertex is on the same horizontal line as (2, 1), so it has the same y-coordinate, 1. It is on the same vertical line as (6, 4), so it has the same x-coordinate, 6.

This means that the length of one leg of the triangle is $6 - 2$, the difference in the x-coordinates of the original two points. The length of the other leg is $4 - 1$, the difference in the y-coordinates of the original two points. Now apply the Pythagorean Theorem to find the length of the hypotenuse.

$$d^2 = (6 - 2)^2 + (4 - 1)^2$$

$$d^2 = 4^2 + 3^2$$

$$d^2 = 25$$

$$d = \sqrt{25} = 5$$

Use the Pythagorean Theorem to find the distance between the following pairs of points in the coordinate plane. Draw a sketch in each case, and give the coordinates of the vertex of the right angle.

1. $(0, 0)$ and $(5, 12)$

2. $(8, 3)$ and $(2, 10)$

3. $(-4, 1)$ and $(5, -5)$

You will see many uses for the Pythagorean Theorem as you learn more about mathematics and science. It is fundamental to any technological or industrial society. In fact, many years ago there was a plan to use it to try to communicate with life on other planets by drawing a *very* large copy of the figure with the triangle and the three squares, many miles wide in a desert. The theory was that any advanced civilization, regardless of how they communicated, would have to know the idea of the Pythagorean Theorem. They would recognize the figure and know that there is intelligent life on this planet, too.

Problem Set: 1.8

1. According to the Pythagorean Theorem, if you draw squares on the sides of a right triangle, the sum of the areas of the squares on the legs will be the same as the area of the squares on the hypotenuse. Does that also work with shapes other than squares? This problem asks you to explore a part of that question. Your teacher will give you a copy of a right triangle with squares drawn on its sides to help you answer the following questions. Use the centimeter as your unit of length.

(a) Measure the sides of $\triangle ABC$. Then measure the sides of the squares on each side and calculate their areas. In this case, is it true that $a^2 + b^2 = c^2$?

(b) Extend each square by 2 cm along the dashed lines to form a rectangle. The dimensions of your rectangle on side BC should be a and $a + 2$.

  (i) In terms of b and c, what are the dimensions of the rectangles on the other two sides?

  (ii) Calculate the areas of these three rectangles. Is it true that the sum of the areas of the rectangles on the legs equals the area of the rectangle on the hypotenuse?

(c) Extend each of these rectangles further along the dashed lines, so that the long side of each is twice as long as the side of the original square.

  (i) In terms of a, b, and c, what are the dimensions of these new rectangles?

  (ii) Calculate the areas of these three rectangles. Is it true that the sum of the areas of the rectangles on the legs equals the area of the rectangle on the hypotenuse?

(d) Try to generalize these examples to make up a rule that describes when the area-sum property holds for rectangles on the sides of a right triangle. If you're really feeling adventuresome, try to prove your rule algebraically, based on your expressions for the dimensions of the rectangles in parts (b) and (c).
Hint: It has something to do with the Distributive Law.

2. Two empty lots have been put up for sale, and Ms. Bocciarelli is thinking about buying them. The real estate agent said they are both rectangular lots. He claimed the small lot is 50 feet wide by 120 feet long and the large lot is 320 feet wide by 400 feet long. Ms. Bocciarelli went out and checked the measurements. They were what the agent said. She also measured the distance from one corner of each lot to the opposite corner. She got 130 feet for the small lot and 540 feet for the large lot. Then she knew something was wrong. What is it? How is it likely to affect the value of the property?

3. A right triangle has legs of lengths 8 mm and 15 mm long. How long is the hypotenuse? Find the area and the perimeter.

4. A right triangle has one side 27 yd. long and a hypotenuse 40 yd. long. How long is the other side? Round your answer to one decimal place. Find the area and perimeter.

5. In the western flatlands there is a rectangular tract of prairie bounded on all four sides by almost perfectly straight dirt roads. Two roads run north–south; two run east–west.
    The tract of land measures 10 miles by 12 miles. A car and a horseback rider start from its southeast corner at the same time, both headed for its northwest corner. The car must drive on the dirt roads and can average about 35 mph. The horse can cut across the prairie and can average about 25 mph. Who will get to the northwest corner first, and by how much time?

6. Ms. Bocciarelli is building a two-story house. The second floor is 8 feet above the first floor. She plans a staircase from the first floor to the second that would cover 11 feet horizontally.

    (a) How long does the banister for the staircase need to be?
    (b) The lumberyard works in inches. How much banister stock should Ms. Bocciarelli order at the lumberyard? Make careful calculations; banister stock is expensive.

7. Can there be a Pythagorean triple with 1 in it? If so, find one. If not, explain why not.

8. Prove that, if n is a natural number and a, b, c is a Pythagorean triple, then na, nb, nc is also a Pythagorean triple. *Hint:* Use the Distributive Law.

9. A triangle in the coordinate plane has vertices (1, 2), (7, 10), and (26.2, –4.4). Is it a right triangle? Why or why not? Find its perimeter and its area. *Hint:* Start by finding the lengths of its sides.

10. Over the centuries, the Pythagorean Theorem has been proved in hundreds of different ways. Here is a proof from about 900 A.D. by an Arab scholar. The main idea of the proof, illustrated by Display 1.72, is this.

    Starting with a square on the side of the hypotenuse, cut away two copies of the original right triangle. Then glue them back on to the remaining odd pentagon in such a way that they clearly form the shape of the other two squares, side by side.

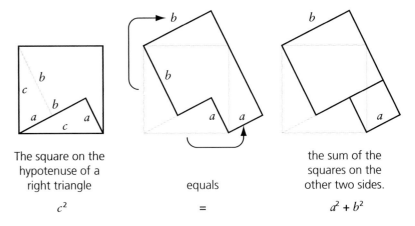

The square on the
hypotenuse of a
right triangle

c^2

equals

$=$

the sum of the
squares on the
other two sides.

$a^2 + b^2$

The Pythagorean Theorem

Display 1.72

(a) Your teacher will give you a sheet of paper with two square figures on it. The top one is for this part. It shows two congruent copies of a right triangle inside a square with side length the same as the hypotenuse of the triangle. Cut out the two triangles. Then reassemble the three pieces to form the sum of the squares on the other two sides of the triangle, as shown in Display 1.72.

(b) Is the cut-and-paste demonstration of part (a) a convincing proof of the Pythagorean Theorem? There is a danger in believing such things without checking the details. For instance, look at the bottom square of the handout sheet. It is an 8 by 8 square, measured in half-inches that are clearly marked all the way around it. Cut out the square. Then cut it carefully along the dotted lines to make four pieces. Reassemble the four pieces into a 5 by 13 rectangle. Then explain what's wrong with what you just did. *Hint:* What is the area of the square? Of the rectangle?

1.9 It Varies With the Square

Mrs. Chi is preparing a birthday party for Fan. She knows that he and his friends are really crazy about Cliff's Famous Homemade Chocolate Ice Cream. It's pretty expensive and comes only in pints, but birthdays are special occasions. Mrs. Chi figures a pint will serve two hungry teenagers.

1. How many hungry teenagers can be served with 10 pints of ice cream? With 12 pints? With 15 pints?

2. Write an equation for the number, T, of hungry teenagers that can be served with p pints of Cliff's Famous Homemade Chocolate Ice Cream.

3. Graph this equation on your calculator. What shape do you get? Describe its location in the coordinate plane.

You have just seen a typical example of direct variation, a particularly nice relationship between two variables. As one variable increases, so does the other, and they increase "in step," so to speak. Similarly, as one variable decreases, so does the other. In the ice cream example, for instance, if you double the number of people, you double the number of pints you need; if you triple the number of people, you triple the number of pints you need, and so on.

> **Phrases to Know:** A variable y **varies directly as** a variable x if there is a positive constant k, such that $y = kx$. This situation is also described by saying that y is **directly proportional** to x. The number k is called the **constant of proportionality.**

Sometimes the constant of proportionality is called the *scaling factor*, particularly when we are talking about changing the size of a picture or a geometric figure. This simpler phrase will appear often in the next chapter, where we talk about scaling geometric shapes.

Learning Outcomes

After studying this section, you will be able to:

Recognize situations in which one variable varies directly or inversely as another or as the square of another;

Express direct and inverse variations algebraically;

Describe real world situations using direct or inverse variation.

a

1. What shape is the graph of a direct variation equation? Describe its position in the coordinate plane as specifically as you can.

2. What is the constant of proportionality in the ice cream example?

3. Does the perimeter of a square vary directly as its side length? If so, what is the constant of proportionality? If not, why not?

4. Does the side length of a square vary directly as its perimeter? If so, what is the constant of proportionality? If not, why not?

5. Does the area of a square vary directly as its side length? If so, what is the constant of proportionality? If not, why not?

6. For a given number *n* of sides, is the perimeter of a regular *n*-gon directly proportional to its side length? If so, what is the constant of proportionality? If not, why not?

Are Fahrenheit degrees directly proportional to Celsius degrees? Why or why not?

A close relative of direct variation is important in dealing with variables, particularly in geometric settings involving area. Here is a simple example.

b

The legs of an isosceles right triangle are the same length.

1. What is the area of an isosceles right triangle with leg length 4 cm? 5 cm? 7 cm? 10 cm? 20 cm? 100 cm? Make a small table of these data.

2. Write a formula for the area, *A*, of an isosceles right triangle with leg length *x*.

3. Graph your formula on your calculator. Is it a straight line? Where does it touch the axes?

4. As *x* gets larger, does *A* get larger? Does *A* vary directly as *x*? If so, what is the constant of proportionality? If not, why not?

In this latest example, *A* (which is measured in square units) is equal to a constant times the *square* of *x* (which is measured in units of length). This kind of situation comes up often enough to have a name of its own.

> **Phrases to Know:** A variable y **varies directly as the square** of a variable x if there is a positive constant k, such that $y = k \cdot x^2$. This phrase is sometimes shortened to "y *varies directly as* x^2." The number k is again called the **constant of proportionality**.

1. Write a formula expressing the length d of the diagonal of a square in terms of its side length s.

2. Does the diagonal vary directly as the side length, or does it vary directly as the square of the side length? What is the constant of proportionality? Explain.

In some situations, as one variable increases, another *decreases*. This often comes up in a situation where the variables represent conflicting goals. As temperature decreases, the cost of heating increases; as the price of a product increases, demand for it (usually) decreases. In a state lottery, it is attractive to have as many prizes as possible and prizes as large as possible. However, it is difficult to increase the number of prizes without reducing their value!

> **Phrases to Know:** A variable y **varies inversely as** a variable x if there is a positive constant k, such that $y = \frac{k}{x}$. This situation is also described by saying that y is **inversely proportional** to x. As before, the number k is called the **constant of proportionality**.

You are the director of a state lottery. In a typical week, ticket sales total \$6 million. Of that, \$3 million goes to the state budget and \$1 million goes toward the expenses of running the lottery, leaving the state with \$2 million to give away each week. You are considering various ways of splitting up the prize money. Your goal is to sell as many tickets as possible.

1. One plan is to give five prizes of equal value. If you follow that plan, what will each prize be worth?

2. You are also considering seven other plans, each with prizes of equal value. How large can each prize be if you give 1, 2, 10, 50, 100, 1000, or 10,000 prizes? Make a table of these data.

3. Which of these eight plans would *you* find most attractive if you were thinking of buying a ticket?

4. Define some variables and write an equation describing these situations.

5. Graph the equation on graph paper using the same scale on both axes. Try letting both variables vary between 0 and 10,000. You may need to compute more data points.

6. Can you find any symmetry in the graph?

7. Make the same graph on your graphing calculator. Is this graph better or worse than the one you made by hand for studying this function? Explain.

Sometimes as one variable increases, its square determines the rate at which another decreases. This often comes up in a situation where something—such as light, sound, or magnetic attraction—spreads out from a source.

Phrases to Know: A variable y **varies inversely as the square** of a variable x if there is a positive constant k, such that $y = \frac{k}{x^2}$. This phrase is sometimes shortened to "y *varies inversely as* x^2." The number k is called the **constant of proportionality.**

The amount of light from a point source varies inversely as the square of the distance away from the light source. Have you ever seen anyone trying to take flash pictures at a school play or graduation? The flash on a simple camera provides the right amount of light about 8 feet from the camera. For a particular flash, the law is

$$L = \frac{256,000}{d^2}$$

where L is the amount of light (in units of light) and d is the distance (in feet) from the flash to the subject.

1. How much light is available at 8 feet? Assume that this is just the right amount of light for taking pictures with this camera.

2. How much light is available at 6 feet, the minimum recommended distance for this flash? What percent is this of the amount available at 8 feet? How do you think a picture taken at 6 feet will look?

3. How much light is available at 10 feet, the maximum recommended distance for this flash? What percent is this of the amount available at 8 feet? How do you think a picture taken at 10 feet will look?

4. Suppose you take this camera to your friend's graduation and from 50 feet away, take a picture of her receiving her diploma. How much light is available at 50 feet? What percent is this of the amount available at 8 feet? How do you think a picture taken at 50 feet will look? What's the message here?

Problem Set: 1.9

1. Display 1.73 shows a spring. If you pull on the ends of the spring, the amount the spring stretches varies directly as the force with which you pull. Springs like this are used to make simple scales. (Some scales for weighing fish or produce are made like this.) If you turn the spring vertically and hang a weight on one end, the amount it stretches is directly proportional to the weight. This enables us to read the weight on a length scale.

Display 1.73

(a) A particular spring stretched 1.28 inches when we hung a 32 pound weight on it. Find the constant of proportionality.

(b) How far would the spring stretch if you hung a 50 pound weight on it?

(c) We want to make a scale with this spring with marks every 5 pounds. How far apart should the marks be, in inches?

(d) The scale is 4 inches long. What is the heaviest weight the scale will measure?

2. The amount of fuel needed to keep a house warm in winter is directly proportional to the difference in temperature between the inside and outside. We shall measure fuel usage in terms of dollars of fuel cost. (Assume that the price of fuel stays the same all winter.) It costs $4 per day to heat a particular house when the inside temperature is 68°F and the (average) outside temperature is freezing (32°F).

    (a) Write an equation for the relationship between the fuel cost per day, c in dollars, and the difference between the indoor and outdoor temperatures, d in degrees Fahrenheit. (You will have to find the constant of proportionality from the data given.)

    (b) What will it cost for a day when the average outside temperature is 0°? 50°? –10°? Round your answers to the nearest cent.

    (c) Copy the table in Display 1.74. In the second column, fill in the costs that you calculated in part (b). Then calculate and fill in the costs for the indoor temperatures of 62° and 72°.

    (d) If you were living in this house and paying for the fuel, what temperature would you maintain indoors? Why?

Outdoor Temp.	Indoor Temperature		
	68°	62°	72°
50°			
32°	$4.00		
0°			
−10°			

Daily heating cost

Display 1.74

3. (a) Explain the following two statements:

    (i) Saying that y varies directly as x is the same as saying that $\frac{y}{x}$ is a fixed number.

    (ii) Saying that y varies inversely as x is the same as saying that xy is a fixed number.

    (b) Write the analogous two statements for direct and inverse *square* variations.

4. If you ignore air resistance, the distance that a free falling object travels varies directly as the square of the time that it is falling. This basic law of physics was discovered by Galileo in the 17th century. In particular, a rock dropped from the top of a 19.5 meter tower will hit the ground in exactly 2 seconds.

   (a) Write an equation for this relationship between the distance fallen, in meters, and the time of the fall, in seconds. Be sure to define the variables you use. (Find the constant of proportionality from the data given.)

   (b) The tallest unbroken vertical drop of Niagara Falls is 51 meters. How long does it take a drop of water to fall from the edge of the Falls to the pool at its base? Round your answer to the nearest tenth of a second.

   (c) Victoria Falls, on the Zambezi River in south central Africa, was discovered by a European, David Livingstone, in 1855. To estimate the height of the Falls, Livingstone might have timed how long it took a log going over the falls to drop from the edge to the river below. It would have taken the log $4\frac{3}{4}$ seconds. How high is this waterfall? Round your answer to the nearest meter.

   (d) Write an equation for the relationship between distance fallen, *in feet*, and the time of the fall, *in seconds*. Be sure to define the variables you use. Round your value for the constant of proportionality to the nearest integer. One meter equals 39.37 inches.

   (e) A careless mechanic leaves a small wrench in the wheel well of a cargo plane. As the plane is flying at 30,000 feet, the wrench falls out. How far (in feet) does the wrench fall in 5 seconds? In 10 seconds? How long does it take to hit the ground? Round your answer to the nearest tenth of a second.

5. A special case of Newton's Law of Gravity says that the weight of an object on Earth varies inversely as the square of its distance from the center of the Earth. For this problem, assume that the distance from sea level to the center of the Earth is 4000 miles. It actually varies from place to place on the globe, but this estimate will work well enough for us.

(a) Mount Everest, located in the Himalayas between Nepal and Tibet, is the world's tallest mountain. Its top is 29,028 feet above sea level. Kumar weighs 200 pounds at sea level. If he is transported to the top of Mount Everest (so that he doesn't burn off any weight getting there), how much less will Kumar weigh at the top of this mountain? Round your answer to the nearest tenth of a pound.

(b) A rocket at Cape Canaveral is starting to lift a 900 pound lunar satellite into space. The farther up it goes, the less the satellite will weigh. How much will the satellite weigh 50 miles up? 100 miles up? 200 miles up? Round your answers to the nearest pound.

(c) How high above the Earth will the satellite of part (b) weigh only 100 pounds?

1.10 Volume

A building has been demolished, leaving a big hole in the ground. Measuring the perimeter of the top of the hole tells you how far it is to walk around the hole. Measuring the area of the top of the hole tells you how much plywood you would need to cover the hole so that no one falls in. Measuring the *volume* of the hole tells you how much stuff you need to fill it up. We use a unit segment to measure length, a unit square to measure area, and a unit cube to measure volume.

The size of a unit cube depends on the unit of length you choose. A **unit cube** is a cube that measures one unit of length along each edge. A **cubic inch** is a cube with each edge one inch long, a **cubic meter** is a cube with each edge one meter long, and so on. The **volume** of a three dimensional object is the number of unit cubes (of some unit length) needed to fill up the space the object occupies.

1. How many unit cubes does it take to fill each of the boxes with the dimensions (in cm) given in Display 1.75? Copy and complete that table.

a

2. Which of the five boxes in the table of Display 1.75 is pictured in Display 1.76?

3. Use the data from your table to determine the number of cubes that are needed to fill a box of any dimensions. You may want to build boxes of other dimensions for additional data.

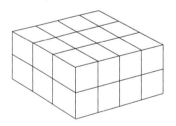

Display 1.76

Box	Length	Width	Height	No. of Cubes
A	4	2	2	
B	4	3	2	
C	4	4	2	
D	4	4	3	
E	4	4	4	

Display 1.75

Will your formula tell you how many unit cubes it takes to fill a box even if the dimensions of the box are not whole numbers? Explain.

b

EXPLORATION

We shall explore how volume is related to area by designing cake pans.

SETUP

Take out a sheet of graph paper and cut out an 18 by 18 square, as shown in Display 1.77. Don't worry about the corner markings yet. This represents a piece of sheet metal, 18 inches on a side. The Kingpin Cakepan Company (KCC) wants to make cake pans out of these sheets of metal. They want the pans to hold as large a volume as possible. They are not sure how to do this, so they have hired your class to help them figure it out.

To make a cake pan, you cut out a square at each corner, then fold up the four sides to make the pan. Display 1.77 shows the sheet marked for cutting four different sizes of squares out of the corners: 1 by 1, 2 by 2, 3 by 3, and 4 by 4. Your teacher will divide the class up into teams. Team 2 will cut out a 2 by 2 square, make a pan, and find its volume. Team 3 will cut out a 3 by 3 square, make a pan, and find its volume—and so on. We'll be Team 1, to provide examples for you along the way. We'll refer to you as Team n, where n is a number from 2 through 8.

QUESTIONS

1. What is the perimeter of the entire metal sheet? What is its area?

2. Cut an n by n square out of each corner. What is the perimeter of the sheet that's left? What is its area? Team 1 cut a 1 by 1 square out of each corner. The area that's left is 320 sq. in.

3. Fold up the sides of the pan. What is the height of each side? What is the length? What is the area of the bottom of the pan? Each side of Team 1's pan is 1 inch high and 16 inches long. The area at the bottom of its pan is 256 sq. in.

4. How many 1 inch cubes can fit into your cake pan? This is its volume. Team 1's pan holds 256 1 inch cubes.

5. If your pan were filled with unit cubes, how many layers would there be? How many cubes would be in each layer? Team 1's pan contains one layer of 256 cubes.

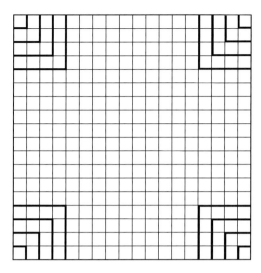

Display 1.77

Make a table of the results from the whole class. Include the side length, height, bottom area, and volume of each cake pan. Do you find any patterns in the table? Which team has the pan with the largest volume?

You probably have a winning team—one team with the biggest pan volume. However, before you turn the results in to KCC, you want to check and make sure they are correct. After all, if one of the results is really just a big mistake, it may seem like the biggest volume. Besides, you haven't checked cutout sizes that are not integers. Maybe one of them gives you a bigger volume.

One way to check your results is to make a graph. If the points lie on a line or a smooth curve, that gives you more confidence that your results are correct. If you find a pattern with one exception, you may want to check the exception.

To make the graph with your graphing calculator, you need to express the volume as a function of one variable, x. In this case, let x be the side length of the cutout squares.

1. **Express the height of the cake pan in terms of x.**

2. **Express the length of the cake pan in terms of x.**

3. **Express the width of the cake pan in terms of x.**

4. **Express the volume of the cake pan in terms of x.**

5. Now graph the volume function on your calculator. Use the information that the class collected as a guide for setting your window.

6. Does the volume that your team got agree with the graph? Check by using a menu choice on the calculator to find the value for your *n*.

7. Does there appear to be a maximum volume? For what value of *x*? Does it agree with what one of your teams got?

REFLECT

This chapter traced the study of geometry back to its roots. The tap root—the most basic root of all—is the idea of a line segment and a unit of length. Everything has grown from that central, fundamental idea. Except for this last section, you have studied *plane* geometry, the geometry of flat surfaces. You learned how to make and measure polygons, and how to classify them by symmetry. You saw how areas can be described in terms of unit squares, which are based on unit lengths. The huge variety of polygons became more manageable when they were broken into triangles by triangulation. This made it important to know how to find areas of all kinds of triangles, which we did by constructing altitudes and finding a formula: $A = \frac{1}{2} bh$, where h is the length of an altitude and b is the length of its base. You learned about the *Pythagorean Theorem*, one of the oldest and most powerful statements in all of mathematics; and finally, you saw how measuring volume in three dimensional space is based on unit lengths and unit squares.

The next chapter is about changing size without changing shape. It shows how proportionality is the key to understanding angles and how to measure them. We shall take closer looks at scaling figures to different sizes, at congruence of triangles, and at the relationship between angles and parallel lines. Triangulation will allow us to extend our results about triangles to other polygons, and you will see how unit squares and cubes help us understand how scaling affects the areas and volumes of two and three dimensional shapes.

Problem Set: 1.10

1. You now have a long-term consulting contract with Kingpin Cakepan Company. They have a new loaf pan that measures 4 inches by 5 inches by 9 inches.

   (a) Find the volume of this new pan in cubic inches.

   (b) KCC needs your result in quarts. There are 57.75 cubic inches in a quart. How many quarts will the pan hold? Round your answer to two decimal places.

   (c) KCC is still not satisfied. To get the best results, you should only fill the cake pan three-quarters full. If you do that, how many quarts will the new cake pan hold? How many cubic inches?

2. KCC needs a cake pan that holds 200 cubic inches when filled to the top.

   (a) Find five possible length, width, and height combinations that could be used for such a pan. For simplicity of design, stay with measurements in whole numbers of inches.

   (b) For each possibility you consider, find the size of the rectangular piece of sheet metal you would need to make the pan and the size of the corners that must be cut out before it is folded up.

   (c) Which of your five designs uses the least sheet metal? Who would be interested in this question?

   (d) Do you think there is an even smaller sheet size that will give you the same volume? Why or why not?

3. In the text you saw that the volume of a rectangular cake pan can be expressed in terms of the area of its base,

$$V = lwh \text{ or } V = Ah$$

   where A is the area of the bottom of the pan. This second formula extends to cake pans (and similar shapes) whose bases are not rectangular.

   (a) KCC makes heart shaped cake pans for Valentine's Day. The area of the bottom is 85 square inches. The pan is 1.5 inches deep. What is its volume? How many quarts of batter will the pan hold when it is three-quarters full? (See problem 1.) Round your answers to two decimal places.

   (b) KCC also makes small cake pans in the shape of triangular prisms, for use by pastry chefs who need parts for special order cakes with fancy designs. The bottom of the pan is an isosceles right triangle with

4 inch legs, and the pan is 3 inches high. What is its volume? How many quarts of batter will it hold when it is three-quarters full? (See problem 1.) Round your answer to two decimal places.

4. The Fixit family renovated an old part of their house. They had a trailer full of old plaster, lath, wood ends, and wallboard pieces to dispose of. Their trailer is 5 ft. by 8 ft. with 2 ft. high sides, and it was completely filled.

   (a) When they got to the town waste disposal center, they found out that it costs $15 per cubic yard (or fraction thereof) to dump this trash. How much did they have to pay?

   (b) After the Fixits dumped their trash, they picked up a load of cut and split firewood, which sells for $120 a cord. The woodcutter filled their trailer completely and charged them $80. A cord of wood is usually measured as a 4 ft. by 4 ft. by 8 ft. stack. Did the Fixits get a good deal, a fair deal, or a poor deal?

5. The Armstrong Aquarium has a dolphin tank that is 40 ft. by 30 ft. by 15 ft. deep. Its owners need to clean it out and repaint it. The directions on the cleaner say that they should completely fill the tank with water and add one box of cleaner for each 10,000 gallons of water in the tank.

   (a) Find the volume of the tank in cubic feet.
   (b) How many inches are in a foot? How many square inches are in a square foot? How many cubic inches are in a cubic foot?
   (c) How many cubic inches are in the dolphin tank?
   (d) A gallon contains 231 cubic inches. How many boxes of cleaner should the Armstrong Aquarium owners buy?
   (e) After cleaning the tank, they want to paint its inside walls and floor. Find the area they want to paint.
   (f) The paint they need is sold only in gallons. One gallon covers 400 sq. ft. How many gallons must they buy?

Brad Bower
Movie Magic

They have been seen in almost all action movies ever made. They even star in music videos. Months are spent making sure they look as real as they can. And then, in a flash, most are trashed, smashed, sunk, run over or blown up. Ah, the life of a motion picture special effects created model.

Brad Bower is manager of the Creative Studio Model Shop for Universal Studios Recreation Group. He has been building models professionally since 19. "I look forward to every day on the job," says Brad. "After all, who doesn't like entertainment?"

Brad started out building models at the Walt Disney Company. He rose to manager of their special effects department, then was hired by Universal. "Models can be created to replicate existing structures and environments. Or, they can be three dimensional blueprints of future projects," Brad explains. "But in both cases, precision is the key and math is the tool."

Every Universal Studio's model starts its "life" on paper, in the design department. Next, rough drawings of the design concept are sent to the Creative Studio Model Shop. Here's where Brad's group of model-builders, painters and sculptors start their creative work. Often, the model-builders are working from drawings that are still in progress. "As the design becomes more fully developed, they produce more accurate scale models that include more details."

"Math is something I enjoyed in school from the start," says Brad. "We use math every day in all different forms. Each scale model must be a perfectly accurate representation of its full-sized counterpart. Its dimensions, proportions, location and function must be precise."

"The challenge for the model-builder," Brad continues, "is to maintain the intent of the original design throughout the project."

Even if that means hearing the director yell "ACTION!" and watching your prized creation go up in smoke!

106

Similarity and Scaling: Growing and Shrinking Carefully

CHAPTER **2**

2.1 The Same Shape

"One side will make you grow taller, and the other side will make you grow shorter."

"One side of *what*? The other side of *what*?" thought Alice to herself.

"Of the mushroom," said the Caterpillar, just as if she asked it aloud; and in another moment it was out of sight.

Alice remained looking thoughtfully at the mushroom for a minute, trying to make out which were the two sides of it; and, as it was perfectly round, she found this a very difficult question. However, at last she stretched her arms round it as far as they would go, and broke off a bit of the edge with each hand.

"And now which is which?" she said to herself and nibbled a little of the right-hand bit to try the effect: the next moment she felt a violent blow underneath her chin; it had struck her foot!

She was a good deal frightened by this sudden change, but she felt that there was no time to be lost, as she was shrinking rapidly; so she set to work at once to eat some of the other bit. Her chin was pressed so closely against her foot, that there was hardly room to open her mouth; but she did it at last, and managed to swallow a morsel of the left hand bit.

—Lewis Carroll, Alice in Wonderland

This section is about growing and shrinking. More precisely, it is about similarity. A dictionary defines the geometric meaning of *similar* as "having the same shape, but not [necessarily] the same size or position." This isn't a bad description of the idea, *provided that* you know what "same shape" means. Do you?

What do *you* think it means to say that two things "have the same shape"? Test your opinion with these examples.

1. Do all triangles have the same shape? If you say Yes, explain why. If you say No, draw two triangles that have different shapes. Also draw two triangles with the same shape but different sizes.

2. Do all rectangles have the same shape? If you say Yes, explain why. If you say No, draw two rectangles that have different shapes. Also draw two rectangles with the same shape but different sizes.

3. Do all squares have the same shape? If you say Yes, explain why. If you say No, draw two squares that have different shapes. Also draw two squares with the same shape but different sizes.

4. Do all automobile tires have the same shape? Defend your answer.

5. Do all boxes of Kellogg's Corn Flakes have the same shape? Go to a supermarket and look at the 12 oz., 18 oz., and 24 oz. boxes of this cereal. Measure them, if you like. Then explain whether or not these boxes have the same shape.

In some sense, these questions are unfair. The idea of "same shape" has not been carefully defined, so there is no reliable way for you to justify your answers. But that was the point of asking. We want you to see the need for a careful definition of *similar figures*.

Look at Carroll's description of Alice nibbling on the magic mushroom. How does your imagination picture the shrinking Alice? Which part of Display 2.1—(a) or (b)—comes closer to what you "see" in your mind's eye? Do you see her squashed down as in (a), almost all head and feet? Do you think that was what Carroll imagined when he wrote,

"Her chin was pressed so closely against her foot, that there was hardly room to open her mouth"?

From these words, it seems so. But that would be a strangely distorted Alice, hardly fit for her next adventure, in which she is an ordinary little girl—except that she's 9 inches tall! In spite of his chin and foot comment, Carroll probably imagined something more like Display 2.1(b). He probably thought of Alice as growing and shrinking "proportionally," so that she always stayed the same shape. In this case, her chin would be just as far from her foot, relatively speaking, as it had been when she was large. That is, if the distance from her chin to her foot was twice her arm's length when she was big, then that distance should still be twice her arm's length when she was small!

(a)

(b)

Display 2.1

About Words

The Latin term *per cent* expresses a ratio; it means for each hundred or: out of one hundred.

To make the idea of same shape precise, we need to begin with the idea of a **ratio**, which is a way of measuring one quantity in terms of another. A ratio is usually (but not always) expressed as a fraction. For example, if Pat Pivot, the star center on the basketball team, has made 42 of her 60 foul shots, we say that she is "42 for 60." We can express this relative measurement as a fraction, $\frac{42}{60}$, or as a *percent*, which is just a special kind of fraction—a fraction with an implied denominator of 100.

1. Express Pat Pivot's foul shot record of 42 out of 60 as a percent. Then explain how your process can be used to express any fraction as a percent.

2. Jeannie Jumpshot has made 28 of her 49 foul shot attempts. At this rate, if she has a total of 91 attempts during the season, how many would she make? Explain how to find this number *without* expressing her foul shot ratio as a percent.

Here is an example of how ratios are used. Display 2.2 from the March 1994 issue of *Railroad Model Craftsman* is a drawing of a boxcar. Notice what it says in the lower left corner.

$$\text{O scale: } \tfrac{1}{4}" = 1' - 0"; 1 : 48$$

This line explains O *scale*, a size ratio used by many model railroaders. The scale factor $\frac{1}{4}" = 1' - 0"$ part tells you that $\frac{1}{4}$ inch in the model represents 1 foot in real life. The next part, 1 : 48, actually says the same thing. Because there are 48 quarter-inches in 1 foot, each quarter-inch of the model represents 48 quarter-inches of the real boxcar. That is, the model-to-real-length ratio is 1 to 48. The numbers of a ratio may be written with a colon between them or in fraction form. Both 1:48 and $\frac{1}{48}$ represent the ratio 1 to 48.

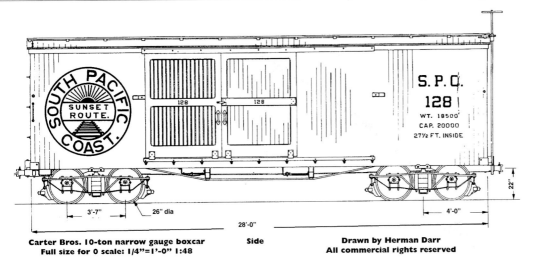

Carter Bros. 10-ton narrow gauge boxcar
Full size for O scale: 1/4"=1'-0" 1:48

Side

Drawn by Herman Darr
All commercial rights reserved

Display 2.2

"Carter Bros. 10-ton Narrow Gauge Boxcar (side view)," drawn by
Herman Darr, page 66. Copyright © March 1994 by *Railroad Model
Craftsman*, Carstens Publications Inc. Reprinted with permission.

The measurement given in the drawing states that the
boxcar shown in Display 2.2 is 28 feet long.

1. How long is an O scale model of this boxcar?

2. If HO scale is defined by the ratio 1 : 87, how long
   is an HO scale model of this boxcar? (Round your
   answer to the nearest 10th of an inch.)

3. If N scale is defined by the ratio 1 : 160, how long
   is an N scale model of this boxcar? (Round your
   answer to the nearest 10th of an inch.)

If you were building an O scale model of the boxcar in
Display 2.2, you'd need to know how wide to make the sliding
double door. That's not one of the measurements marked on
the drawing. How can you figure it out from the picture?
An easy way is to use a **proportion**, an equality between
two ratios, like this:

- From the answer to question 1, just before this, we know that
  an O scale model of this boxcar would be 7 inches long.

- Measure that length on the picture in the book (which is
  not a full-size picture of the model). Using a ruler marked
  in centimeters and millimeters, find the length of the boxcar
  in the picture, about 12.4 cm.

- Next measure the double door width in the picture. It is about 4.1 cm. This means that the ratio of the double-door width to the boxcar length is 4.1 : 12.4; in fraction form, it is $\frac{4.1}{12.4}$.

- Now because the ratio $\frac{\text{door width}}{\text{boxcar length}}$ should be the same in the model as it is in the picture, set up the equation

$$\frac{\text{door width}}{\text{boxcar length}} = \frac{4.1}{12.4} = \frac{x}{7}$$

The solution to this equation is the proper door width *in inches* for the O scale model.

Solving this equation depends on a fact about fractions that you probably already know. Two fractions are equal if, and only if, you get the same product both ways when you "cross multiply."

For example,

$$\frac{2}{3} = \frac{6}{9} \text{ because } 2 \cdot 9 = 3 \cdot 6$$

Using this process on our proportion, we get

$$\frac{4.1}{12.4} = \frac{x}{7}$$
$$12.4x = 4.1 \cdot 7$$
$$x = \frac{28.7}{12.4}$$
$$x = 2.3 \text{ inches (approx.)}$$

Cross multiplication is a handy way to test whether or not two fractions are equal. Why does it work? That is, how is this process related to the equality of two fractions? (*Hint:* Start by answering these simpler questions.)

1. How do you know whether or not two fractions with the *same denominator* are equal?

2. What's a sure way to find a common denominator (not necessarily the least) for two fractions?

1. Suppose you compute the width of the sliding double doors by repeating the process just described, but use a ruler marked in inches (and fractions of inches), rather than in centimeters. Will you get the same final answer? Why or why not? Try it. Does it come out the way you thought it would?

2. What is the width of the sliding double doors on the real boxcar?

3. Use the method just described to figure out the height of the sliding door on the O scale model, and also on the real boxcar. Can you use either a centimeter-marked or an inch-marked ruler?

4. How high off the rails will the top of the boxcar's roof be in O scale? In real life?

Now we are ready to tackle the question of describing more carefully the idea of *similar* objects. You go first.

How can the ideas of ratio and proportion be used to make a useful definition of what it means to say that two shapes are similar? Once you have a definition you like, test it by looking at Display 2.3. Are any of the figures (b), (c), or (d) similar to (a)? Are more than one of them similar to (a)? What does *your* definition tell you?

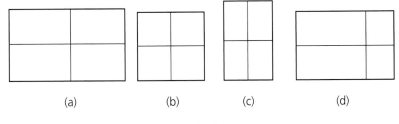

Display 2.3

Now it's our turn. First, here is a useful term that occurs often in mathematics— *constant*. A **constant** is a particular number that doesn't change throughout an entire example or discussion. Sometimes we know that a number is a constant, but we don't know or don't want to write down its exact value. In such cases, we can represent it by a letter and just say that this letter is a constant.

A Word to Know: Two objects are **similar** if there is a constant k such that the distance between any two points of one object is k times the distance between the corresponding two points of the other.

We call the constant k a **scaling factor.** Sometimes it is also called the *constant of proportionality.* Similar objects are also said to be in *proportion* to each other. The scaling factor tells you the relationship between the two different sizes. For example, the note at the bottom left of Display 2.2 says that the scaling factor for an O scale model of the boxcar is $\frac{1}{48}$. This means that the distance between any two points of the model should be exactly $\frac{1}{48}$ times the distance between the corresponding two points of the real boxcar.

Look at Display 2.2.

1. **What is the scaling factor for an HO scale model of this boxcar?**

2. **Think of the O scale model of the boxcar as the first object in the definition of *similar* and think of the real boxcar as the second. What is the scaling factor?**

Here's a simple example: The two rectangles in Display 2.4 are similar. Because a rectangle is determined by its four vertices (corner points), we can check similarity just by comparing the distances between corresponding vertices. In this case, the distance WX must be k times the distance AB for some scaling factor k and the distance XY must be k times the distance BC for the same k.

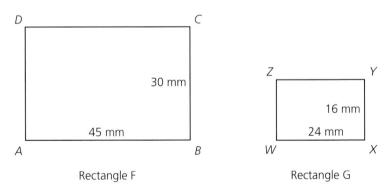

Rectangle F   Rectangle G

Display 2.4

Using the measurements (in millimeters) from Display 2.4, we have

$$24 = k \cdot 45 \quad \text{and} \quad 16 = k \cdot 30$$

That is, the ratios $\frac{24}{45}$ and $\frac{16}{30}$ both must equal the same number, k. Do they? You can check this in either of two ways:

1. simplify the two fractions and see that you come out with the same value for k; or

2. check that the two fractions are equal by cross-multiplying.

The second way often is more efficient, particularly when you don't need to know the value of the scaling factor. Here we see that

$$\frac{24}{45} = \frac{16}{30}$$

because

$$24 \cdot 30 = 45 \cdot 16$$

(Did you check our arithmetic to make sure?) In other words, the ratios of the corresponding side lengths form a proportion.

These questions refer to Display 2.4.

1. Use the Pythagorean Theorem to compute the length of the diagonal *AC* of rectangle *F*. Check your answer with a ruler.

2. Use a proportion to compute the length of the diagonal *WY* of rectangle *G*. Check your answer with a ruler.

3. Use the Pythagorean Theorem to compute the length of the diagonal *WY* of rectangle *G*. Compare your answer with your answer for part 2.

4. Because these two rectangles are similar, you can multiply the distance between two points of rectangle *F* by a scaling factor to find the distance between the corresponding two points of rectangle *G*. What is the numerical value of this scaling factor?

5. You can also multiply the distance between two points of rectangle *G* by a scaling factor to find the distance between the corresponding two points of rectangle *F*. What is the numerical value of this scaling factor? How is it related to your answer for part 4?

Problem Set: 2.1

1. A photocopier has reduced a diagram by a scaling factor of 60%.

   (a) If two points are 5 inches apart on the original diagram, how far apart are they on the copy?

   (b) If two points are 1 inch apart on the original diagram, how far apart are they on the copy?

   (c) If two points are 2 inches apart on the original diagram, how far apart are they on the copy?

   (d) If two points are 3 inches apart on the copy, how far apart are they on the original diagram?

   (e) If two points are 1 inch apart on the copy, how far apart are they on the original diagram?

   (f) If two points are 2 inches apart on the copy, how far apart are they on the original diagram?

   (g) The person who received the reduced copy of the diagram wants to blow it back up to its original size. What scaling factor should she use?

2. Both American football and Canadian football are played on rectangular fields, but the sizes of the fields are different:

   - The American field is $53\frac{1}{3}$ yards wide, 100 yards long from goal line to goal line, and has an extra 10 yards of end zone at each end.

   - The Canadian field is 65 yards wide, 110 yards long from goal line to goal line, and has an extra 10 yards of end zone at each end.

   (a) Make a sketch of each field and label it with the appropriate dimensions.

   (b) The two playing fields, without the end zones, are not proportional. How wide would the 100 yard American field have to be in order for it to be proportional to the Canadian field?

   (c) Are the two playing fields, including the end zones, proportional? Justify your answer.

   (d) The end-zone sizes are not proportional when compared with the lengths of the playing fields between them. How long would the Canadian end zone have to be in order for it to be proportional to the American one?

(e) How might the differences in field sizes affect the strategy of the game? Do you know of any major rule differences between the two games? How (if at all) are they related to the different field sizes?

3. Display 2.5 shows scale drawings of the front and side views of the Snydertown, PA, railroad depot. The drawing shows the length, width, and height of the real depot, and the scaling information is given in its upper right corner.

(a) If you were building an HO scale model of this depot and working with a metric ruler, what would be the length, width, and height of your model? Round your answer to the nearest millimeter.

(b) If you were building an HO scale model of this depot and working with a ruler marked in inches, what would be the length, width, and height of your model? Round your answer to the nearest 100th of an inch.

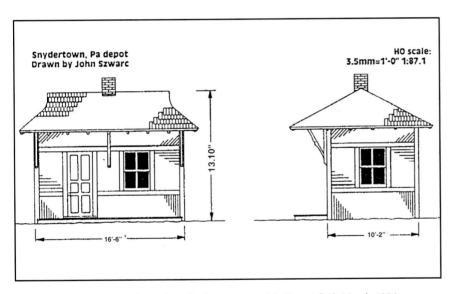

"Snydertown, PA depot," drawn by John Szwarc, page 85. Copyright© March 1994 by *Railroad Model Craftsman*, Carstens Publications, Inc. Reprinted with permission.

Display 2.5

4. Many model railroaders think of HO scale as "half-O."

   (a) Using this meaning, what is the scaling factor for HO scale? Express it as a ratio and also as a fraction.

   (b) What is the difference in length between a scale model of a 40 foot boxcar using the half-O ratio versus a model of the same boxcar using the other HO scale ratio, 1:87?

5. You have completed a precision drawing that just fits on an 11 by 17 inch piece of paper, with no room to spare on any edge.

   (a) You need a reduced copy that will fit inside a 6 by 10 inch box in a report that is being prepared. What is the largest scaling factor you can use when setting the copying machine? Round your answer down to the nearest percent. Why round *down*?

   (b) Your drawing is so well liked that it's going to be made into a wall poster. The shorter side of the rectangular poster must be 2 feet long; the other length can be cut exactly to your specifications. If you don't want to leave any extra margin, what scaling factor should you use? How long will the longer side of the poster be? Round your answer to the nearest tenth of an inch.

6. This problem refers to Display 2.4. Begin by tracing or copying this figure on a plain piece of paper.

   (a) On side *DC* of rectangle F, mark the point that is 30 mm to the right of *D*. Call this point *P*. Then find and mark the corresponding point, *P′* ("*P* prime"), on rectangle G.

   (b) On side *DA* of rectangle *F*, mark the point that is 15 mm below *D*. Call this point *Q*. Then find and mark the corresponding point, *Q′*, on rectangle G.

   (c) Use the Pythagorean Theorem to compute the distance between *P* and *Q* on rectangle *F*. Round your answer to the nearest mm. Check your result by measuring. Do you get the same answer? If not, explain what went wrong.

   (d) Find the distance between *P′* and *Q′* on rectangle G in three different ways,
   - using the Pythagorean Theorem,

   - using the scaling factor, and

   - by measuring.

   Round your answer to the nearest mm. Which way was easiest for you? Which way do you think is the most accurate? Which way do you like best? Why?

   (e) On side *ZY* of rectangle G. mark the point that is 10 mm to the right of *Z*. Call this point *R′*. Then find and mark the corresponding point, *R′*. on rectangle *F*.

   (f) On side *YX* of rectangle G. mark the point that is 12 mm below *Y*. Call this point *S′*. Then find and mark the corresponding point, *S*. on rectangle *F*.

   (g) Find the distance between *R* and *S* by measuring and by one other way. Round your answer to the nearest mm. Do you get the same answer both ways? If not, explain what went wrong.

7. Is the drawing of Alice in Display 2.6 out of proportion? How can you tell? Relate your explanation to our mathematical definition of proportion.

Display 2.6

2.2 Similar Triangles and Rectangles

There's a lot of information packed into the definition of similarity, along with a hidden difficulty. Let's unpack it carefully. Do you remember what it says? Here it is again, with two key words missing. Can you fill them in?

> Two objects are **similar** if there is a constant k such that the distance between _____ two points of one object is k times the distance between the _____ two points of the other.

The first missing word is *any*. It means that you can't control the choice of points when you apply this definition. No matter which two points *anybody* picks, the same constant k must work for them. The difficulty is hiding in the second missing word. Do you know what the word is? Can you describe the difficulty? Try to figure it out as you answer the following questions.

These questions refer to the two triangular regions, *F* and *G*, in Display 2.7.

1. Can you tell just by looking at these triangular regions *exactly* which point of region *F* should correspond to point *A* of *G*? What about point *B*?

2. Find one point of *G* for which, just by looking, you know the exact corresponding point of *F*. Can you find two points of *G* for which you know the corresponding points of *F*? Three? Four? Explain your answers.

3. Suppose you know that these two triangular regions are similar. How can you find which point of *F* corresponds exactly with point *A* of *G*? Do it if you can, and describe your method. Will your method work for point *B*? Why or why not?

4. What is the difficulty in applying the definition of similarity?

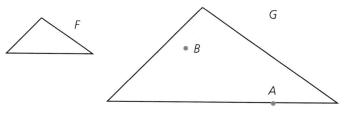

Display 2.7

Two drawings are shown in Display 2.8. Make a copy of each one that is twice the size of the original. That is, make copies that have a scaling factor of 2. Which one is easier to do, (a) or (b)? Why?

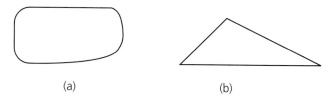

(a)   (b)

Display 2.8

Did the questions about Displays 2.7 and 2.8 help you to see the difficulty in using the definition of similar figures?

The problem is deciding which points of one figure really correspond to which points of the other.

For triangles, the process is easy. A triangle is determined by its vertices (its corners). Once you know where all three vertices are, only one triangle will fit. But sometimes figuring out which vertices of one polygon correspond to which vertices of another is not so simple. In many situations you just have to be told what the correspondence is. There are two common ways to do this.

• Corresponding vertices of two figures often are labeled with the same letter, but with different subscripts to indicate which figure the vertex is in. For instance, when we write two triangles as $\triangle A_1B_1C_1$ and $\triangle A_2B_2C_2$, we mean that the vertex A_1 of the first triangle corresponds to the vertex A_2 of the second triangle, B_1 corresponds to B_2, and C_1 corresponds to C_2.

• Sometimes the order in which the vertices are listed is intended to tell you the correspondence between the vertices of two polygons. (This often is the case on standard tests.) For instance, if two similar triangles are written as $\triangle ABC$ and $\triangle DEF$, you are expected to assume that A corresponds to D, B corresponds to E, and C corresponds to F.

The first of these ways is clearer, but the second way is simpler. This book usually uses the simpler method, unless it is likely to be confusing. Unless you are told otherwise, assume that the order in which the vertices of two polygons are listed tells you the correspondence between them.

Because the vertices of a triangle determine its size and shape, two triangles are similar if the distances between the vertices of one triangle are proportional to the distances between the corresponding vertices of the other. That's a lot of words to express a very simple idea. It's easier and clearer with symbols, as follows.

> **Triangles $A_1B_1C_1$ and $A_2B_2C_2$ are similar if all three ratios of the lengths of their corresponding sides are equal. In symbols,**
>
> $$\frac{A_1B_1}{A_2B_2} = \frac{B_1C_1}{B_2C_2} = \frac{A_1C_1}{A_2C_2}$$

To show you how assuming the correspondence of vertices from their listing order makes it easier to read and write such expressions, we restate this important principle without using subscripts.

$$\triangle ABC \text{ and } \triangle DEF \text{ are similar if } \frac{AB}{DE} = \frac{BC}{EF} = \frac{AC}{DF}$$

Which of these two forms do *you* think is easier to understand?

1. Are all three of the triangles in Display 2.9 similar? Use a ruler to help you justify your answer.

2. Can you draw two triangles, *ABC* and *DEF*, for which
   $$\frac{AB}{DE} = \frac{BC}{EF}$$
   but the triangles are *not* similar? If you can, do it. If not, explain why it cannot be done.

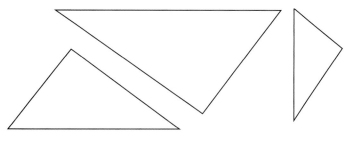

Display 2.9

For rectangles, there is an even easier test for simplicity. Two rectangles have the same shape if the ratio of their lengths equals the ratio of their widths. In symbols, two rectangles *ABCD* and *EFGH* (as shown in Display 2.10) are similar if

$$\frac{AB}{EF} = \frac{BC}{FG}$$

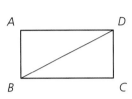
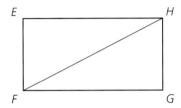

Display 2.10

 The test for similar rectangles checks only three of the four corner points. What about the fourth one? Refer to Display 2.10 as you answer these questions.

1. Suppose $\frac{AB}{EF} = \frac{BC}{FG} = k$ (where k is the scaling factor). Why must the ratios of corresponding sides that meet at *D* and *H* also equal k?

2. Why must the lengths of the corresponding diagonals also have the same ratio?
   Hint: Use the Pythagorean Theorem.

- In each row, the lengths of some of the sides have been given (in inches). Find values for the missing entries so that $\triangle 1$ and $\triangle 2$ are similar. Also find the scaling factor (from $\triangle 1$ to $\triangle 2$) in each case. You may copy the table onto your own paper and fill it in, if that helps you organize your work. Use your calculator whenever you want.

| | Triangle 1 | | | Triangle 2 | | | Scaling Factor |
	a	b	c	d	e	f	
(a)	8	10	14	32			
(b)		5.5	6.4	4.5	20.625		
(c)	20.5			90.2	121.44	198	
(d)	3.58		6.08		25.764	34.352	
(e)		10.85		24.2875	36.3475	52.0925	
(f)	12.5	4.8	8		3		

Display 2.13

3. The Make More Money Dept. of the U. S. Postal Service has decided to market a set of commemorative ceramic tiles displaying popular stamp designs of the 1990s. The tiles will be 6 inch squares, suitable for decorating kitchen counters, shower stalls, patio walks, etc. The stamps to be copied come in 4 different sizes (including allowance for a border).

   (a) regular issue: 20 x 22 mm
   (b) standard commemorative: 42 x 22 mm
   (c) oversize commemorative: 28 x 36 mm
   (d) special issue (love stamps, etc.): 27 x 20 mm

   For each stamp size, find the scaling factor that will make its design as large as possible on the tile. Then find the dimensions of the scaled tile design. Round your final answers to the nearest tenth of an inch. (*Hint:* In each case, one of the dimensions should be 6 inches.)

4. Little League baseball is similar to major league baseball in many ways. A major league baseball diamond is a square 90 feet on a side and the distance from the pitcher's mound to home plate is 60.5 feet. A Little League baseball diamond is a square 60 feet on a side.

   (a) Using your ruler, draw a square to represent a major league baseball diamond and then draw a proportional square representing a Little League baseball diamond.

(b) Use your calculator to find the proportional distance from the pitcher's mound to home plate in Little League, assuming that the two diamonds are in proportion.

(c) Another baseball league is called the Intermediate League. This league's diamond is a square 75 feet on a side. Using your ruler, draw a square representing an Intermediate League diamond that is proportional to your drawings of the other two diamonds.

(d) Use your calculator to find the proportional distance from the pitcher's mound to home plate in the Intermediate League, assuming that its diamond is proportional to the major league diamond.

(e) The official distances from the pitcher's mound to home plate are 46 feet in Little League and 54 feet in Intermediate League. They should *not* agree with the answers you got in parts (b) and (d). Are the official distances longer or shorter than the proportional ones? Why do you think this is the case?

5. The General Crunchies Co. is beginning a series of cutout models for the back of its breakfastfood boxes, starting with a camping theme. The first cutout is to be for a pup tent 7 feet long, 4 feet wide at the base, and 3 feet high at the peak. A sketch of the cutout pattern for this pup tent is shown in Display 2.14. The dashed lines are for folds, and the striped pieces are tabs for gluing the model together.

Unfortunately, the person who made this sketch was not very careful; some of the lengths and corners are not exactly right. Your job: Make an accurate pattern for this cutout, to a scale of $\frac{1}{2}$ inch to 1 foot. The measurements shown give you enough information to determine the rest of the shape. A ruler and a compass are the only tools you should need. Here are some questions to help you as you make your drawing.

(a) What is the scaling factor for this model?
(b) What are the dimensions of each slanted wall of the tent? How can you figure that out?
(c) Each front flap is a right triangle. If they are cut and folded accurately, they will close the front of the tent with no overlap. What are the side lengths of these triangles? How do you know?

(d) How can you use a compass to find the correct position of the right angle corners of the front flaps?

(e) How wide should you make the glue tabs? This is a free choice, within reason.

(f) Will your pattern fit on the back of a cereal box? What are its maximum length and width?

Draw your pattern on a plain piece of paper. Then cut it out, fold it up, and glue or tape it together. Does your pattern work?

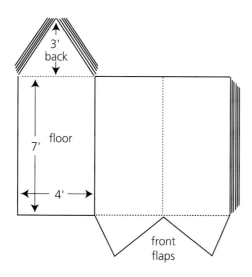

Display 2.14

6. The second in the series of General Crunchies cutout models is a lean-to. It is 8 feet from side to side, 7 feet from front to back, with a low back wall 3 feet high. The front opening is 6.5 feet high, and the roof overhangs about 6 inches in each direction. A sketch of the cutout pattern for this lean-to is shown in Display 2.15. The dashed lines are for folds, and the striped pieces are tabs for gluing the model together.

Using ruler and compass, make an accurate pattern for this cutout on a sheet of plain paper, to a scale of $\frac{1}{2}$ inch to 1 foot. Draw your pattern on a piece of plain paper. Then cut it out, fold it up, and glue or tape it together.

If your pattern were to be put on the back of a cereal box, how big would that back have to be?

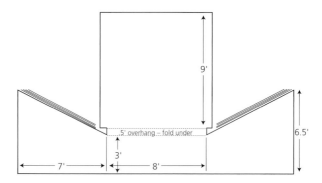

Display 2.15

7. Suppose you are drawing a new triangle that is similar to one you are given.

(a) If the scaling factor is greater than 1, will the new triangle be larger or smaller than the given one?

(b) If the scaling factor is positive but less than 1, will the new triangle be larger or smaller than the given one?

(c) If the scaling factor is 1, what will the new figure look like?

(d) If the scaling factor is 0, what will the new figure look like?

(e) Does it make sense to have a negative scaling factor? Why or why not?

8. Show that the similarity test for rectangles,

$$\frac{AB}{EF} = \frac{BC}{FG}$$

does not work for all quadrilaterals. That is, draw two quadrilaterals, *ABCD* and *EFGH*, that are not similar, but for which this equation is true. Verify these conditions by measuring your drawing.

9. Give a convincing argument to justify the following statement. Two right triangles are similar whenever the ratios of the lengths of *any two* pairs of their corresponding sides are equal.

2.3 How to Measure Angles

You have seen that similarity depends on knowing corresponding points of objects. You have also seen that the easiest corresponding points to identify are the "corner points," the vertices of angles. Usually, all the vertices (and some other points) in a diagram are labeled with letters. This makes it easy to name and keep track of angles. Sometimes the vertex alone is enough to identify the angle. When several different angles have the same vertex, other points are used to identify the sides, as you saw in Chapter 1.

You also saw that two angles are **congruent** if one can be placed on top of the other so that their vertices match and their corresponding sides lie along the same rays.
(A **ray** is part of a line that starts at a particular point and extends infinitely far in one direction.)

In Display 2.16, ∠A is congruent to exactly one of the other angles. Which one is it? How would you convince a friend who doesn't believe you that your choice is correct?

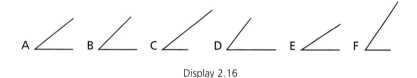

Display 2.16

Why do you think we say *ray*, instead of *line*, in the description of congruent angles? If we substitute *line* for *ray* in this description, can you find a counterexample? That is, can you find an example of two angles that fit the new description, but obviously are not the same size?

Comparing angles by placing one on top of the other is a simple and clear idea, but it's not always practical. The corner of a building, the peak of a roof, and a switch in a railroad track are just a few of the many, many cases of angles that can't just be traced or picked up and superimposed. To compare angles like that, we need a way to measure them.

Learning Outcomes

After studying this section, you will be able to:

Identify and construct congruent angles in various ways;

Measure angles in several different ways using degrees and slope;

Describe, construct, and measure angles in terms of rotation.

About Words

The word *angle* comes from the Latin word for corner, which is *angulus*.

About Words

The prefix *super-* means *above* or *over*. The verb *impose* means *put on*. So *superimpose* means put on from above.

But what shall we measure? To compare the angles, the important thing to measure is how fast the rays from the sides of the angle diverge (move away from each other). For instance, picture two mice walking along the (inner) rails away from the vertex of a railroad switch. How fast are they moving away from each other?

Railroads actually measure the angles of their switches this way. (They don't use mice, of course!) They measure the distance, say y, between the inner rails at some point and then they measure the distance, say x, from that place to the vertex of the switch. The ratio $\frac{x}{y}$ is called the *number* of the switch. It's the number of feet of track *for each foot of separation*, assuming that the tracks keep running straight away from the turnout in each direction. For instance, a #12 switch is an angle that provides 1 foot of separation for every 12 feet of track. The diagram in Display 2.17 shows how switch size is determined. (In this display, the switch is called a "turnout" because it comes from a model railroading book. Track switches are called turnouts by model railroaders to distinguish them from electrical switches.)

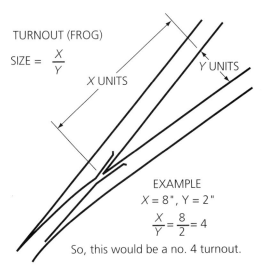

TURNOUT (FROG)

SIZE $= \dfrac{X}{Y}$

X UNITS

Y UNITS

EXAMPLE
$X = 8"$, $Y = 2"$
$\dfrac{X}{Y} = \dfrac{8}{2} = 4$

So, this would be a no. 4 turnout.

DETERMINING
TURNOUT SIZE

From *Practical Guide to HO Model Railroading* by *Model Railroader Magazine*.
Copyright © 1986 by Kalmbach Publishing Company. Reprinted with permission.

Display 2.17

The Moosehead Lake Railroad wants to lay new track near its eastern terminal. They want a side track to run parallel to the main line, but 20 feet away from it, to bypass a loading platform.

1. If they use a #12 switch, how far will it be from the vertex of the switch until the inner rails are 20 feet apart?

This switch is on a main track for express trains. This railroad, like many others, uses the number of a switch as a guide for the maximum safe train speed through that switch—double the switch number, in miles per hour. This means that the maximum safe train speed over a #12 switch is only 24 mph. They would like the switch to handle trains safely at about 40 mph.

2. What number switch do they need?

3. How far would it be from the vertex of the switch until the inner rails are 20 feet apart?

Their surveyors say that the distance from the end of the platform to the switch vertex cannot be more than 360 feet.

4. What is the largest size switch they can use?

5. What is the maximum train speed over this switch?

Using a ratio to measure the rate of separation between lines should sound familiar. That's what *slope* is about. The slope of the wheelchair ramp at the Fuzzy Friends Toy Co. built earlier in **MATH** *Connections* measures its height relative to the horizontal distance from its low end. This rise-over-run ratio measures how fast the ramp line diverges from the parking lot level, the horizontal axis.

Display 2.18 is a diagram of the wheelchair ramp. It is a straight ramp that rises 4 feet and has a horizontal length of 32 feet. The vertical line segments are the eight ramp supports. Each ordered pair tells you the location and length of a support. The first number is its horizontal distance from the left end of the ramp; the second number is its vertical length. If this ramp diagram is cut off at any one of these eight vertical segments, you have a right triangle.

1. Are all eight triangles similar? Justify your answer.

2. What does this have to do with the slope of the ramp line?

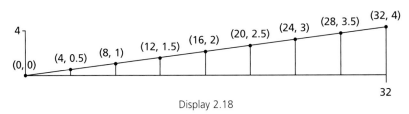

Display 2.18

The slope of a line in a coordinate system is a measure of the angle it makes with the horizontal axis. We can borrow that idea to measure angles, whether or not they are in a coordinate system. We can pick a point on one ray of an angle, measure the distance from that point to the vertex, and also measure the perpendicular distance from that point to the other ray. The ratio of that perpendicular distance divided by the distance to the vertex will be the same, no matter which point you pick. That makes the ratio a good measure of angle size; we'll call it the *slope measure* of the angle.

For instance, to find the slope measure of the angle made by the ramp and the ground in Display 2.18, we could begin by picking a point P on the ground under the ramp. If P is the point 16 feet to the right of the vertex, for example, then the slope measure of this angle is

$$\frac{\text{perpendicular distance from } P \text{ to ramp}}{\text{distance from } P \text{ to vertex}} = \frac{2}{16} = \frac{1}{8}$$

Here's another example. This one refers to Display 2.19. To find the (approximate) slope measure of $\angle AVB$, we can use a ruler to measure the segments AV and AB. Now, AV is about 3 inches long and AB is about 0.5 inches long, so

$$\text{approximate slope measure of } \angle AVB = \frac{AB}{AV} = \frac{0.5}{3} = \frac{1}{6}$$

We say approximate because the answer depends on measuring with a ruler, which is always only an approximation of actual length.

These questions refer to Display 2.19.

1. Use a ruler to find the approximate slope measures of ∠AVC, ∠AVD, and ∠AVE.

2. Find the approximate slope measures of ∠BVC and ∠DVE. (Watch out! What do you have to measure? Measure carefully.)

3. How are the slope measures of ∠AVD and ∠AVE related?

4. When you add the slope measures of ∠AVD and ∠DVE, do you get the slope measure of ∠AVE? Do you think you should? Why or why not?

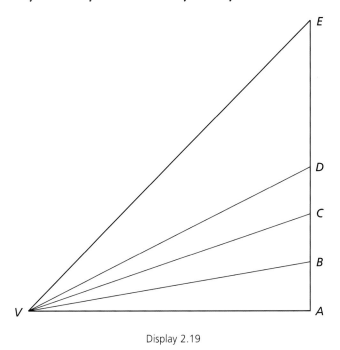

Display 2.19

The slope measure of an angle is very much like the way railroads measure switches, but it's not quite the same. What's different? (Look carefully at Displays 2.17 and 2.19.)

There are times when slope is a useful way to measure angles, but it applies easily only to angles smaller than a right angle. Also, as you may have noticed, slope measure does not behave very well with respect to addition and subtraction. We need to find a better way to measure angles.

Earlier in Chapter 1, you saw that any measurement system starts with choosing a *unit of measure*. Then everything is measured in terms of that unit. What shall we choose as a unit of measure for angles?

 Make up two different units of angle measure that nobody in the class has ever heard of before. Then decide which one you think is better. Give reasons to support your opinion.

To measure angles, one unit of measure we might choose is a right angle. Right angles are easy to make, so there would be no confusion about how big the unit is. But a right angle is bigger than a lot of angles we might want to measure; we ought to make the unit smaller. How about using some fraction of a right angle as the unit? That's exactly what the French Academy of Sciences started to do back in 1791, when they were setting up the metric system. The metric system was based on powers of 10, so they thought about making $\frac{1}{100}$th of a right angle the unit of angular measure. They called this unit a *grade*. Thus, a right angle would be a 100 grade angle; folding a right angle in half, we would get two 50 grade angles; and so on.

Instead, the French Academy decided to measure angles with a different unit—the *radian*. We shall see more about radian measure later, after studying circles in Chapter 4. You will see then why the radian is such a useful unit for measuring angles.

For now, we'll use a unit of angle measure that comes from the Babylonians, several thousand years ago. That unit is the *degree*. The Babylonians divided a right angle into 90 equal parts.[1] Each of these 90 parts is a **degree**. We abbreviate "degree" with the same symbol used for temperature degrees, a small raised circle. Thus a right angle is a 90° angle; half of a right angle is a 45° angle; and so on. Display 2.20 shows you the size of a degree.

---

[1]For reasons related to astronomy, their calendar, and their system of counting, they divided the four right angles made by two perpendicular lines into a total of 360 equal parts.

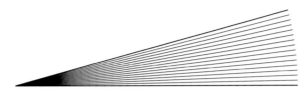

A 15° angle, measured in 1° steps.

Display 2.20

Display 2.21 shows ten angles. Estimate in degrees the measure of each one. (See if you can come within 5° of the exact size.)

a

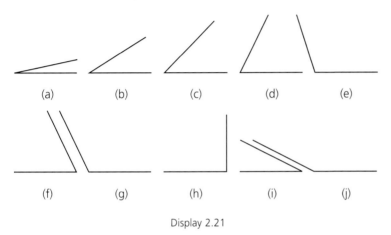

Display 2.21

Phrases to Know: The measures of some of the angles in Display 2.21 are less than one right angle. Such angles are called **acute angles**. Angles that have measure more than one right angle, but less than two, are called **obtuse angles**.

About Words

The words *acute* and *obtuse* come from the Latin words for sharpened and blunted, respectively.

1. Which of the angles in Display 2.21 are acute? Which are obtuse?

2. Restate the definitions of *acute* and *obtuse* angles in terms of degrees.

b

3. Here are some other angle measures. Which of these angles are acute? Which are obtuse?

   (a) 48° (b) 84° (c) 148° (d) 95° (e) 3° (f) 180° (g) 179°

How would you describe an angle of exactly 180°? What do you think it should be called? Is it really an angle? Why or why not?

To check your size estimates of the angles in Display 2.21, we need to measure the angles. The simplest tool for measuring angles is a **protractor**. Display 2.22 shows a picture of a protractor. Its basic shape is a semicircle resting on a straight base. The semicircle its divided into 180 equal (small) arcs, each one representing 1 degree. To measure an angle, put the center of the base at the vertex and align one side of the angle with the base line. The place at which the other side of the angle crosses the semicircle tells you the measure of the angle in degrees.

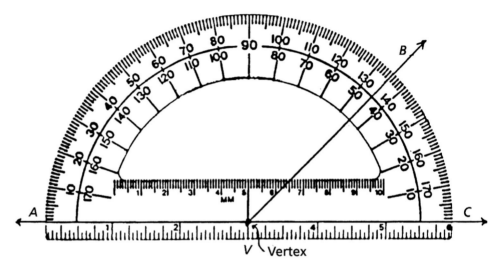

Measuring a 135° Angle and a 45° Angle With a Protractor

Display 2.22

Many protractors number the degree scale from both sides, so that an angle can be measured from either direction. That is, a side of the angle can be aligned with the base line either to the left or to the right of the vertex. In Display 2.22, for instance, the inner arch of numbers is used for measuring angles with base side to the right, while the outer arch of numbers measures angles with base side to the left. We sometimes say that the angles "open" to the right or to the left, depending on this alignment with the base. Thus, the ray that is heading up to the right (through B) is one side of a 45° angle, ∠BVC, that opens to the right; it is also one side of a 135° angle, ∠AVB, that opens to the left.

1. Use a protractor to measure, to the nearest degree, the ten angles shown in Display 2.21. Compare your measurements with your earlier estimates. Did you come within 5° each time?

   Hint: If you don't have a protractor handy, use tracing paper to copy the angles of Display 2.21 and lay them out, one by one, on top of the protractor picture in Display 2.22. You may have to extend the sides of the angles a bit to make this work.

2. Use a protractor to draw an angle of each of these sizes.

   (a) 48°   (b) 84°   (c) 148°
   (d) 95°   (e) 3°   (f) 179°

   This question can also be answered by using tracing paper and Display 2.22.

   In English, the verb *protract* means "draw out or pull out." Explain why *protractor* is a good name for the tool shown in Display 2.22.

Sometimes it is useful to think of angles in terms of rotation. That is, if we think of the sides of an angle as two arrows that pivot on the same endpoint (like the hands of a clock), then the size of an angle measures how far one arrow has rotated away from the other. It is customary to treat counterclockwise rotations as positive and clockwise rotations as negative.

From this viewpoint, there is no reason to stop measuring angles at 180°. We can measure all the way around the circle counterclockwise, getting larger and larger angles, until we get back to where we began. In fact, this is what the Babylonians had in mind when they defined the degree. They divided the entire circle into 360 equal parts. By rotating clockwise, we can get angles with negative measures. You might think of measuring such angles by using a double protractor, as in Display 2.23.

A Phrase to Know: An angle with a measure of more than 180° but less than 360° is called a **reflex angle.**

About Words

The root *flex* comes from the Latin word for bend, and the prefix *re-* means back. Thus, a *reflex* angle is one that bends back.

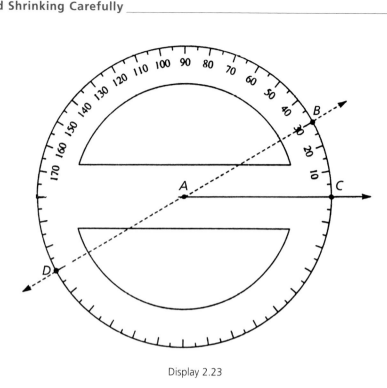

Display 2.23

 These questions refer to Display 2.23. Think of ray *AC* as the starting side of each angle.

1. What is the measure of the counterclockwise angle with other side *AB*?

2. What is the measure of the counterclockwise angle with other side *AD*?

3. What is the measure of the clockwise angle with other side *AD*?

4. What is the measure of the clockwise angle with other side *AB*?

5. What is the measure of the counterclockwise angle with other side *AC*?

6. What is the measure of the clockwise angle with other side *AC*?

7. Which of the six angles just described are reflex angles?

8. What numbers should be used to label the next three of the longer hash marks beyond point *D* in the counterclockwise direction?

9. What numbers should be used to label the next three of the longer hash marks beyond point *D* in the clockwise direction?

A review of angle terminology using degree measure follows.

- An angle of measure less than 90° (but more than 0°) is an **acute angle**.

- An angle of measure 90° is a **right angle**.

- An angle of measure more than 90°, but less than 180°, is an **obtuse angle**.

- An angle of measure 180° is a **straight angle**.

- An angle of measure more than 180°, but less than 360°, is a **reflex angle**.

Problem Set: 2.3

1. (a) Copy Display 2.24a, add letters to it, and name all the angles. How many angles do you find?
   (b) Copy Display 2.24b, add letters to it, and name all the angles. How many angles do you find?
   (c) Copy Display 2.24c, add letters to it, and name all the angles. How many angles do you find?
   (d) If you were to copy Display 2.24d, add letters to it, and name all the angles, how many angles do you think you would find?
   (e) What would be the next step in this pattern?
   (f) Try to describe how this pattern works in general.

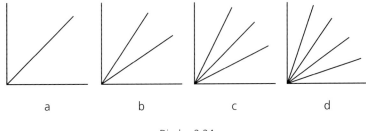

Display 2.24

2. Trace Display 2.24b on a piece of patty paper. Extend the four lines so that each one is at least 3 inches long. Label the vertex V, and label the other ends of the segments P, Q, R, and S in clockwise order, starting from the top.

   (a) There are five acute angles in this figure. List them in a column, using their three-letter names. Then measure each one with a protractor and write its degree measure next to its name. Round to the nearest degree.

   (b) Using a ruler, find the slope measure of each of these

five angles, and write that next to its degree measure. Round to two decimal places.

(c) How are $\angle QVR$ and $\angle RVS$ related to $\angle QVS$? How are their degree measures related? How are their slope measures related?

(d) What angle is formed by putting together $\angle PVQ$, $\angle QVR$, and $\angle RVS$? What is the sum of their degree measures? Do you get a similar result when you add their slope measures? What do we mean by similar?

(e) Write a paragraph comparing degree measure and slope measure. Which system is easier to use? Which behaves better in relation to arithmetic? Which do you like better? Give reasons to support your opinions.

3. Using just a pencil and a ruler, draw your best estimate of an angle of each of the following sizes. Try to get within 5° of the correct size. When you are finished, measure with a protractor to see how close you came. How many were within 5°? How many were within 3°? Did you get any to within 1°?

   (a) 90°   (b) 45°   (c) 30°   (d) 60°   (e) 10°
   (f) 180°   (g) 135°   (h) 100°   (i) 52°   (j) 175°
   (k) 270°   (l) 225°   (m) 240°   (n) 300°   (o) 359°

4. Assume here that we are referring to a standard 12 hour clock and that the answers to these questions are not reflex angles.

(a) When a clock reads 3 p.m., what is the measure of the angle between the hour hand and the minute hand?

(b) When a clock reads 5 p.m., what is the measure of the angle between the hour hand and the minute hand?

(c) When a clock reads 6:30 p.m., what is the measure of the angle between the hour hand and the minute hand? Explain your answer.

(d) When a clock reads 9:30 p.m., what is the measure of the angle between the hour hand and the minute hand? Explain your answer.

(e) Is the process of finding the (nonreflex) angle between the hands of a clock a function? If so, what are its domain and range? If not, why not?

5. Assume here that we are referring to a standard 12 hour clock.

   (a) If the angle between the hour hand and the minute hand of a clock is 180°, what time is it? Can there be more than one correct answer to this question? Can there be more than two? Explain your answer.

   (b) If the angle between the hour hand and the minute hand of a clock is 120°, what time is it? Can there be more than one correct answer to this question? Can there be more than two? Explain your answer.

   (c) Is the process of finding the time from the (nonreflex) angle between the hands of a clock a function? This process is the reverse of the one described in question 4(e). If so, what are its domain and range? If not, why not?

6. (a) Draw five different triangles. For each one, measure its angles and add up the three numbers you get. Are your five sums related in any way? If so, how? Compare your results with those of two classmates.

(b) Draw five different quadrilaterals (four-sided polygons). For each one, measure its angles and add up the four numbers you get. Are your five sums related in any way? If so, how? Compare your results with those of two classmates.

(c) What should be the next group of questions in this sequence? Answer them.

(d) Can you see any sort of pattern here? If so, what?

7. (a) The real protractor used to make Display 2.22 was too big to be copied full size, so we reduced it. What scaling factor did we use (approximately)? How do you know?

(b) If we measured the angles of Display 2.21 using the real protractor instead of the one in Display 2.22, would we get different answers? If you say Yes, describe a way of converting one set of answers to the other. If you say No, explain why the measurements shouldn't change.

2.4 Finding Angle Size Efficiently

In Section 2.3 we talked about two ways of measuring angles— by slope and by degrees. Here is an example from house building that shows how they are related.

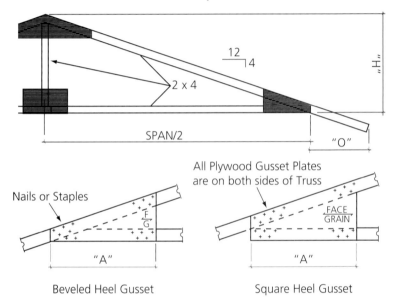

33–11. An example of a nail-glued truss plan for a king-post truss with a 4-in:12 slope. This is one of the designs available from the American Plywood Association.

All Plywood Gusset Plates are on both sides of Truss

Nails or Staples

Beveled Heel Gusset

Square Heel Gusset

From *Carpentry and Building Construction*, 5th edition, page 483, by John L. Feirer, Gilbert R. Hutchings and Mark D. Feirer. Copyright © 1997 by Glencoe/McGraw-Hill. Reprinted with permission.

Display 2.25

Learning Outcomes

After studying this section, you will be able to:

Use the calculator functions TAN and TAN[-1] to convert angle measures from degrees to slope, and vice versa;

Explain the meanings of the terms *supplementary* and *vertical* angles;

Apply the defining properties of vertical and supplementary angles in various settings.

Display 2.25 shows a diagram for a king-post truss— a type of roof support. The diagram contains most of the information needed for building this truss once you know the width of the house (the *span*). In particular, it tells you that the slope of the roof is 4 : 12. That is, the roof rises 4 inches for every 12 inches of span from side to center. This is the meaning of

in the upper part of the diagram.

If the house is 30 feet wide (measured from the outsides of the walls), about how long is the vertical center post? Answer to the nearest foot. In actual construction, you would have to allow a few inches for the width of the beams. Along the sloped top beam, about how far is it from the peak to the outside wall? Don't include the overhang ("O" *as in Display 2.25*). Explain how you found your answers.

The lower half of Display 2.25 shows the shape of the *gussets*. These are the plywood supports that go on the sides of each joint. As you can see, the top edge of each gusset should be cut on an angle to match the slope of the roof. Often the gussets are cut from plywood sheets before assembling the trusses, using a table saw or a radial arm saw in a woodworking shop.

Here's the problem. Table saw settings for angle cuts are marked in degrees, not by slope. You need to know what degree setting corresponds to the roof slope. But that's OK—your calculator can tell you the degree value for any slope! You just have to know how to ask for it.

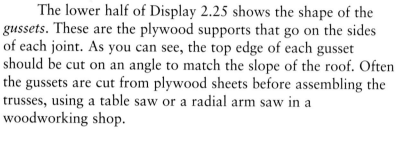

Display 2.26

The correspondence between the degree measure of an angle and its slope measure is a function. Each degree measurement has exactly one slope value. And if we restrict ourselves to angles that are less than 90° (as we would when building a roof), the opposite is also true. Each slope measurement has exactly one degree value.

- The process that turns the degree measure of an angle into its slope measure is called the **tangent function**; its calculator key is marked TAN.

- The reverse process, which turns slope measure into degree measure, is called the **inverse tangent function**; its calculator key is marked TAN^{-1}.

In general, a function that reverses the correspondence process of another function is called the **inverse** of that other function. Later you will see how trigonometry gives us an explanation of how the calculator is able to get each of these measurements from the other. You will also see then why the name *tangent* is used for this function. For now, we will concentrate on ways of using this handy tool.

To make the gusset shown in Display 2.26 with a table saw, we would need to know the measure of ∠V in degrees. To find this with your calculator, answer the following questions. (Before you start, make sure that your calculator is in Degree mode. This means that the calculator is using the degree as its unit of angle measure.)

1. What is the slope measure of ∠V?

2. Before calculating the degree measure of ∠V, estimate it by relating the picture to your idea of a right angle, as follows:

   (a) Is ∠V more or less than half a right angle?

   (b) Do you think that ∠V is more or less than a quarter of a right angle?

   (c) What is your best estimate of the degree measure of ∠V?

3. Which calculator function converts slope to degree measure? Use it to find the degree measure of ∠V to the nearest tenth of a degree. How does your answer compare with your estimate? If there is a difference of more than 10°, which answer do you trust more, the estimate or the computation?

4. Which calculator function converts degree measure to slope? Use it to check your answer. Do you get back the original slope? If not, what do you think went wrong?

1. Draw a horizontal line on a piece of paper. Then use a protractor to draw a line that makes a 30° angle with your first line.

a

2. Use your calculator to find the slope of the second line relative to the horizontal line. Explain how you do this.

3. How can you check this answer by measuring your drawing? Do it. Do your results agree? If not, can you explain what's wrong?

4. Draw a 30° angle on your calculator by graphing an appropriate equation. Does the angle in your graph look to be the same size as the one you drew? If not, can you explain what's wrong and how to fix it?

5. Is the slope made by a 60° angle double the slope made by a 30° angle? Check by whatever method you choose.

6. Think of a question related to this exercise that you would like to have answered.

Angles often occur in related groups, so that you can find the size of two or more angles by measuring just one of them. Here's a case where the measure of one angle determines the measure of four! When you draw two crossing lines to make an angle, you actually make four angles. (See Display 2.27.) The measures of each pair of these angles are related in one of two special ways. Can you see how?

Choose any two of the four numbered angles shown in Display 2.27. In what way are their measures related? Give a reason to justify your answer.

b

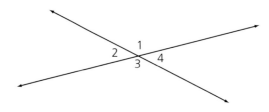

Display 2.27

A Phrase to Know: Two angles that are formed by two intersecting lines and do not have a side in common are called **vertical angles**.

How many pairs of vertical angles can you find in Display 2.27? What are they?

a

A Phrase to Know: Two angles with measures that add to 180° are called **supplementary angles**.

How many pairs of supplementary angles can you find in Display 2.27? What are they?

b

Each of these special pairs of angles has a useful property.

- Supplementary angles placed alongside one another so that their vertices and a single side coincide to form a straight angle (a straight line).

- The measures of vertical angles are equal.

We know that the first statement is true because the measure of a straight angle is 180°. The second statement can be approached in several ways. One simple way is to try an experiment. Draw two crossing lines at random on a sheet of scrap paper; then fold it through the crossing point so that the rays of the two different lines coincide. You will see that the vertical angles are congruent; they match exactly.

Here's another way of seeing that the measures of vertical angles are equal. It's a little more formal, but it's more reliable because it doesn't depend on a particular pair of lines or on your paper folding skill.

Form any pair of vertical angles—say ∠1 and ∠3, as in Display 2.27. Notice that ∠1 and ∠2 are supplementary, and ∠2 and ∠3 are also supplementary. That is,

$$\angle 1 + \angle 2 = 180° \text{ and } \angle 2 + \angle 3 = 180°$$

This means that the two sums equal each other:

$$\angle 1 + \angle 2 = \angle 2 + \angle 3$$

Subtracting ∠2 from both sides of this equation, we get

$$\angle 1 = \angle 3$$

That is, the measures of the vertical angles must be equal.

1. How many pairs of supplementary angles can you find in Display 2.28? What are they? Justify your answer.

2. How many pairs of vertical angles can you find in Display 2.28? What are they? Justify your answer.

3. Draw a picture of vertical angles that are supplementary. What other property *must* such angles have? Justify your answer.

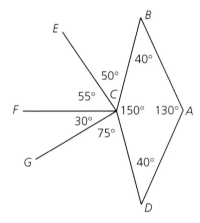

Display 2.28

Problem Set: 2.4

1. In this section you learned how to use the TAN and TAN⁻¹ functions of your calculator to convert the measure of an angle from degrees to slope and vice versa. Use your calculator to make the following conversions. Round your answers to two decimal places.

   (a) Convert from degrees to slope measure:

       30°   65°   46°   12°   89°   89.5°   1°

   (b) Convert from slope measure to degrees:

       $\frac{1}{2}$ 2 $\frac{6}{7}$ 1.25   23   1   10,000

2. Answer these questions *without* using your calculator. Choose the larger angle in each of the following pairs. Give a reason to justify your choice.

   (a) $\angle A = 42°$; the slope measure of $\angle B$ is $\frac{7}{6}$

   (b) $\angle C = 53°$; the slope measure of $\angle D$ is 0.985

   (c) $\angle E = 100°$; the slope measure of $\angle F$ is 250

   (d) $\angle G$ is a right angle; the slope measure of $\angle H$ is 9000.09

   (e) $\angle J = 47°$; the slope measure of $\angle K$ is $\frac{7}{3}$

   (f) $\angle L = 73°$; $\angle M$ is its supplement

   (g) $\angle N = 98°$; $\angle P$ is its supplement

   (h) The slope measure of $\angle Q$ is 98; $\angle R$ is its supplement

3. Mr. Santos is painting his house. He needs to be able to rest the top of his ladder on the roof edge, which is 18 feet above the ground. His ladder, fully extended, is just 20 feet long, but it carries this warning.

   Do not exceed 70° angle of elevation between ladder and ground.

   (a) Why do you think the ladder carries this warning?

   (b) Can Mr. Santos safely use his ladder if it rests on the roof edge? Explain, using a mathematical argument. *Hints:* Draw a sketch. Use the Pythagorean Theorem. Think about the TAN function of your calculator.

   (c) If you were preparing a report for a consumer research group, what would you give as the maximum safe height (to the nearest inch) that this 20 foot ladder can reach? Why?

   Problems 4 and 5 are about sundials. The sundial is civilization's oldest timekeeping device. It doesn't require any moving parts, batteries, or electronics, and—unlike modern clocks—it constantly reminds us that time, as we humans define it, is based upon the movement of the Earth relative to the Sun. As the Earth rotates on its axis, the Sun appears in different places in the sky, causing the shadow of a fixed object on the Earth to change. This change is what marks the hours on a sundial.

For more than 4000 years, sundials in many shapes and sizes have graced courtyards and cities, inspiring their users with such inscriptions as:

Carpe Diem (*Seize the day!*)

Tempus Fugit (*Time flies.*)

Utere, Non Numera (*Use them, don't count them.*)

Omnes Vulnerant, Ultima Necat (*Each one wounds, the last one kills.*)

Una Ex His Erit Tibi Ultima (*One of these will be your last.*)

Mach' es wie die sonnenuhr, zähl' die heiteren stunden nur (*Do as the sundial: count only the bright hours.*)

All but one of these quotes are shown in their original Latin.[1] Which one is the exception? In what language is it written?

The most surprising thing about sundials is that they work at all! As the seasons change, the sun rises and sets at different times and takes a higher or lower path across the sky. The daily shadow patterns are always changing. But *they change in a predictable way* that can be used to tell time! You just have to make exactly the right triangular shape and put it in exactly the right position, like this:

- Cut a right triangle (out of wood or metal or anything else rigid) so that the measure of one of its angles is exactly the latitude of the place where you are on the Earth. Do you know what *latitude* means? If not, look it up.

- Place the triangle upright on a flat surface in a sunny location, with its hypotenuse slanting upward, away from its latitude-angle vertex and headed toward the North Star.

Then the shadow cast by the slanted edge of the triangle at a particular time of day will lie along the same line on the surface every day of the year! It sounds like magic, but it's science. If you study astronomy, you'll see why this works as it does[†]. Sundials like this have the hours marked as lines on the

---

[1]Source: *Sundials: History, Theory, and Practice*, by René J. Rohr, (Toronto: University of Toronto Press, 1970).

[†]If you can't wait until then, you might look at *Sundials, Their Theory and Construction*, by Albert E. Waugh, (New York: Dover Publications, 1973).

flat (horizontal) surface. The upright triangular piece is called a **gnomon**. For a sundial to work properly, the shape and position of its gnomon must be exactly right.

About Words

Gnomon is derived from the Greek word meaning one who knows.

2.4 Finding Angle Size Efficiently

4. (a) Hartford, Connecticut, is near 42° N latitude. The proper angle and position for a gnomon there is shown in Display 2.29 as ∠ BAC. Calculate the height of this gnomon for each of these horizontal (base) dimensions:

    (i) 4 in.　　(ii) 7 in.　　(iii) 11 in.

    Round your answers to the nearest tenth of an inch.

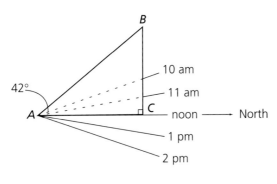

Display 2.29

(b) Using an 8.5" × 11" sheet of thick paper or cardboard, cut out a gnomon that would work for a sundial in Hartford.

(c) Find out the latitude of your home town (look on the edges of a road map) and make a sundial gnomon that will work there. Choose whatever base size you want.

(d) Repeat part (a) above for locations in Fairbanks, Alaska, at 65° N latitude and Miami, Florida, at 25° N latitude.

5. (a) The Big Ben Sundial Co. exports sundials to major cities around the world. Their basic model has a right triangular gnomon with a 24 cm horizontal side. What is the proper height for this gnomon in each of the following cities? (Do you know the country of each one?)

Athens	Beijing	Berlin
Cairo	Calcutta	Lagos
London	Moscow	Mexico City
Panama City	Paris	Rome
San Juan	San Salvador	Singapore
Stockholm	Tel Aviv	Tokyo

Round your answers to the nearest mm. (You'll need to start with a globe, a world atlas, an encyclopedia, or a good map of the northern hemisphere.)

(b) Where in the northern half of the world are accurate gnomons shaped like *isosceles* right triangles? Locate at least one town or city in North America for which this is true.

(c) What would an accurate gnomon at the equator look like? What about at the North Pole?

2.5 Parallel Lines and the Angle Sum of a Triangle

In Section 2.4 you saw some properties of angles formed by intersecting lines. Now we look at the case of lines that do not intersect. They don't form any angles by themselves, of course, but angles formed by crossing such lines with another line have some useful relationships. Let's begin with a reminder of a few basic facts that you may already know.

- In a plane, straight lines that never intersect, no matter how far they are extended, are called **parallel**.

- The perpendicular distance between two parallel lines is the same everywhere, no matter where you check it.

- If we put a coordinate system on the plane, parallel lines will always have the same slope.

Display 2.30(a) shows a line, *t*, that intersects two parallel lines, making eight angles. Which of these angles do you think are equal? Give reasons to support your answers.

Learning Outcomes

After studying this section, you will be able to:

Explain the meaning of the terms *corresponding*, *alternate interior*, and *complementary* angles;

Recognize and apply the equality of corresponding angles and alternate interior angles in relation to parallelism of lines;

Use in various settings the fact that the angle sum of any triangle is 180°.

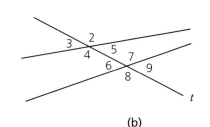

(a)   (b)

Display 2.30

The situation pictured in Display 2.30(a) is sometimes described as "parallel lines cut by a *transversal*". A **transversal** is a straight line that intersects two or more other straight lines at distinct points; *t* is the transversal in this figure.

About Words

Transversal is related to the verb *traverse*, which means go across. Traverse City is in northern Michigan. Can you find out how it got its name?

The key to understanding parallel lines cut by a transversal is seeing that an angle at one crossing point should have the same measure as the angle in the same relative position at the other crossing point. For instance, in Display 2.30(a), ∠1 and ∠5 should have the same measure. In Display 2.30(b), ∠1 and ∠5 do not have the same measure because the two lines are not parallel. (Measure them with a protractor to convince yourself.)

One way to convince yourself of this fact is to make a picture on your graphing calculator. Set the window to include X from 1 to 10, Y from -5 to 5. Then graph the equations

$$y_1 = x - 3 \text{ and } y_2 = x - 6$$

The picture you get should look something like Display 2.30(a), with the *x*-axis as the transversal. The slope of each of the two parallel lines measures the angle it makes with the *x*-axis. But both lines have the same slope! (What is it?) Thus, they are congruent angles; they have the same measure.

A Phrase to Know: When two lines are crossed by a transversal, the two angles that are in the same relative position at the two crossing points are called **corresponding angles.**

Name the four pairs of corresponding angles in Display 2.30(a). Are the same pairs corresponding angles in Display 2.30(b)? Why or why not?

One use of corresponding angles is to see if two lines actually are parallel.

A Fact to Know: Two lines crossed by a transversal are parallel *if and only if* the measures of any pair of corresponding angles are equal.

A Phrase to Know: The phrase **if and only if** means that the two statements it connects are logically equivalent. If either one is true, so is the other.

If we know that two lines are parallel, then the corresponding angles formed by any transversal *must* be equal. In Display 2.30(a), the two unlabeled lines are parallel, so ∠1 = ∠5, ∠2 = ∠6, and so on.

On the other hand, if two lines crossed by a transversal have an equal pair of corresponding angles, then the lines *must* be parallel. In Display 2.31(a), we can check to see if the lines are parallel by finding out if the two marked angles (or any other corresponding pair) are equal. In other words, knowing that two corresponding angles have the same measure guarantees that, no matter how far you extend these two lines in either direction, the distance between them will stay the same.

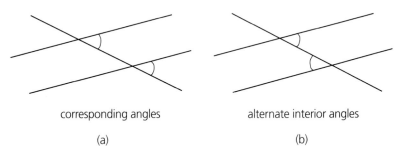

corresponding angles   alternate interior angles

(a)   (b)

Display 2.31

Display 2.31(b) illustrates another useful pair of angles that occur when two lines are crossed by a transversal.

A Phrase to Know: When two lines are crossed by a transversal, two angles with different vertices that are between the two lines and on opposite sides of the transversal are called **alternate interior angles.**

1. Name all the pairs of alternate interior angles in Display 2.30(a).

2. What do you think *alternate exterior angles* are? Make a sketch to illustrate your answer. Then name at least one pair of alternate exterior angles in Display 2.30(a).

Alternate interior angles can also be used to determine if two lines actually are parallel.

A Fact to Know: Two lines crossed by a transversal are parallel *if and only if* the measures of any pair of alternate interior angles are equal.

The parallel lines in Display 2.30(a) guarantee that ∠1 = ∠7 and ∠4 = ∠6. In Display 2.31(b), we can check to see if the lines are parallel by finding out if the two marked angles are equal.

How can the statement that relates alternate interior angles to parallels be derived from the statement that relates corresponding angles to parallels?

Let's pull together what we know so far about parallel lines and the angles formed by a transversal. For any two lines in a plane, the following statements are **equivalent**. That is, if we know that *any one* of them is true, then we know that *all* of them are true.

1. The lines are parallel.

2. The lines never meet, no matter how far they are extended.

3. The distance between the lines is the same everywhere.

4. For some transversals, two corresponding angles are equal.

5. For any transversal, all pairs of corresponding angles are equal.

6. For some transversals, two alternate interior angles are equal.

7. For any transversal, all pairs of alternate interior angles are equal.

A very important fact about triangles follows from 7.

A Fact to Know: The angle sum of any triangle is 180°.

That is, if we draw *any* **triangle** of *any* shape and add the measures of its three angles, the sum of the angles will *always* be 180°.

If a triangle contains a right angle, the sum of its other two angles must also be a right angle. Two angles that are related to each other in this way have many interesting, useful properties. This special case arises often enough to have a name of its own.

Words to Know: Two angles with measures that add to 90° are called **complementary angles**. Each one is called the **complement** of the other.

Answer these questions to see why the sum of the angles of a triangle is *always* 180°, regardless of the shape of the triangle. The questions refer to Display 2.32, which shows a triangle with a line through its top vertex, parallel to its base line.

1. Which three angles must you add to form the sum of the angles of this triangle?

2. What can you say about the two angles labeled 1? Why?

3. What can you say about the two angles labeled 2? Why?

4. What can you say about the angle formed by angles 1, 2, and 3 at the top of the figure? Why?

5. Are we done? Why or why not?

6. Do your answers to any of the preceding questions depend on knowing the measures of angles 1, 2, and 3?

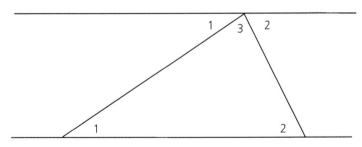

Display 2.32

In an earlier chapter you saw that polygons could be triangulated (subdivided into triangles). Use this fact to help you answer these questions.

1. What is the angle sum of a quadrilateral? Do all quadrilaterals have the same angle sum? Justify your answers.

2. What is the angle sum of a pentagon? Do all pentagons have the same angle sum? Justify your answers.

3. What is the angle sum of a hexagon? Do all hexagons have the same angle sum? Justify your answers.

4. If someone who was hiding a polygon told you the number of sides of that polygon, could you discover its angle sum? Would you bet $100 that you were right without seeing the polygon first? Explain.

1. When you cross parallel lines with parallel transversals, what kind of figure do you get? What is it called?

2. When this figure was defined in Chapter 1, did the definition use parallel lines? How would you define it, if you were making up your own definition?

3. Do you think that your definition and the definition in Chapter 1 always refer to exactly the same figures? Explain.

Problem Set: 2.5

1. (a) Draw a capital letter of the alphabet that is formed by a pair of alternate interior angles and one that is formed by a pair of vertical angles.

   (b) Why does each of these statements about some angle, ∠A, *not* make sense by itself? *Hint:* It's the same reason in each case.

   ∠A is a vertical angle.

   ∠A is an alternate interior angle.

   ∠A is a corresponding angle.

   ∠A is a supplementary angle.

2. These questions refer to the roof truss diagrams in
    Display 2.33.

    (a) Truss B outlines two right triangles. To the nearest tenth
        of a degree, what is the size of each angle in these right
        triangles? Explain how you got your answers.

    (b) Suppose the vertical center post in Truss B is 5 feet
        long. Find the lengths of the other two sides of each
        right triangle. Round your answers to the nearest inch.

    (c) The top part of Truss C outlines two right triangles.
        To the nearest tenth of a degree, what is the size of
        each angle in these right triangles? Explain how you
        got your answers.

    (d) Suppose the vertical center post in Truss C is 9 feet
        long. Find the lengths of the other two sides of each
        right triangle. Round your answers to the nearest inch.

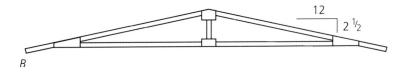

B

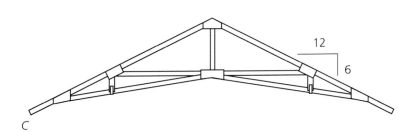

C

From *Carpentry and Building Construction*, 5th edition, page 487, by John L. Feirer,
Gilbert R. Hutchings and Mark D. Feirer. Copyright © 1997 by Glencoe/McGraw-Hill.
Reprinted by permission.

Display 2.33

3. The diagram in Display 2.34 is a puzzle that has these properties,
   - *CDJK* is a rectangle.

   - ∠*F* and ∠*G* are right angles.

   - Triangles *ABN* and *HLN* are equilateral.

   - ∠*AML* and ∠*MLB* are supplementary angles.

   In this figure, 14 of the angles are congruent to ∠*BEH*, which is marked by a star. Without measuring anything, find at least five of them. Can you find ten? Can you find them all? Justify each angle you pick.

   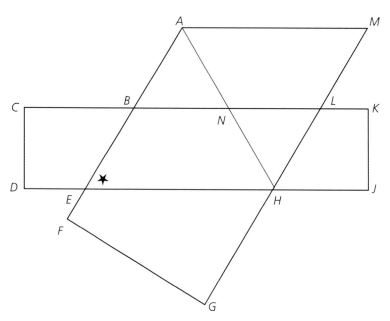

   The measurements in this figure are not exact.

   Display 2.34

4. (a) ∠*A* and ∠*B* have slope measures $\frac{2}{5}$ and $\frac{5}{2}$, respectively. Find their degree measures, rounded to one decimal place. Then find the sum of their degree measures and the product of their slope measures. How are ∠*A* and ∠*B* related?

   (b) ∠*C* and ∠*D* have slope measures 6.25 and 0.16, respectively. Find their degree measures, rounded to one decimal place. Then find the sum of their degree measures and the product of their slope measures. How are ∠*C* and ∠*D* related?

(c) $\angle E = 33°$ and $\angle F = 57°$. Find their slope measures, rounded to two decimal places. Then find the sum of their degree measures and the product of their slope measures. How are $\angle E$ and $\angle F$ related?

(d) What pattern do you see in the information from parts (a) − (c)? Make up a general rule based on that pattern.

(e) What angle should be paired with a 72° angle to fit the pattern you see? Does your general rule work for these two angles? Explain.

(f) An angle has slope measure $\frac{3}{7}$. What is the slope measure of its complement? You should be able to find this *without* finding the degree measure of the angle.

(g) An angle has slope measure 3.58. What is the slope measure of its complement? You should be able to find this *without* finding the degree measure of the angle.

5. In Chapter 1 we saw that some figures can be used to tile an area. That is, copies of a figure can fill in an area completely, with no gaps between edges.

(a) Extend the top and bottom parallel lines in Display 2.32 to form a long strip. Then describe how the triangle in the figure can be used to tile the strip as far as you like in either direction. Draw a sketch to illustrate your description.

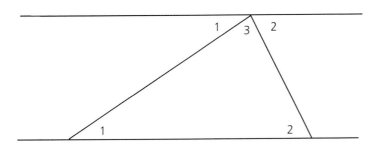

Display 2.32

(b) Draw a triangle of any shape you choose. Make it as weird as you like! Then show how the process you described in part (a) guarantees that your triangle can be used to tile a strip between two parallel lines.

(c) Explain and justify this statement. If you can tile a strip, you can tile a plane.

(d) Strips between parallel lines can be placed side by side in many different ways. Draw a picture of at least three of your triangle strips, running horizontally and arranged so that the corresponding vertices of the triangles are aligned vertically.

(e) Draw another picture of at least three of your triangle strips, running horizontally and arranged so that each side of each triangle lines up along a straight line with a side of another triangle.

(f) Parts (d) and (e) illustrate two different ways of using your triangle to tile a plane. Can you think of a third way? Which do you like best? Why?

6. Two English words that are pronounced in the same way but have very different meanings are *complement* and *compliment*. Look up these two words in a dictionary and write out a definition for each one (as a noun). Then explain why it makes sense to apply one of these words, but not the other, to angles.

2.6 Parallelograms and Congruent Triangles

Polygons are figures made up of line segments and angles. In earlier chapters, we examined their side lengths and their symmetries. Now it is time to see what useful things can be said about the angles of polygons. There are many, many things that we *could* say about them—some interesting, some not, some useful, some not. To keep this section and the next two from being a hopeless clutter of details, they are built around a single theme question.

How much information is enough to determine a polygon?

This section and the next one focus on triangles. Section 2.8 extends our explorations and findings to other polygons.

In Chapter 1 you found that the lengths of the three sides are enough to determine a triangle—not its exact location, but its size and its shape. That is, any two triangles with sides of the same lengths must be congruent. This principle is abbreviated as SSS— which stands for side-side-side.

A Fact to Know: (SSS) If the three sides of one triangle have the same lengths as the three sides of another triangle, then the triangles are congruent.

So determine really should be understood in terms of congruence. A figure is **determined** if there is no doubt or ambiguity about its size or shape. Sometimes this is called "determined up to congruence". If a figure is determined by some information, there should be a way to find *any other* fact about its size or shape from that information. The way may not be obvious or easy, but if the figure is determined, *there has to be a way*!

Learning Outcomes

After studying this section, you will be able to:

Find the measures of all sides and all angles of a triangle if you know two sides and the included angle;

Find the measures of all the angles of a triangle if you know all three of its sides;

Explain and use a formula for finding the area of a parallelogram.

By SSS, there is only one triangle (up to congruence) with side lengths 4, 5, and 7 inches. Find each of the following facts about this triangle. Do as little drawing and measuring as possible, but do as much as you feel you need. In each case, explain your approach to the question. Find

1. its perimeter;

2. the length of the altitude from the 7 inch side to its opposite vertex;

3. the area enclosed by the triangle;

4. the size of each angle.

Why do you think we want you to do as little drawing and measuring as possible?

For part 2 of the previous question, how did you find the altitude of the triangle? Did you draw a diagram and measure it? That's OK, if you have a sharp pencil and are careful, but what if the triangle were 4 by 5 by 7 *miles*, instead of inches? Or, what if you don't have good measuring tools, or if you want a very precise answer? There is a way to find that altitude exactly, without measuring anything. Here's how.

1. Start with a sketch. You can draw your own or look at Display 2.35. Draw the altitude you want and call its length a. The foot of this altitude divides the 7 inch side into two pieces. If you call the length of one piece x, then the length of the other is $7 - x$.

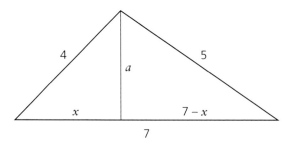

Display 2.35

2. Apply the Pythagorean Theorem on the two right triangles formed by this altitude.

$$x^2 + a^2 = 4^2 \quad \text{and} \quad (7 - x)^2 + a^2 = 5^2$$

3. Each of these equations can be rewritten as
   $a^2 = $ [something].

   $$a^2 = 4^2 - x^2 \quad \text{and} \quad a^2 = 5^2 - (7-x)^2$$

4. You have two things equal to a^2, so they must equal
   each other.

   $$4^2 - x^2 = 5^2 - (7-x)^2$$

5. Now just work out the arithmetic and solve for x.

   $$4^2 - x^2 = 5^2 - (7^2 - 14x + x^2)$$

   $$4^2 - x^2 = 5^2 - 7^2 + 14x - x^2$$

   $$4^2 = 5^2 - 7^2 + 14x$$

   $$16 - 25 + 49 = 14x$$

   $$\frac{40}{14} = x$$

6. Now you can find a just by substituting $\frac{40}{14}$ for x in
   one of the first equations.

   $$a^2 = 4^2 - \left(\frac{40}{14}\right)^2$$

Compute the numerical side of this equation with your
calculator. Then take its square root to get a. What do you get?
Does it agree with what you got before?

The problem about *The Daily Planet's* real estate taxes,
at the end of this section, will give you a chance to use this
technique in a real world situation.

The SSS test for congruent triangles can be used to get
a handy formula for finding the area of a parallelogram.

1. Suppose that *ABCD* is a parallelogram, as in
   Display 2.36. Use SSS to make a convincing argument
   that the diagonal *BD* divides the parallelogram into
   two congruent triangles. *Hint:* Recall the definition
   of a parallelogram given in Chapter 1.

2. If the length of *BC* is 7 and the vertical distance
   from *BC* to *D* is 4, what is the area of triangle *BCD*?
   What is the area of triangle *ABD*? What is the area
   of the parallelogram *ABCD*? How do you know?

3. If the length of *BC* is *b* and the vertical distance from *BC* to *D* is *h*, what is the area of triangle *BCD*? What is the area of triangle *ABD*? What is the area of the parallelogram *ABCD*? How do you know?

4. Write a general formula for the area of a parallelogram. Be sure to say what the letters in your formula represent.

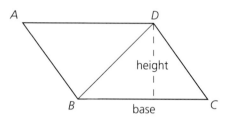

Display 2.36

Thinking Tip

Visualize. A mental picture often can lead you through an example more reliably than memorized steps or formulas.

Sometimes other combinations of three, or even two, pieces of information are enough to determine a triangle. Here are some examples to help you see which combinations work that way. As you work through them, try to visualize the given pieces of the triangle in your mind's eye.

In each of the following cases,

• If you think the given facts determine a particular triangle, draw it.

• If you think the given facts can be true for more than one triangle, draw two different (noncongruent) triangles that fit those facts.

• If you think that no triangle fits the given facts, explain why.

1. Two of the sides are 6 cm and 8 cm long, the included angle (the angle between them) is 40°.

2. Two of the sides are 6 cm and 8 cm long; an angle not between them is 40°.

3. Two of the angles are 30° and 45°; the included side (the side between them) is 5 cm long.

4. Two of the angles are 30° and 45°; a side not between them is 5 cm long.

5. The three angles are 50°, 60°, and 70°.

6. The three angles are 60°, 70°, and 80°.

7. It is equilateral and has perimeter 21 cm.

Here's an example of how a situation like question 1 above might turn up in real life.

Smalltown owns part of Puddle Lake, including a shallow, sandy cove. The Recreation Department wants to put a float line across the cove to mark off a wading area for children, as is shown in Display 2.37. How long must the float line be?

We can't answer this question yet, of course, because we don't have any measurements. The cove could be only a few feet wide (unlikely) or several miles wide (also unlikely) or any size in between (far more likely). How can you attack the problem?

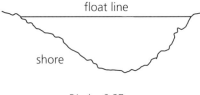

Display 2.37

One way is to get wet. Wade across the cove, stretching a long string from one shore point to the other. But today the water is much too cold. Another way is to think of the float line as part of a triangle that has two dry sides. Call the float line *AB* and pick a point *C* on shore so that the straight paths from *C* to both *A* and *B* are completely on dry land, as in Display 2.38. Now we can measure directly *AC*, *BC*, and the included angle, ∠*ACB*.

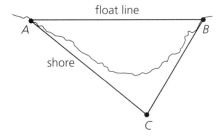

Display 2.38

Once you know two sides and the included angle, a triangle is determined (up to congruence). Only one triangular shape and size will fit that description because the positions of the "free" ends of the two sides are fixed exactly by their distances from the vertex of the included angle. The line segment between those two fixed points is the third side of the triangle. In this case, the measurements for the dry sides of the float line triangle are: AC is 135 feet long, BC is 93 feet long, and $\angle ACB$ is 72°. Now what?

1. **How long is the float line? Explain how you got your answer.**

2. **Is your answer *exactly* accurate? Do you think it is within a foot of being exact? Is it accurate enough for making the float line? Explain.**

3. **Which do you think is easier to measure in this situation—the lengths of the sides or the included angle? Why?**

Here is a way to find the length of the float line without actually having to measure the angle between AC and BC.

- Extend AC through C along a straight line to a point A' such that $A'C$ is equal in length to AC. Do the same thing with BC, making $B'C$ equal to BC, as shown in Display 2.39.

- Notice that $\angle A'CB' = \angle ACB$. Why? This means that two sides of triangle ABC and the angle between them have the same measures as two sides of triangle $A'B'C$ and the angle between them.

- Since two sides and the included angle determine a triangle up to congruence, triangles ABC and $A'B'C$ must be congruent. This means that the float-line side, AB, must have the same length as the dry side $A'B'$. So, to find the length of the float line, you just have to measure the distance between A' and B'.

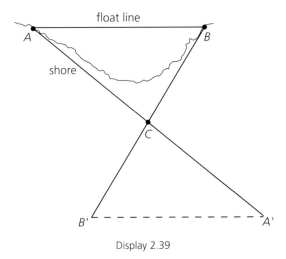

float line

A   *B*

shore

C

B' – – – – – – – – – *A'*

Display 2.39

The example we have just done illustrates a basic principle determining triangles: The measures of two sides of a triangle and the included angle are enough to determine the size and shape of the triangle. This principle is abbreviated as SAS—which stands for side-angle-side.

A Fact to Know: (SAS) If two sides and the included angle of one triangle have the same measures as two sides and the included angle of another triangle, then the triangles are congruent.

In Display 2.40, point *E* is the midpoint of *AC*, point *F* is the midpoint of *AB*, and *DE* is exactly half as long as *AB* and parallel to it. The exact size and shape of △ *ABC* are not known.

1. Use SAS to explain why all four of the following triangles must be congruent.

   △ *AFE*   △ *EDC*   △ *DEF*   △ *FBD*

2. Explain why *D* must be the midpoint of *BC*.

3. If the area of △ *ABC* is 150 sq. in., what is the area of △ *DEF*?

4. Do the answers to questions 1, 2, and 3 depend on knowing the exact size of the individual sides or individual angles of ABC? Justify your answer.

5. If you also know that the perimeter of △ ABC is 60 in., can you find the perimeter of △ DEF? If so, do it. Explain.

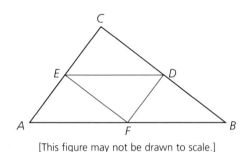

[This figure may not be drawn to scale.]

Display 2.40

Problem Set: 2.6

1. (a) Find the areas of these two parallelograms.
   (i) base = 13 ft., height = 5.2 ft.
   (ii) base = 19.7 m, height = 6.5 m

   (b) Find the areas of a parallelogram with sides of 12 ft. and 8 ft. and one angle of 45°. (*Hints:* Make a sketch. Apply the Pythagorean Theorem to find the height.)

2. In downtown Metropolis, land is expensive and taxes are high. When the new highway went through, the surveyors took a narrow triangular piece of land from *The Daily Planet*'s property. The sides of this triangular piece are 110 ft., 300 ft., and 400 ft. Since taxes are based on the square footage of the land, *The Daily Planet*'s management needs to know exactly how many square feet of land they lost, so that they can appeal to the City Assessor's Office for a reduction in their taxes. How much land did they lose? (*Hint:* Use some algebra and your calculator.)

3. Ripoff Realty Co. is selling riverfront lots along a straight stretch of the Rocky River. They are priced at $250 per front foot (measured along the riverbank), and the company says that they extend 250 feet back from the river along their other boundary lines. They advertise the land at "only $1 per square foot." Display 2.41 is a tracing from the town tax map, showing some of the lots. As you can see, the boundary line does not go back from the shore at right angles.

(a) Is the price of the land $1 per square foot, more than that, or less than that? Explain.

(b) By measuring the diagram carefully, find the height of Lot 1. Use the riverfront as the base. Then find the area of this lot.

(c) What is the price of Lot 1? How much is its cost per square foot?

(d) Find the area of Lot 2. What is its price? What is its cost per square foot?

(e) Write a function that gives you the area of a lot with x feet of riverfront.

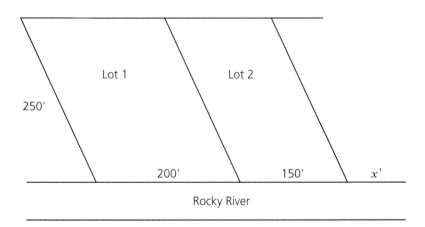

Display 2.41

4. Scientists want to know if the universe is expanding, contracting, or staying the same size. To do this, they need to know where each of the stars are. If the distances between stars get smaller, then the universe is contracting and will someday collapse. If the distances stay the same, then the universe is not getting larger or smaller. If the distances are increasing, then our universe is expanding.

How do you find the distance between two stars? You can't measure it directly. No one has ever been to another star; no one knows how to build a machine to get there. (But that may be only a matter of time.) So we have to do it from here. First, you need to know the distance from Earth to each of the stars. (A problem in the next section shows you how to do that.) Then you need to know the angle between them when you view them from Earth. For instance, if we want to know the distance between Zuben Eljanubi (pronounced "zoo bin ell juh *noo* bee") and Aldebaran (pronounced "all *deh* buh rahn"), you need to observe each star, get their distances from Earth, and measure the angle between the two sighting lines. (See Display 2.42.) In this case, the angle of separation is 122°, the distance to Zuben Eljanubi is 61 light-years, and the distance to Aldebaran is 60 light-years.

Explain why these measurements are enough information to determine the distance between Zuben Eljanubi and Aldebaran. What geometric principle in this section guarantees that these measurements are enough? Outline as clearly as you can the process of finding this distance. If you can find the distance, do it. If you can't, describe what part(s) of the process you don't yet know how to do.

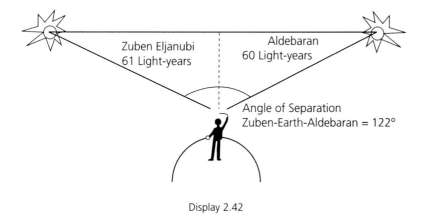

Zuben Eljanubi
61 Light-years

Aldebaran
60 Light-years

Angle of Separation
Zuben-Earth-Aldebaran = 122°

Display 2.42

5. In Chapter 1, you saw that the diagonals of a rhombus are perpendicular bisectors of each other. What about the converse of this statement: If the diagonals of a quadrilateral are perpendicular bisectors of each other, must that quadrilateral be a rhombus? Justify your answer either by giving a counterexample or by proving it (giving a logical argument that works in every case).

(*Hints:* Start by making sure you recall what *rhombus* and *perpendicular bisector* mean. Then sketch what you know about the diagonals. Does that determine the rest of the figure? Can you turn what you see into a logical argument?)

6. Suppose that the perpendicular distance from one of two lines to the other is the same in two different places. Must the lines be parallel? Give a logical argument to justify your answer.

(*Hint:* Draw a diagram of what it would look like if the lines were not parallel. Then label your diagram with letters to help you clarify your thinking and writing.)

2.7 Other Tests for Congruent Triangles

Learning Outcomes

After studying this section, you will be able to:

Find the measures of all sides and all angles of a triangle if you know two angles and one side;

Give examples to show that knowing two sides and an angle *not* between them does not determine a triangle;

Give examples to show that three angles do not determine a triangle;

Describe the relationships between the sides and the angles of an isosceles triangle.

In the previous section you saw that a triangle is determined by any two of its sides and the angle between them. But sometimes only one side of a triangle can be measured. If the angles at either end of it can be measured, too, that's enough to determine the triangle, as you can see from Display 2.43. Because the measures of the angles are known, the other two sides of the triangle must lie along the dotted lines. But two lines that are not parallel must cross at one (and only at one) point; that point is the third vertex of the triangle.

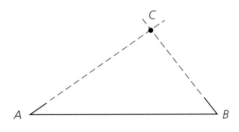

Display 2.43

Here is an example of how this fact can be used.

Two land developers are standing in a flat field at the base of a small mountain. They plan to put a ski lift on the side of the mountain, that is too rugged for a ski trail. To estimate the length of the main cable, they want to know the approximate straight-line distance from the mountaintop to the spot at which they are standing. How can they find out?

 Can you describe a strategy for this problem based on the idea that two angles and the included side determine a triangle? How would you start to attack this problem? Does Display 2.44 help?

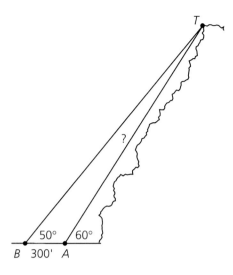

Display 2.44

Does Display 2.44 suggest a strategy to you? Here is the approach we were thinking of when we drew the picture.

- The developers are standing on flat ground at point *A*. Using a surveyor's tool, they can find the angle between the ground and a sight line from *A* to the mountaintop, *T*. That angle measures 60°. They want to know the length of *AT*.

- They move away from the mountain another 300 feet (to point *B*) and measure the angle between the ground and this sight line to the mountaintop; this angle measures 50°.

- Now they know two angles and the included side of a triangle, *ABT*: Side *AB* is 300 feet long, ∠*ABT* measures 50°, and they know the measure of ∠*BAT*, too. What is it? This means that the triangle is determined; they can easily find the approximate length of *AT* just by making a scale drawing and measuring that side.

> Finish the developers' problem for them. Find the approximate distance from point *A* to the mountaintop. How close do you think your measured approximation is to the actual distance?

The ski lift example illustrates that the measures of two angles of a triangle and the included side are enough to determine the size and shape of the triangle. This principle is abbreviated as ASA— which stands for angle-side-angle.

A Fact to Know: (ASA) If two angles and the included side of one triangle have the same measures as two angles and the included side of another triangle, then the triangles are congruent.

The ASA principle is the basis for **triangulation**, a location finding process used by surveyors, navigators, search and rescue teams, and others. The following problem shows you how it works for fire wardens in the north woods.

The lookout towers on Mt. Abraham and Snow Mountain are 29 miles apart. A fire warden in each tower watches for forest fires. When smoke rises above the trees, each warden measures the angle between the direction of the smoke and the line between the two towers. From the two angles and the distance between the towers, the wardens know exactly where to send the firefighters.

1. One day the wardens spot a column of smoke. From Mt. Abraham, the angle to the smoke is 44°. From Snow Mountain, the angle to the smoke is 37°. (See Display 2.45.) Make a scale drawing of the resulting triangle, and measure the approximate straight-line distance from each fire tower to the smoke.

About Words

The literal meaning of *trigonometry* is measurement of triangles.

Of course, the wardens don't draw and measure the triangle to find the location of the smoke. They use tools from trigonometry that you haven't learned yet. You can use your graphing calculator and linear equations to find the other vertex of the triangle (the smoke). Start by imagining that Mt. Abraham is at the origin of a coordinate system and Snow Mountain is on the *x*-axis at (29, 0). Refer to Display 2.46 for this setup and the following questions.

2. What is the slope of line L_1? What is its equation?

3. What is the slope of line L_2? What is its equation? Be careful; use some common sense here.

4. Graph lines L_1 and L_2 on your calculator. Then use TRACE to find their approximate intersection point.

5. Calculate the distances between this intersection point and the points for the two mountain towers. Do these answers agree (approximately) with your answers to part 1? If not, what explains the difference?

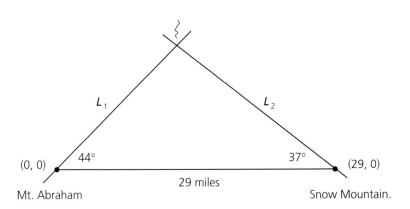

Display 2.45

Display 2.46

If you know the measures of *any* two angles of a triangle, you also know the measure of the third angle, by subtraction. The angle sum of a triangle is 180°, so the measure of the third angle is 180° minus the measures of the other two angles. So, if you know one side and *any* two angles of a triangle, you actually know the angles at each end of the known side. This allows us to extend the ASA principle to a closely related case— often called angle-angle-side.

A Fact to Know: (AAS) If two angles and a side not between them in one triangle have the same measures as the corresponding two angles and a corresponding side in another triangle, then the triangles are congruent.

1. In Display 2.46, what is the measure of the angle at the smoke? How do you know?

2. A long distance hiker with a cellular phone falls in the woods and badly sprains her ankle. She can see the fire towers at Mt. Abraham and Snow Mountain, but neither warden in either tower can see her. She calls the warden at Snow Mountain and tells him that by using her compass she determined that the angle between her lines of sight to these two towers is about 105° and that she is directly between the Snow Mountain tower and a third fire tower that both she and the warden can see.

   (a) The Snow Mountain warden knows that the Mt. Abraham tower is 29 miles away. How can the warden figure out where to send the paramedics?

   (b) The angle between the sight lines from Snow Mountain to the Mt. Abraham tower and to the tower beyond the hiker is 60°. By making a scale drawing, locate the hiker by finding how far she is from each tower.

State a congruence principle that you think would be abbreviated as SSA. Look at Display 2.47; then explain how this figure shows that SSA is *not* a valid principle for determining a triangle. How close can you come to determining a triangle using SSA?

You know the SSS principle, that the lengths of all three sides determine exactly one triangular shape and size. What about AAA? Does knowing the three angles determine the size and shape of a triangle?

Choose three angle sizes that add to 180°. Then, using a protractor and a ruler, draw four triangles that have these angle sizes. Make the triangles as different as you can. Then do it again—pick three other angle sizes that add to 180° and draw four more triangles.

Write a paragraph describing what you observe, and propose a general principle for AAA. Explain how your principle relates to the triangles you drew.

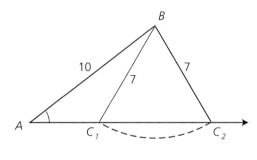

Display 2.47

In Chapter 1 you examined isosceles and equilateral triangles, using symmetry. You also worked with a straightedge (an unmarked ruler) and a compass to make accurate drawings. We're going to take another look at these things, but from a different point of view. We'll use just a ruler and a compass to construct these figures and explore their properties.

Why just a ruler and a compass? Because they're *simple*. Often, the simpler the tools you use, the clearer the underlying ideas become. In fact, we won't even use the markings on the ruler, just the straightness of its edge. We don't need to bother with measuring lengths or angles. All we really need are tools for making straight lines and circles. (If you're stuck on a desert island with just a board and a piece of string, you can still scratch these figures in the sand!) Using these tools, you'll be able to see clearly how the angle properties of isosceles and equilateral triangles relate to the principles of this section.

Thinking Tip

Take a simple approach.
Using simple, basic tools to attack a question sometimes reveals its connections to other ideas. Even when they don't work, seeing why not can be helpful.

Let's begin with isosceles triangles. Recall that a triangle is **isosceles** if two of its sides have the same length. Often an isosceles triangle is drawn with the third side at the bottom, and that side is called the **base**. Display 2.48 shows an isosceles triangle. The base is *RS*; the sides *RT* and *ST* are equal in length. The dashes form the line of symmetry. If you fold the triangle along the line of symmetry, the equal sides will match, and vertices *R* and *S* will match.

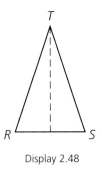

Display 2.48

Use a straightedge and a compass to draw an isosceles triangle without measuring, like this.

- Use your straightedge to make two line segments that meet at a point. Call that point *A*.
- Put the point of your compass at *A*, and draw a circular arc that intersects both line segments. Call these intersection points *B* and *C*.
- Connect *B* and *C* by a line segment.
1. Which two sides of △*ABC* are the same length? How do you know?

Now construct the line of symmetry, like this.

- Put your compass pivot point at *B*, make the compass opening span more than halfway to *C*, and draw a circle.
- Without changing the compass opening, move the pivot point to *C*, and draw a circle.
- Pick one of the two intersection points of the two circles and call it *D*. (The point farther from *A* will probably be easier to work with, but it doesn't really matter.)
- Draw the line *AD*.
2. Is *AD* *really* the line of symmetry? How can you be sure?

In the previous question, we said that *AD* is the line of symmetry for your isosceles triangle, △*ABC*. That is, *AD* divides △*ABC* into two congruent halves. How can we be so sure? After all, different people in your class started by drawing different angles, and this was written long before any of you drew your diagrams. We couldn't know in advance exactly what your triangle would look like, yet we predicted that *AD* would work for you. Here's how we knew.

> In your diagram, draw segments *BD* and *CD*. Then label as *E* the crossing point of *AD* and *BC*. Now your diagram should look like Display 2.49. It might be turned differently, and it might be fatter or thinner than our diagram, but the letters show you how your diagram should match up with ours.

> Do you remember how point *D* was constructed? What guarantees that *BD* and *CD* have the same length? Now look at the other sides of △*ABD* and △*ACD*. Sides *AB* and *AC* have the same length because the original triangle was made that way, and side *AD* is common to both triangles. Therefore, by SSS, △*ABD* and △*ACD* are congruent. This means that

$$\angle BAD = \angle CAD$$

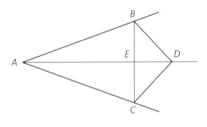

Display 2.49

That is, *AD* divides ∠*A* exactly in half. That's why *AD* is called the **angle bisector** of ∠*A*.

> Now look again at how *AD* divides the original isosceles triangle, △*ABC*, into △*ABE* and △*ACE*. Sides *AB* and *AC* are equal in length (why?), and side *AE* is common to both triangles. We know that ∠*BAD* and ∠*CAD* have the same measure (see above), so △ *ABE* and △*ACE* must be congruent (by what principle from this section?). In other words, *AD* is the line of symmetry for the original isosceles triangle, △*ABC*.

We didn't do all that work just to convince you that we had the right line of symmetry all along. An important result follows from what we just did. In an isosceles triangle, the angles opposite the two equal sides are called the **base angles** of the triangle. In Display 2.49, the base angles of $\triangle ABC$ are $\angle ABE$ and $\angle ACE$. Because the two triangles formed by the angle bisector are congruent, we know that

The base angles of an isosceles triangle are equal.

The converse of this statement is also true. That is,

A triangle that has two equal angles *must* be isosceles.

Problem 5 at the end of this section asks you to prove that this is true. Think about it.

These facts about isosceles triangles apply easily to the special case of equilateral triangles. Since all three sides of an equilateral triangle have the same measure, we can apply the equal base angles idea to the angles opposite any two sides. Doing this twice (with different pairs of sides) tells us that all three angles must have the same measure. You can also see this from the triangle's three axes of symmetry. Since the angle sum of any triangle is 180°, each angle of an equilateral triangle must be 60°.

 Write a detailed explanation of why all three angles of an equilateral triangle must be equal. Start with an equilateral triangle, $\triangle ABC$, and lead your reader step by step to the conclusion that $\angle A = \angle B = \angle C$.

A review of congruence tests for triangles.

- **SSS.** If the three sides of one triangle have the same lengths as the three sides of another triangle, then the triangles are congruent.

- **SAS.** If two sides and the included angle of one triangle have the same measures as two sides and the included angle of another triangle, then the triangles are congruent.

- **ASA.** If two angles and the included side of one triangle have the same measures as two angles and the included side of another triangle, then the triangles are congruent.

- **AAS.** If two angles and a side not between them in one triangle have the same measures as the corresponding two angles and a corresponding side in another triangle, then the triangles are congruent.

Problem Set: 2.7

1. For each part,

   - If you think the given facts determine a triangle, draw it.

   - If you think the given facts can be true for more than one triangle, draw at least two non-congruent triangles that fit these facts.

   - If you think that no triangle fits the given facts, explain why.

   (a) A triangle with sides 4, 7, and 5 cm.

   (b) A triangle with sides 3, 4, and 7 cm.

   (c) A triangle with sides 5 cm and 7 cm, and a 30° angle.

   (d) A right triangle with two 5 inch legs.

   (e) A right triangle; two of its sides are 8 cm and 10 cm.

   (f) An isosceles right triangle with hypotenuse 13 cm and a 50° angle.

   (g) An isosceles triangle containing angles of 50° and 80° and a 12 cm side.

   (h) An isosceles triangle containing angles of 50° and 60° and a 10 cm side.

   (i) An isosceles right triangle with a hypotenuse of 15 cm.

2. Earlier in this section you were asked to find the distance of an injured hiker from the Mt. Abraham and Snow Mountain lookout towers by making a scale drawing. Check the results of your drawing by using a coordinate system, writing two linear equations to describe the sight lines from the hiker to the towers, and using the TRACE function of your graphing calculator to find where the graph lines cross.

3. How far away is the star you saw last night? We can't travel there and measure the distance, so we have to be able to measure it from here. We *can* measure the angle made with the Earth's surface when we sight the star and the angle made again six months later, when the Earth is on the opposite side of its orbit. These two Earth orbit points and the star form an isosceles triangle (approximately). (Display 2.50) The base of this large triangle measures about 186,000,000 miles across. Orbits are nearly ellipses, so their bisector length changes with time, but we can choose sighting times for which this is approximately true. Then, using ASA, we can derive the distance between our solar system and the star, like this.

- For a particular star, suppose that the angle in June is 89.9999°. The angle measured in December is 89.9999°. (Notice that rounding off these measurements is *not* appropriate here.)

- The distance between the measurements (across the Earth's orbit around the Sun) is 186,000,000 miles. Half of this (93,000,000 miles) is the distance from either base angle to the perpendicular bisector of the base. This distance times TAN of the angle (89.9999° in this case) is the perpendicular distance from the center of the base to the opposite vertex. That perpendicular distance is the distance between our Sun and that star.

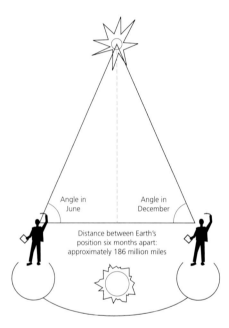

Display 2.50

(a) What is the approximate distance, in miles, between our Sun and this star?

(b) Light can travel 5,865,696,000,000 miles in a year; this length is called a **light-year**. How many light-years away from our Sun is this star?

(c) In June or December, approximately how many miles away from Earth is this star? How many light-years?

(d) Similar sightings are taken for another star, at different months (a half-year apart). Each angle is 89.99995°, and the Earth-orbit diameter for these months is

184,000,000 miles. In miles and light-years, how far away is the star?

(e) Similar sightings are taken for a third star, at different months (a half-year apart). This time each angle is 89.999992°, and the Earth-orbit diameter for these months is 183,000,000 miles. In miles and light-years, how far away is the star?

4. One night in 1798, Captain Hardtack was sailing his American privateer northward, parallel to the east coast of Spanish Florida. To avoid the risk of capture by the Spanish, he had to stay out of their territorial waters, which extended 3 miles from shore. To check his location, Captain Hardtack sighted the beacon at Lighthouse Point at a 30° angle to the west of his course. (Display 2.51.) One mile further on, he sighted the same beacon at a 36° angle west of his course. Was he in Spanish waters or in international waters? How far offshore was he?

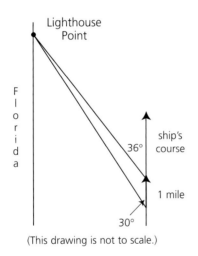

(This drawing is not to scale.)

Display 2.51

5. Suppose you have a triangle, $\triangle ABC$, in which $\angle A = \angle B$. Justify the claim that $\triangle ABC$ must be isosceles. (*Hint:* Draw an angle bisector and think about the AAS principle.)

2.8 Other Polygons

Learning Outcomes

After studying this section, you will be able to:

Describe the size and shape of a polygon by using triangulation;

Find the sum of the interior angles and the sum of the exterior angles of any polygon;

Compute the measures of the interior and exterior angles of regular polygons.

There are lots of different types and shapes of polygons. The simplest ones are triangles. Yet we have spent two sections studying them. Did you wonder why? The answer is back in Chapter 1. Do you remember what triangulation was about? Its key idea is,

Any polygonal region can be divided into nonoverlapping triangular regions by adding nonintersecting line segments between vertices of the polygon.

1. Draw a 2 inch by 3 inch rectangle. Triangulate it in as many different ways as you can. How many ways are there? How many triangles do you get each time?

2. Draw a pentagon that looks like home plate on a baseball diamond. Triangulate it. How many triangles do you get? How many different triangulations of this pentagon are there?

Home Plate

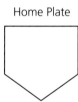

To keep things simple, we'll look mainly at polygons with no reflex angles (polygons in which every angle measures less than 180°). Such polygons are called **convex**. We will eventually get to formulas that apply to *all* polygons. Generalizing our approach to include non-convex polygons will be left as a discussion question for you later.

A polygon with more than three sides can be triangulated in different ways. But, no matter how you do it, the size and shape of the polygon is determined by the size and shape of its triangular pieces. (If you attach to any polygonal frame enough diagonal cross-pieces to triangulate it, the frame will be rigid.) In short, knowing about triangles tells you a lot about other types of polygons.

Here's an example of how this works. Recall the "SSS" test for congruence: When you know the lengths of all three sides of a triangle, you know its shape. Do you think that there is an SSSS test for congruence of quadrilaterals?

What would it mean to say that a quadrilateral is determined by SSSS? Explain how Display 2.52 shows that the "SSSS test" doesn't work.

Display 2.52

As you see, knowing the lengths of four sides does not determine a convex quadrilateral. You can make many different shapes by changing the angles between the sides. But what if *one* of the angles is also fixed? Is that enough information to determine the quadrilateral? The answer is yes, as you'll see from the following description.

Suppose you know the lengths of all the sides of a convex quadrilateral *ABCD*, the order in which they occur, and the measure of one angle, say ∠*A*, as in Display 2.53(a). Then triangulation shows that the measures of *all* the other angles are determined!

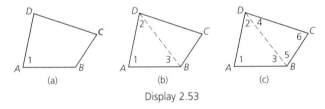

Display 2.53

Here's how.

- Triangulate *ABCD* by drawing segment *BD*.

- You know the lengths of sides *AB* and *AD* and the measure of the angle between them, so △*ABD* is determined by SAS. Therefore the length of *BD* is determined, along with the measures of ∠*ABD* and ∠*ADB*. These are marked as ∠2 and ∠3 in Display 2.53(b).

- Now, since you know the lengths of *BD*, *BC*, and *CD*, △*BCD* is determined by SSS. This means that the measures of ∠*BDC*, ∠*CBD*, and ∠*BCD* are determined. These are marked as ∠4, ∠5, and ∠6 in Display 2.53(c).

- One of the other three angles of the quadrilateral is ∠6. The measures of the other two come from adding ∠2 + ∠4 and ∠3 + ∠5. This means that the quadrilateral is determined (up to congruence).

Explain why a strong diagonal brace across one corner of a screen door will make the entire door rigid.

a

1. Suppose you know the lengths of all the sides of a pentagon and the order in which they occur. How many angles do you have to know to determine the pentagon? One? Two? More? Explain.

2. There is a pattern here, starting with triangles, then quadrilaterals, then pentagons. State the next step in the pattern as precisely as you can. Then try to justify your statement.

Triangulation leads to another interesting, useful property of polygons. We know that the angle sum of any triangle is 180°. We can use this fact and triangulation to show that the angle sum of a polygon is determined by the number of its vertices, according to a simple formula.

1. Draw a convex pentagon (any way you want). Call its vertices *A*, *B*, *C*, *D*, and *E*. Then triangulate your pentagon by drawing diagonals from *A*. How many triangles do you get?

b

2. What is the sum of the angles in *all* the triangles? Is each angle of each triangle at a vertex of the pentagon? What is the angle sum of the pentagon?

3. Draw a convex hexagon (any way you want). Call its vertices *A*, *B*, *C*, *D*, *E*, and *F*. Then triangulate your hexagon by drawing diagonals from *A*. How many triangles do you get?

4. What is the sum of the angles in *all* the triangles? Is each angle of each triangle at a vertex of the hexagon? What is the angle sum of the hexagon?

5. Suppose you were to triangulate a convex dodecagon (a twelve-sided polygon) by drawing diagonals from one vertex. How many triangles would you get? What would be the angle sum of the dodecagon?

6. Can you see a general formula for the angle sum of an n-sided polygon? Try to write one down, as precisely as you can. Check your formula to see if it holds for triangles ($n = 3$) and quadrilaterals ($n = 4$).

Let's look carefully at the key ideas behind the questions you just worked through.

- When you triangulate a polygon, every angle of each triangle is part of some angle of the polygon, and there is no overlap. Thus, the angle sum of the polygon is the same as the sum of the angles of *all* the triangles—the number of triangles times 180°.

- If a convex polygon is triangulated with diagonals from a single vertex, the number of triangles depends only on the number of vertices, not on the shape of the polygon.

- From a single vertex, A, you can draw diagonals to every other vertex except the two vertices immediately on either side of A. Thus, if the polygon has n vertices, you can draw $n - 3$ diagonals. (Did you draw 2 diagonals in your pentagon and 3 diagonals in your hexagon?)

- As you draw the diagonals from A to successive vertices around the polygon, each one cuts out a single triangle. The last diagonal drawn cuts out its triangle from a quadrilateral, making one extra triangle. In other words, you get $n - 3$ triangles (one for each diagonal) plus one more a total of $n - 2$ triangles. Putting all these ideas together, we get:

A Fact to Know: The angle sum of an n-sided polygon is
$$(n - 2) \cdot 180°$$

The angle-sum formula is true for all *n*-sided polygons, but our explanation only works for convex polygons. How can the justification be extended to include nonconvex polygons?

Hint: Try drawing an example of a simple case. Can you use a diagonal to cut a nonconvex polygon into convex polygons? How do the angle sums of the pieces relate to the angle sum of the whole thing?

The angles we have been talking about are the ones that open to the inside of the polygon, of course. These are called the **interior angles** of the polygon. When we talk about the angle sum of a polygon, we mean the sum of the interior angles. Sometimes it is useful to look at the angle formed by one side of a polygon and the extension of a side next to it. This is called an **exterior angle**. (Display 2.54.)

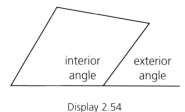

Display 2.54

Imagine yourself walking around the perimeter of a convex polygon. The measure of an exterior angle is the amount you have to turn when you turn the corner at a vertex. For instance, if you're walking along side *AB* of the pentagon in Display 2.55 (from *A* to *B*), ∠1 is the amount you have to turn at *B* to get onto side *BC*.

 Suppose you are walking along a convex polygon. As you go around it, how much do you have to turn to get back onto the side you started from? That is, what is your total number of degrees of turning? Does the number of vertices matter? (Display 2.55 might help you to visualize this.)

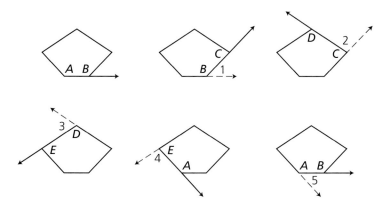

Display 2.55

If you walk around a typical city block, you make four 90° turns to get back to your original direction, a total of 360°. If you walk a convex polygonal path around a statue, it takes you the same total amount of turning to get back to your original direction, no matter how many corners you turn. This should make the following fact easy to remember.

A Fact to Know: The sum of the exterior angles of any convex polygon is 360°.

Here's a slightly more formal explanation of the exterior angle sum—one that doesn't depend on imagining that you're walking around a diagram. The interior and exterior angles at a vertex are supplementary (see Display 2.54). That is, their sum is 180°. So if we sum the interior-exterior pairs for all the vertices of an n-sided polygon, the total is $n \cdot 180°$. But the interior angles add to $(n-2) \cdot 180°$, so the exterior angles must add to the rest. That's 360°, no matter what n is.

If all the sides of a polygon have the same length and all its angles have the same measure, we call that polygon *regular.* An equilateral triangle is an example of a regular polygon.

1. What is the measure of an interior angle of an equilateral triangle? What is the measure of one of its exterior angles? How do you know?

2. What is the measure of an interior angle of a square? What is the measure of one of its exterior angles? How do you know?

3. What is the measure of an interior angle of a regular pentagon? What is the measure of one of its exterior angles? How do you know?

4. What is the measure of an interior angle of a regular polygon with 100 sides? What is the measure of one of its exterior angles? How do you know?

5. What patterns do you see here?

Since all n interior angles of a regular n-sided polygon must be equal, the measure of any one of them can be found by dividing the sum of the interior angles by n. That is,

The measure of an interior angle of a regular

$$n\text{-gon} = \frac{(n-2) \cdot 180°}{n}$$

Since all n exterior angles of a regular n-sided polygon must be equal, the measure of any one of them can be found by dividing the sum of the exterior angles by n. That is:

The measure of an exterior angle of a regular n-gon $= \dfrac{360°}{n}$.

 Display 2.56 is an illustration from a woodworking book. How are the angle cuts shown there related to their corresponding geometric shapes? How are they related to interior or exterior angles?

Miter box settings, left and right, for making various geometric constructions *(Stanley Tools)*

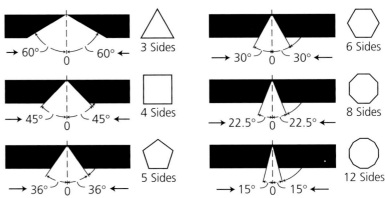

From page 203 of *Complete Book of Woodworking*, by Rosario Capotosto (New York: Harper & Row, 1975).

Display 2.56

A review of important facts

The sum of the interior angles of an *n*-sided polygon is

$$(n-2) \cdot 180°$$

The measure of an interior angle of a regular *n*-gon is

$$\frac{(n-2) \cdot 180°}{n}$$

The sum of the exterior angles of any convex polygon is 360°.

The measure of an exterior angle of a regular *n*-gon is $\frac{360°}{n}$.

Problem Set: 2.8

1. Display 2.57 shows the lengths of the four sides of a quadrilateral *ABCD*. For each of the following sizes for ∠*B*, draw the quadrilateral *ABCD*.

    (a) 45°   (b) 90°   (c) 120°   (d) 30°   (e) 60°   (f) 10°

Side	Length
AB	7 cm
BC	10 cm
CD	8 cm
AD	5 cm

    Display 2.57

2. Display 2.58 is a table of angle measures for regular polygons. Copy it and fill it in.

Number of Sides *n*	Sum of Interior Angles	Sum of Exterior Angles	Measure of 1 Interior Angle	Measure of 1 Exterior Angle
6				
7				
8				
10				
12				
16				
17				
24				

    Display 2.58

3. A common pattern on soccer balls is a black regular pentagon surrounded by five white regular hexagons.

   (a) Draw this pattern.

   (b) What is the ratio of hexagons to pentagons in this pattern?

   (c) Get a soccer ball to examine. How many black pentagons are on the ball? How many white hexagons are on the ball?

   (d) What is the ratio of white hexagons to black pentagons on the ball? Why isn't this answer the same as your answer for part (b)?

   (e) What is the sum of all the interior angles of all the black pentagons on the ball?

   (f) What is the sum of all the interior angles of all the white hexagons on the ball? What is the ratio of this number to your answer for part (e)?

   (g) When you divide the ratio in part (d) by the ratio in part (f), what number do you get? How does this relate to the angle sums of a pentagon and a hexagon? Is this a coincidence? Explain.

4. Polygons that are not convex are called concave. Write a direct definition of *concave polygon* in terms of angle measure.

5. Fenway Park, home of the Boston Red Sox, is a unique ballpark built in 1912. Unlike many modern ballparks, it is not symmetrical in the layout of its playing field, shown in Display 2.59. Using strong, but expensive, lightweight plastic, it might be possible to cover the entire playing field (both infield and outfield) when it rains. To estimate the cost of such a cover, the head groundskeeper needs a close approximation of the area of the playing field.

   (a) Explain how the head groundskeeper could use what you have learned about polygons to compute the area of the Fenway Park playing field.

   (b) Do the measurements shown in Display 2.59 give you enough information to determine the area of the playing field? If so, do it. If not, describe what other measurements you need.

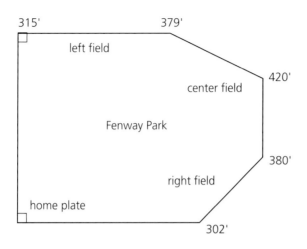

315'   379'

left field

420'

center field

Fenway Park

380'

right field

home plate

302'

(All measurements shown are direct distances from home plate.)

Display 2.59

6. Why do you think we limited our explanation of exterior angles to convex polygons? How can you change the explanation to make the exterior angle sum of *any* polygon equal 360°? Write one or two paragraphs explaining your thoughts about this.

2.9 Stretching and Shrinking Angles and Areas

Learning Outcomes

After studying this section, you will be able to:

Use the fact that scaling preserves angle size and explain why it is true;

Use the fact that two triangles with all corresponding angles congruent must be similar;

Compute the area of a scaled figure from its original area and the scaling factor;

Find the scaling factor for a scaled figure from its original area and its scaled area.

In this chapter we have been talking about scaling and about angles. Do you think that scaling changes angle size?

In Display 2.60, $\triangle A$ and $\triangle B$ are similar.

1. What is the scaling factor? Do some measuring.

2. What are the slope measures of $\angle 1$ and $\angle 2$? How are they related?

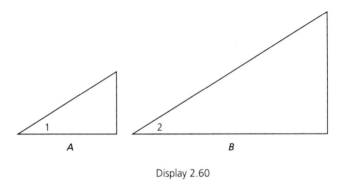

Display 2.60

Scaling always preserves angle size. To see why this must be true, think in terms of slope measure. Whenever two figures are similar, there is a scaling factor, k, such that each length in one figure is k times the corresponding length in the other. Now, the slope measure of an angle is the ratio of two lengths, say $\frac{a}{b}$. Then the slope measure of the corresponding angle in the similar figure is $\frac{ka}{kb}$ as in Display 2.61. But $\frac{ka}{kb} = \frac{a}{b}$, so the angle size must be the same in both figures.

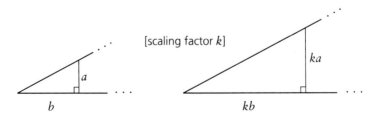

Display 2.61

A Fact to Know: Corresponding angles of similar polygons are congruent.

The previous fact can be stated in this form.

If two polygons are similar, then their corresponding angles must be congruent.

What is the converse of this statement? Give an example to show that the converse is *not* true.

In general, two polygons with congruent angles may or may not be similar. For triangles, however, the situation is more predictable.

A Fact to Know: (AAA) If the three angles of one triangle are congruent to the three angles of another triangle, then the triangles are similar.

Often the AAA statement is combined with its converse (which is true for all polygons) in this form.

Two triangles are similar if and only if their corresponding angles are congruent.

Do two angles determine the shape of a triangle? In particular, are all triangles that contain angles of 50° and 75° similar? Why or why not? Does one angle determine the shape of a triangle? Why or why not?

The previous facts about angles depend on knowing that if k is the scaling factor relating some figure A to a similar figure B, then every length in B is k times the corresponding length in A. For instance, if a side of A is 3 units long, then the corresponding side of B is $3k$ units long. But what about area? The area of a figure is measured in *square* units, not linear ones. Does the scaling factor affect areas in a predictable way? If so, how? The following example should help you see the answers to these questions.

Movie star Monica Rich has tiled the 8 by 12 foot patio by her swimming pool with the pattern shown in Display 2.62. She used two kinds of custom made tiles. The plain ones are solid gold in color, and the others have a green dollar sign inlay. Each tile is one foot square and costs $100, with or without the inlay.

1. How much did the tiles for Monica's patio cost? How many tiles were used?

Monica's next door rival, Glenda Greenback, decides to build a much larger patio. Because she thinks that she is three times as rich as Monica, she plans to build a patio three times as long and three times as wide, using exactly the same kinds of tiles and the same pattern to cover it.

2. What are the dimensions of Glenda's patio?

3. The two rectangular patios are similar. What is the scaling factor?

4. How much will the tiles for Glenda's patio cost? How many tiles will be used?

5. Will Glenda spend three times as much as Monica for her patio tiles? Explain.

Tiles

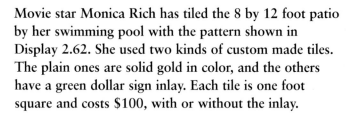

Display 2.62

The story of Monica's and Glenda's patios illustrates a simple, but *very* important, principle of scaling.

If a region is scaled by a factor of k, its area changes by k^2.

That is, if all the linear distances of some figure A are scaled by a factor of k to get a similar figure B, then any area enclosed by B is k^2 times the corresponding area enclosed by A. Let's see why this must always be true.

Area is measured in square units. Once you have chosen a unit length, you can think of the area of any region as made up of little 1 by 1 square tiles (and parts of tiles). You can find the approximate area of the region just by counting the squares. You can make your approximation better by choosing a smaller unit size. Now, what happens to the size of a square if you scale it by a factor of k?

Each side of square A in Display 2.63 is 1 pica long. A pica is a unit length used by printers. All the squares in this figure are similar to A. Why?

1. List the four scaling factors used to get squares B, C, D, and E from A.

2. List the areas of squares B, C, D, and E, in square picas.

3. How are the numbers you listed in part 2 related to the numbers listed in part 1?

4. If you had to add on another square, F, following the pattern of Display 2.63, what would its side length be? What would its area be?

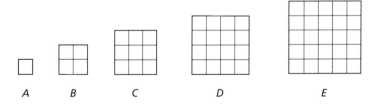

A   B   C   D   E

Display 2.63

Display 2.63 shows how the area of a square is affected by scaling. Algebra lets us express this principle in a way that is easily extended to rectangles and triangles. The area of a square with side length s is s^2. If that square is scaled by a factor k, then the new square has side length ks, so it has area $(ks)^2$. But $(ks)^2 = k^2s^2$, which is just k^2 times the area of the original square.

The same reasoning holds for rectangles. If a rectangle has length l and width w, then the area inside it is lw. Now, if that rectangle is scaled by a factor k, then the new length and width are kl and kw, respectively. Thus, the area inside the scaled rectangle is

$$(kl)(kw) = k^2 \cdot lw$$

which is k^2 times the area of the original rectangle.

1. Write a formula for the area of a triangle with base b and height h.

2. Adapt the reasoning for rectangles to explain,

> If a triangle is scaled by a factor k, then the area of the scaled triangle is k^2 times the area of the original one.

What about regions that are not as nicely shaped as rectangles or triangles? How do we know that the same principle holds? For polygonal regions, there are two ways to answer this. The first uses triangulation. Since any polygon can be triangulated, and since the area of any scaled triangle is changed by the square of the scaling factor, then the area of any scaled triangulated region must also change by the square of the scaling factor.

Write a clear, detailed explanation of how triangulation makes the area scaling principle true for any pentagonal region. Somewhere in your explanation you should need to use a form of the Distributive Law; be sure to state clearly where and how you are using it.

The second approach applies to any planar region, whether or not it is bounded by a polygon. Recall (from Chapter 1) that we can approximate the area of any planar region by a grid of squares. Now, if we scale the region by a factor k, then the sides of each square are scaled by k, so the area of each square changes by k^2. This means that the area of the entire approximation changes by the factor k^2.

For instance, the area inside the irregular hexagon on the left side of Display 2.64 is approximated by 16 squares. The similar hexagon on the right has been scaled by a factor of 2. This means that the area of each of the original squares has become 4 times its original size, so the right hexagon encloses 4 times as much area as the left one does.

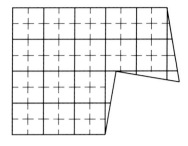

Display 2.64

If we make better and better approximations by choosing smaller and smaller squares, the k^2 factor applies each time, so the area of the region must change by the factor k^2.

A Fact to Know: If a planar region is scaled by a factor k, then the area of the scaled region is k^2 times the area of the original region.

If you know how the area of a figure should be changed by scaling, can you find the scaling factor needed? Yes, you can. Would you ever need to do that? You might. Here's an example of such a situation.

The sailmakers at Easylife Watercraft Corp. have designed a sail in the shape of a right triangle with one leg $1\frac{1}{2}$ times as long as the other. They can make this sail in a variety of different sizes. The sizes are based on area (because the area of a sail determines its wind resistance). Their prototype (model) is 4 ft. by 6 ft., with an area of 12 sq. ft. The boat designer in the next office needs sails of this shape with areas of 75 sq. ft., 84 sq. ft., and 93 sq. ft., for three different styles of a new boat. What are the required dimensions for these sails? How can you help the sailmakers figure this out?

Trying out a lot of different lengths to see if they fit all the conditions might work, if you're lucky, but it could take a long time. There's a faster, easier way, if you use a little algebra. The sailmakers need a scaling factor to use in each case. Now, for any scaling factor k, we know that the original area, A_o, is related to the scaled area, A_s, like this,

$$A_s = k^2 \cdot A_o$$

In this case, the original area is 12 sq. ft. The scaled area is what the designer wants; in the first case, it is 75 sq. ft. Thus, we have

$$75 = k^2 \cdot 12$$

so

$$\frac{75}{12} = k^2$$

That is,

$$k = \sqrt{\frac{75}{12}} = \sqrt{\frac{25}{4}} = \frac{5}{2} = 2.5$$

Actually, there are two square roots of $\frac{25}{4}$, one positive and one negative. We want the positive one here because the scaling factor must be positive.

These questions refer to the sailmakers' problem.

1. What are the dimensions of the sail with area 75 sq. ft.? How did you find them?

2. Find the dimensions of the sails with areas of 84 sq. ft. and 93 sq. ft. Use your calculator, and round your answers to two decimal places.

3. Write the formula for finding the scaling factor as a function of the area needed. Enter it into your calculator. What does X stand for? What does Y stand for?

4. Use your function from part 3 to help you find the dimensions of a sail with 100 sq. ft. of area.

A review of important facts.

- Corresponding angles of similar polygons are congruent.

- (**AAA**) If the three angles of one triangle are congruent to the three angles of another triangle, then the triangles are similar.

- If a planar region is scaled by a factor k, then the area of the scaled region is k^2 times the area of the original region.

Problem Set: 2.9

1. Mathland is having a contest to pick a design for a triangular stamp in honor of Pythagoras. All designs must be enclosed in right triangles with sides of length 24 cm, 32 cm, and 40 cm. When the stamp is issued, the actual side lengths of the triangle will be $\frac{1}{8}$ of the design lengths. Copy and complete the table in Display 2.65. Then answer the following questions.

    (a) How does the perimeter of the design compare to the perimeter of the actual stamp?

    (b) How does the area of the design compare to the area of the actual stamp?

    (c) Why do you think Mathland chose a right triangle with side lengths 24 cm, 32 cm, and 40 cm?

    (d) Has the United States ever issued a triangular stamp? If so, when? Have any other countries issued triangular stamps? If so, can you name any?

	Design	Actual
Side lengths	24 cm, 32 cm, 40 cm	
Perimeter		
Area		

Display 2.65

2. This problem refers to the two pool patios described in this section. When Glenda Greenback designed her patio 3 times as long and 3 times as wide as the one Monica Rich had, she found that the tiles would cost her 9 times as much as Monica's did. Why? How can Glenda change her design so that the tiles only cost her (about) 3 times as much and her patio is still proportional to Monica's? What practical tiling difficulties are caused by your solution?

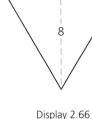

3. Kites come in all shapes and sizes, but any good kite design makes use of this important principle of aerodynamics:

For a given wind speed, the lift (force of air to lift up the kite) is directly proportional to the area of the kite. If the area of a kite is doubled, then its lift is doubled.

A typical kite design has the form of two isosceles triangles, one pointed up and one pointed down, with a common base line, as in Display 2.66. In this case, the base is 10 in., the height of the upper triangle is 6 in., and the height of the lower triangle is 8 in. Make a copy of the table in Display 2.67 to use as you answer parts (a) − (d).

Display 2.66

	Upper Triangle			Lower Triangle			Total Area
	Base	Height	Area	Base	Height	Area	
(a)	10	6		10	8		
(b)							
(c)						490	857.5
(d)			541.875				

Display 2.67

(a) Fill in all blanks in row (a) to find the total area of the kite.

(b) What happens to the total area of the kite when you double all dimensions? fill in row (b) to answer this question.

(c) Given the area of the bottom portion of the kite and the total area, as shown in row (c), fill in row (c).

(d) Given the area of the top portion of the kite, calculate the area of the bottom portion and the total area. Fill in row (d).

As an example of how this information can be used, let's say for a given wind speed the lifting force for the kite described by row (a) is $\frac{1}{4}$ pound. Because the kite dimensions in (b) give us four times the area, the lifting force is four times that of (a). In other words, kite (b) will lift one pound with the same wind speed.

(e) Calculate the lift, in pounds, of the kites described by rows (c) and (d).

(f) Design a kite of the same proportions that could lift a human body weighing 100 pounds for this same wind speed. (Find the base length and the two heights.)

4. You are helping to design a large, outdoor concert theater, TriangleWood, in Massachusetts. Its floor plan is a large equilateral triangle, as shown in Display 2.68. The lengths in the figure are in yards. The triangle at the bottom is the stage and lighting area. Seating is in three sections, proceeding away from the stage so that each section and the stage and any sections before it form a triangle similar to the stage triangle. The sections of seats are priced according to their distance from the stage, with highest priced tickets for section 1, next highest for section 2, and least expensive tickets for section 3.

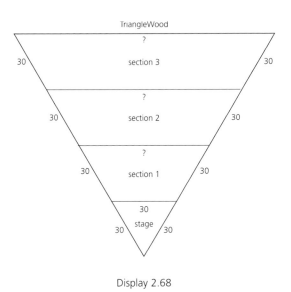

TriangleWood

Display 2.68

(a) Three of the lengths in Display 2.68 are marked "?". What are they? Remember: Each of the following triangles is equilateral:

section 1 + stage,
section 2 + section 1 + stage,
section 3 + section 2 + section 1 + stage

To complete the design of this theater, start by copying the table in Display 2.69. Then fill it in step by step as you work through parts (b)–(h).

	Area (sq. yds.)	No. of Seats	$ per Seat	Total $
stage		0	0	0
section 1		1350	$14	
section 2				
section 3				
Total:				

Display 2.69

(b) Find the area of the stage. Round your answer to two decimal places.

(c) Calculate the total area of the theater by scaling your answer to part (b).

(d) Use scaling and the answer to part (b) to find the area of each seating section. (*Hint:* The area of section 1 is the area of the equilateral triangle made up of section 1 and the stage, minus the area of the stage.) Check your results by comparing the sum of your areas with your answer to part (c).

(e) If section 1 has 1350 seats, calculate the numbers of seats in section 2 and section 3, using proportionality and assuming that each seat requires the same area (How should you round off your answers?)

(f) Find the total number of seats in this theater.

(g) The manager wants a full theater to bring in the same amount of money from the ticket sales for each section. If she prices section 1 at $14 a seat, how much does she charge for a seat in section 2? How much does she charge for a seat in section 3?

(h) If a concert is sold out, what is the total amount of money that the theater collects?

2.10 Stretching and Shrinking Volumes

Just as area is measured in square units, so volume is measured in cubic units. For any unit length, you can think of the volume of something as if it were filled with small 1 by 1 by 1 cubes (and partial cubes). You can find the approximate volume of an object by counting the cubes. You make the approximation better by choosing a smaller cube size. Here's an exercise to help you develop your spatial imagination.

Learning Outcomes

After studying this section, you will be able to:

Compute the volume of a scaled figure from its original volume and the scaling factor;

Find the scaling factor for a scaled figure from its original volume and its scaled volume.

Look at the four boxes in Display 2.70.

1. One of the three taller boxes—A, B, C—is proportional to Box X. Which one do you think it is? Why? What do you think the scaling factor is?

2. If Box X holds a quart of applesauce, how much applesauce do you think Box A holds? What about Box B? Box C? Explain your answers.

3. If Box X measures 4 by 3 by 5 inches, what would be the measurements of a similar box with a scaling factor of 10? What is the volume of Box X in this case? What is the volume of the scaled box?

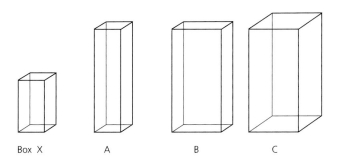

Box X   A   B   C

Display 2.70

Thinking Tip

Use appropriate notation. Sometimes describing a process with an algebraic formula will help you see how and why it works.

The ideas behind Display 2.70 lead to the principle of how volume is affected by scaling. As you know, the volume of a rectangular box is the product of its length, width, and height. If we write this statement algebraically, the formula tells us exactly how the volume of such a box is changed by scaling. Suppose a box has length l, width w, height h, and volume V. Then

$$V = l \cdot w \cdot h$$

If the box is scaled by a factor k, then each of its linear measurements–length l, width w, height h, and volume V is multiplied by k. Thus, the scaled volume, which we'll call V_k, is

$$V = kl \cdot kw \cdot kh$$
$$= k \cdot k \cdot k \cdot l \cdot w \cdot h$$
$$= k^3 \cdot l \cdot w \cdot h$$
$$= k^3 \cdot V$$

That is, the scaled volume is k^3 times the original volume.

Volumes of other figures are affected by scaling in the same way as volumes of boxes. In particular, the volume of a cube of edge length s is s^3, and if the cube is scaled by a factor k, the volume of the scaled cube is

$$(ks)^3 = k^3 s^3$$

That is, the scaled volume is k^3 times the original volume. Now, recall (from Chapter 1) that we can approximate the volume of any three dimensional shape by cubes. If we scale the shape by a factor k, then the volume of each cube changes by the factor k^3. This means that the volume of the entire approximation changes by k^3.

A Fact to Know: If a three dimensional figure is scaled by a factor k, then the volume it encloses is k^3 times the volume enclosed by the original figure.

1. A 2.5 by 8 by 10 foot rectangular bin holds plastic packing peanuts. What volume of peanuts will it hold? If a second bin is built, enlarging the dimensions of the first one by a factor of 3, what volume of peanuts will it hold? What will be the dimensions of the new bin?

2. A company is experimenting with juice cartons of various sizes. Their giant institutional size is 56 cm high and holds 68,600 cc of juice. They want to make a proportionally-sized container only 16 cm high. What scaling factor should they use? What volume will the smaller container hold?

If you know how the volume of a figure should be changed by scaling, can you find the scaling factor needed? Yes, you can. The following problem is an example of such a situation.

Market research tells the Crunchy Cereal Co. that consumers really like the shape of their regular size cornflakes box. The box is 11 inches by 8 inches by 2.5 inches. The company wants to keep this shape for its super-size and its single-serving size boxes.

1. The super-size box must have a volume of 400 cu. in. Rounded to two decimal places, what scaling factor should be used to make a box of the same shape as the regular box? What should the dimensions of the super-size box be?

2. The single-serving box must have a volume of 20 cu. in. Rounded to two decimal places, what scaling factor should be used to make a box of the same shape as the regular box? What should the dimensions of the single-serving box be?

Here is a famous story from ancient history.

In 430 B.C., there was a terrible plague in Athens. The desperate Athenians, seeking a way to stop the plague, appealed to the oracle of Apollo. The oracle told them to double the size of Apollo's cubical altar. They constructed a new altar, a cube with *each edge* twice as long as the edge of the old altar. Of course, this made the new altar eight times the size of the old one. Instead of stopping, the plague got even worse. Realizing their error, the Athenians appealed to Plato for help. After telling them that the oracle had given them this problem "to reproach the Greeks for their neglect of mathematics and their contempt of geometry,"[1] Plato set about finding the proper side length for a new altar whose volume was exactly twice that of the old one.

[1]David M. Burton, *The History of Mathematics* (Boston: Allyn and Bacon, Inc., 1985). P.134.

Explain how this story is related to the material of this section and how to solve the Athenians' problem. If you and your calculator were back in Athens in 430 B.C., do you think you could have solved the problem well enough to satisfy the oracle of Apollo? If so, do it. If not, explain why not.

REFLECT

In this chapter you learned many different facts, all related to similarity, scaling, and angle size.

- You learned about scaling factors for making different-size copies of the same shape.

- You saw two different ways to measure angles, by slope and by degrees, and you learned about the calculator functions that convert from one to the other.

- You saw relationships among the angles formed by parallel lines cut by a transversal, which led to the very important fact that the sum of the angles of *any* triangle is 180°.

- You learned about sets of measurements that determine a triangle up to congruence: **SAS, SSS, ASA,** and **AAS**.

- You saw how facts about triangles can be used to get information about other polygons.

- Finally, you saw how scaling affects areas and volumes of two and three dimensional shapes.

These facts are among the most important building blocks in all of geometry, as you will see in the chapters to come.

In the next chapter we take a much closer look at right triangles. Building on things such as slope measure, it develops and explains some very useful tools for dealing with angles. These tools turn into powerful, important functions that play important roles in many areas of mathematics and science. These ideas are the basis of the subject called *trigonometry*.

Problem Set: 2.10

1. Elka wants to make beanbag chairs for her twins when they go away to college. She has a pattern for a shape like an 18 by 18 by 20-inch rectangular box. Her friend Liz used this pattern to make a chair for her daughter. Elka likes that chair, but doesn't think it is nearly big enough to be comfortable. She is thinking of enlarging the pattern by a factor of 2.

    (a) The amount of filling needed for the chair Liz made was 3.75 cu. ft. How much filling will Elka need for her chair design?

    (b) The beanbag filling comes in packages of 2 cubic feet, for $8.99 a package. How much did it cost Liz to fill the chair she made? How much would it cost Elka to fill the two enlarged chairs for her twins?

    (c) Elka thinks that it will cost too much to make the chairs she had planned. She decides to enlarge the pattern only by a factor of 1.5, instead. How much will the filling cost for these two chairs?

2. SugarSweet Company is making a new, larger sugar cube. They advertise that it contains three times the sugar of the cube that measures 1 by 1 by 1 cm. Calculate the dimensions of the larger sugar cube.

3. Alan Arf, the famous pet sculptor, has been commissioned to carve a large marble dog biscuit for display outside the home office of the Postman's Friend Dogfood Co. To make a preliminary model of his work, Alan started with a 1 by 1 by 2.5 foot wooden block. That turned out to be just the right starting shape, so he wants to start the real sculpture with a block of marble that is proportional to the wooden block. He wants the marble block to be as large as possible. However, it has to be shipped by truck, and the maximum allowable shipping weight is 60,000 pounds. Assuming that the marble weighs 200 lb. per cubic foot, what are the dimensions of the largest marble block he can get?

4. In this section you read this argument.

The volume of a cube of edge length s is s^3, and if the cube is scaled by *a* factor k, the volume of the scaled cube is

$$(ks)^3 = k^3 s^3$$

That is, the scaled volume is k^3 times the original volume.

Rewrite this argument without *using any algebraic symbols or letters that stand for quantities*. Then write a paragraph explaining why letters and other symbols are used in mathematics.

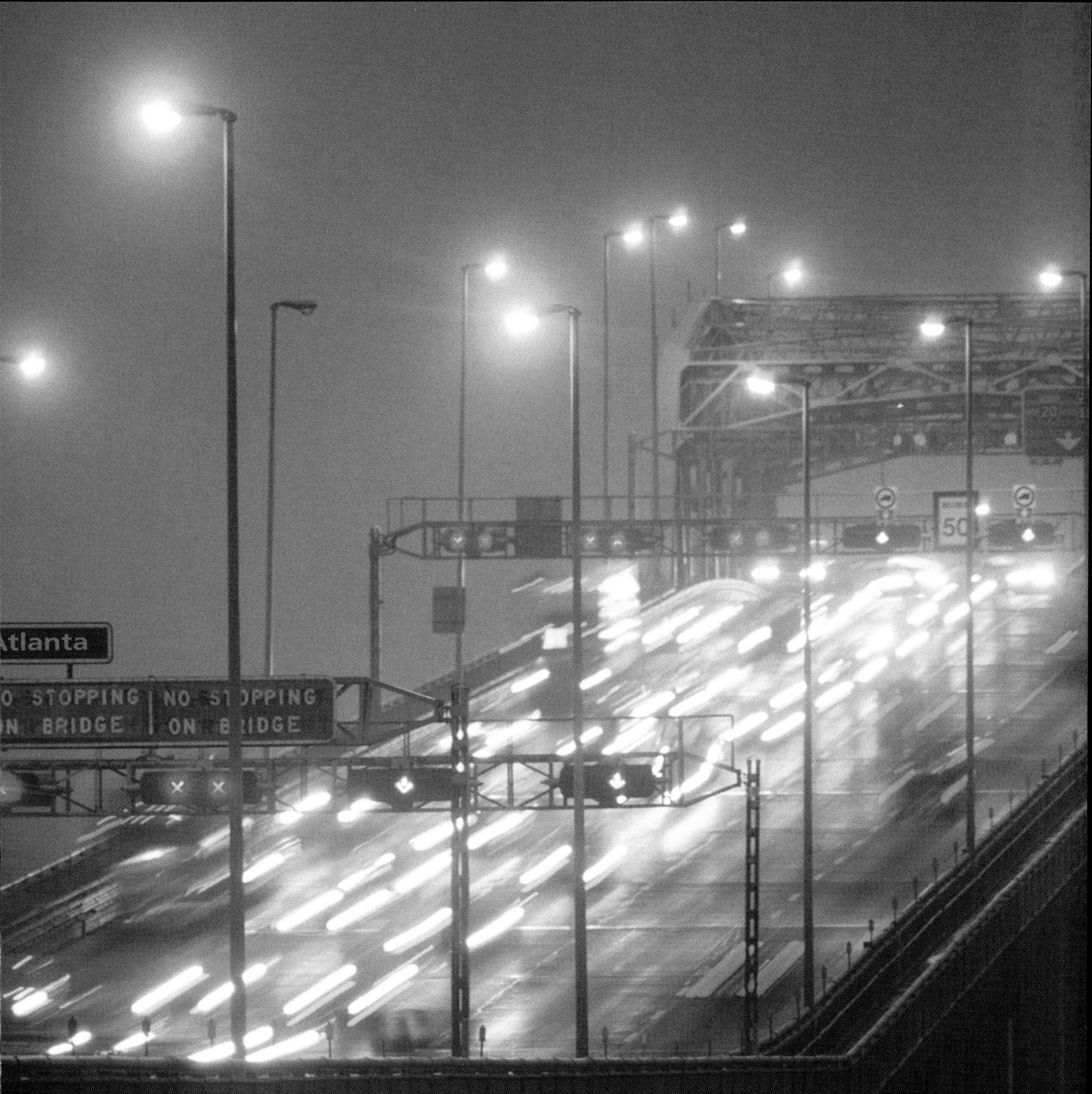
Atlanta
NO STOPPING ON BRIDGE
NO STOPPING ON BRIDGE
50

Farah Brown, M.D., Radiologist
Getting the Inside Story

Farah Brown wanted to be a doctor from high school days. "I always enjoyed science and math," she explains. "Also, my aunt was a nurse. I was very close to her and I admired her greatly. She helped me decide to become a doctor." Today, Farah is the vice chair of Radiology at Southwest Hospital and Medical Center in Atlanta, Georgia.

Farah majored in biology at Bishop College in Dallas, Texas. "At first, I thought I wanted to work in pediatrics, but I also found radiology fascinating." A few years later while attending medical school at Howard University she took an elective in radiology and that set her course. "For me, it's the perfect balance of research, academics and patient care," she explains.

Radiologists need to know how to read and interpret all the various types of imaging media, such as CAT scans, MRIs, as well as X rays. "The calculation of angles is often used to determine the positioning of bones from these images," Farah explains. "For example, with scoliosis, which is when a person's spine is bent in an 'S', the scope of the curvature is determined by a series of X rays that are taken from different angles while the patient is standing up. This is called a scoliosis series. Lines are drawn along the end point of the upper-most vertebra at the top of the curve and also at the end point of the lower-most vertebra at the bottom of the curve.

Second lines are then drawn that are perpendicular to the lines of the upper-most and lower-most vertebrae. The angle between the perpendiculars is the measured angle of scoliosis. These measurements," she continues, "help us to determine if the patient will outgrow the problem or if they will need surgery.

"I think it's important to decide what you want to do in life, and then go for it," declares Dr. Brown. "Be determined, be disciplined and stick to your goal. I hope I stand as a role model for young people in my community."

Introduction to Trigonometry: Tangles With Angles

CHAPTER 3

3.1 The Sine of an Acute Angle

Learning Outcomes

After studying this section, you will be able to:

Write the definition of the sine of an acute angle in a right triangle as a ratio;

Use a calculator to find the sine of an acute angle;

Use the sine of an acute angle as a problem solving tool;

Explain how to estimate the radius of the Earth.

Have you ever flown a kite? If so, did you ever wonder how high the kite was above the ground?

Betty and Jake are on the beach flying kites.

Betty had 200 feet of string and none is left. Jake had 150 feet of string and none is left. A friend estimated the angles that the string made with the ground for each person (Display 3.1).

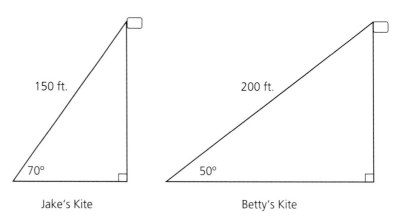

150 ft.   200 ft.

70°   50°

Jake's Kite   Betty's Kite

Display 3.1
Some displays in this chapter might not be to scale.

Which kite do you think is higher Jake's or Betty's? Why?

Determining the height of a kite can be a serious business, as the following example illustrates.

Humans have successfully harnessed the power of the wind for many purposes over the years. Recently, wind power is again being utilized as a source of renewable energy. In the Tehachapi Mountains of California, the wind is being captured by windmills and used to create electricity. One problem that scientists have in making good use of the wind is finding how high they should install the windmills. One easy way to find out at what height the wind is strongest is to fly a kite and measure how much force is on the string. But, how does one determine the height of the kite? Measuring the angle that the string makes with the ground allows them to calculate the height of the kite. The bigger the pull on the string, the stronger the wind.

Here is a typical problem that a "wind prospector" would need to solve: An engineer is flying a kite to measure the wind strength and lets out 39 feet of string. Assuming that the string is in a straight line, and that it makes an angle of 40° with the ground, calculate the height of the kite.

Two students, Rashad and Rolena remember that they studied *scaling* in **MATH** *Connections* and they decide to solve this problem using a scale diagram. Rashad decides to use a scale of 1 inch to each 10 feet and draws a diagram like the one in

Display 3.2(a). He determines that the length of *AC* should be

$$\frac{39}{10} = 3.9 = 3\frac{15}{16} \text{ inches}$$

Then he draws *CB* perpendicular to the ground (*AB*) and measures the length of *BC*.

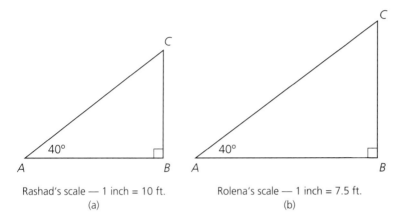

Rashad's scale — 1 inch = 10 ft.

(a)

Rolena's scale — 1 inch = 7.5 ft.

(b)

Display 3.2

1. Draw a right triangle like that in Display 3.2(a) with an angle of 40° and a hypotenuse of $3\frac{15}{16}$ inches. What is the length of *BC* in inches?
2. Using Rashad's scale, what is your estimate for the height of the kite?

a

Rolena uses a similar method, but she chooses a scale of 1 inch to each 7.5 feet (Display 3.2(b)).

1. Using Rolena's scale, draw an appropriate triangle. Using this triangle, what is your estimate on the height of the kite?
2. Do you get the same answer as when you used Rashad's scale? Explain.
3. Find the ratio of *BC* to *AC* for your triangle based on Rashad's scale, and then for your triangle based on Rolena's scale. Do you get the same result? Explain.

b

The key idea here is that the triangles you have drawn are similar, and consequently the ratios of corresponding sides will always be equal. What this means is that for *any* right triangle with an angle measuring 40° the ratio of its sides will be the same.

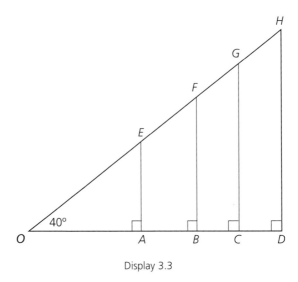

Display 3.3

As you see in Display 3.3, all of the right triangles involved are also similar, so the following ratios of lengths are equal.

$$\frac{AE}{OE} = \frac{BF}{OF} = \frac{CG}{OG} = \frac{DH}{OH}$$

For a 40° angle, mathematicians have found this ratio to be 0.643 (to three decimal places). Does this number agree with (or come close to) your ratios from Rashad's and Rolena's triangles? This ratio is called the sine of 40° and written sin 40°.

You will find a SIN key on your calculator and you will see how this key can help solve many problems without using any scale diagrams. For example, the problem of the wind prospector could be solved by simply noting in Display 3.4 that

$$\frac{opposite}{hypotenuse} = \sin 40° = 0.643$$

$$\frac{BC}{39} = \sin 40° = 0.643$$

or by cross multiplying

$$BC = 39(0.643) = 25.077$$

so the kite is about 25 feet high.

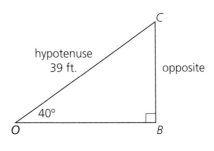

Display 3.4

The same procedure applies to any acute angle θ in a right triangle (Display 3.5). The **sine** of an acute angle θ in a right triangle is the ratio of the length of the side opposite θ to the length of the hypotenuse. That is,

About Symbols

The Greek letter θ, read theta, is frequently used in mathematics books to denote angles. Other Greek letters that are used include α, read alpha, and β, read beta.

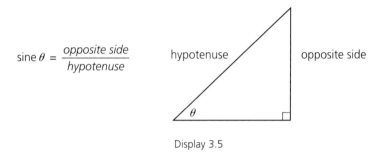

$$\text{sine } \theta = \frac{\textit{opposite side}}{\textit{hypotenuse}}$$

Display 3.5

The purpose of this section is to make you aware of how this ratio sine θ can be used to solve many measurement problems.

Everybody knows what a ball looks like. The word *ball* might bring to mind a baseball, basketball, or a bowling ball.

When viewed from a spaceship far above the Earth, the Earth looks like a ball.

You've probably seen pictures from a spaceship on TV or in magazines. A ball is also called a *sphere*, and the edge of one's view of a sphere or a ball looks like a circle.

This circle has a radius r which is also the radius of the sphere to which it is related.

1. **How would you measure the radius of a baseball?**

2. **How would you measure the radius of the Earth?**

It is interesting to know that a very good estimate of the radius of the Earth was made over 2000 years ago by a Greek astronomer named Hipparchus. He used the following ideas to estimate the radius of the Earth: Climb a mountain, say five miles high, to point A and look toward the horizon at point B, as in Display 3.6. He knew that triangle ABC was a right triangle. (You can learn why this is a right triangle in the Problem Set.)

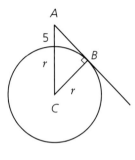

Display 3.6

Let's look at triangle ABC after it has been flipped, enlarged, and put into the position shown in Display 3.7.

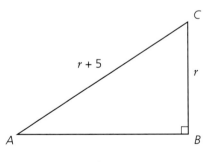

Display 3.7

Using instruments, the angle CAB was measured to be (about) 87.15°. Based on the ideas of our previous example, you should see that

$$\sin 87.15° = \frac{r}{r + 5}$$

or, using a calculator to five decimal places,

$$0.99876 = \frac{r}{r + 5}$$

As a result of cross-multiplying, one obtains

$$0.99876\,(r + 5) = r$$

or

$$0.99876\,r + 4.99380 = r$$

or

$$0.00124\,r = 4.99380$$

thus

$$r = 4027.258065 \text{ miles}$$

That is, the radius of the Earth is approximately 4027 miles.

Assuming a radius of 4027 miles, what is the circumference of Earth at the equator, assuming also that the Earth is round?

Jules Verne wrote the book *Around the World in Eighty Days* in 1873. The travelers in that book did not travel around the equator. However, suppose they did travel around the equator. What average speed, in miles per hour, would they have to maintain in order to go around the world in eighty days? What were the fastest ways to travel in 1873? It is not uncommon for jet planes to maintain an average speed of 550 miles per hour, even with refueling. How long would it take such a plane to go around the Earth? Does it matter that the plane is flying about 6 miles above the Earth?

Problem Set: 3.1

Problems 1–7 will help you become familiar with computing the sine of an angle using your calculator. For each figure, find the value of x to two decimal places.

1.

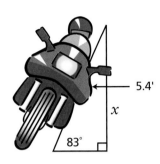

60' x

30°

2.

5.4'

x

83°

3.

6'

x

25°

4.

x

8"

19°

5.

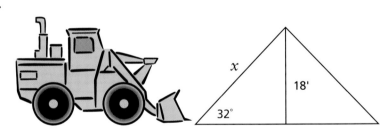

x

18'

32°

6.

17'

x

40°

7.

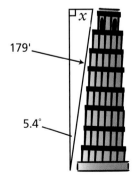

x

179'

5.4°

8. John, a student at Bates School, says that the figure in problem 7 represents the leaning tower of Pisa. Is John correct?

9. On your calculator, press SIN 0 ENTER. Can you explain the answer? What happens when you take the sine of angles that are greater than, but close to 0°?

10. On your calculator, press SIN 90 ENTER. Can you explain the answer? What happens when you take the sine of angles that are less than, but close to 90°?

11. Find the value of r in Display 3.8.

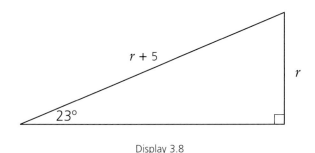

Display 3.8

12. In order to estimate the radius of the Earth, a person climbed a mountain 4 miles high and found that the angle $\angle CAB$ in the diagram below measures 87.4°.

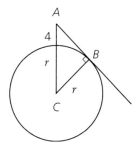

Display 3.9

What estimate of the radius of the Earth did this person get? Is there a mountain somewhere in the world which has a height of 4 miles above the Earth (sea level)?

13. (a) What is the area of the parallelogram in Display 3.10(a)?

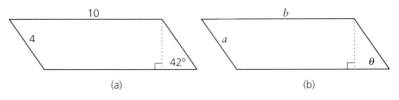

(a)   (b)

Display 3.10

(b) Generalize your solution to find a formula for the area of the parallelogram in Display 3.10(b).

14. (a) What is the area of the parallelogram in Display 3.11(a)?

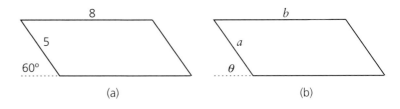

(a)   (b)

Display 3.11

(b) Generalize your solution to find a formula for the area of the parallelogram in Display 3.11(b).

15. Given a right triangle (Display 3.12)

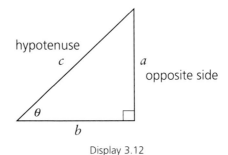

Display 3.12

it is customary to define the **cosecant of** θ, written csc θ, as

$$\csc \theta = \frac{hypotenuse}{opposite \ side} = \frac{c}{a}$$

(a) What is the relation between the sin θ and csc θ?

(b) Explain why there is no need for a **csc** key on a calculator.

16. Explain why one can consider

$$f(\theta) = \sin \theta, \text{ for } 0° < \theta < 90°$$

to be a function.

17. When Hipparchus calculated the approximate radius of the Earth, he used an important fact about tangents to circles.

> The angle made by a tangent line and the radius at the point of tangency is a right angle.

How could he be sure? You actually know the answer, but you may not know that you know. We'll lead you through the reasoning which proves that this is always the case. We'll supply the questions; you supply the answers.

To help keep the notation clear, we have drawn and labeled the diagram in Display 3.13. It shows a line, t, tangent at P to a circle with center C. Now, either the angles made by t and PC are right angles or they're not, right? You will show that "they're not" is impossible. That is, the assumption that they are not right angles leads to a conclusion that can't possibly be true.

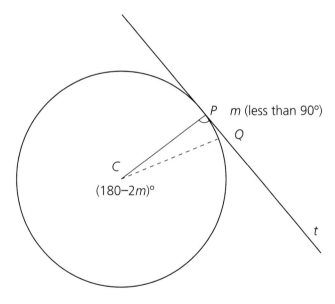

Display 3.13

(a) If the two angles formed by t and PC are not right angles, one of them must measure less than 90°. Why?

(b) If we call the measure of this smaller angle m, then $2m < 180°$. Why?

On the side of the smaller-than-right angle, we've drawn a line segment from C that makes a $(180 - 2m)°$ angle with PC, and extended it until it intersects at some point, Q.

(c) PCQ is a triangle. What is the measure of $\angle CQP$? How do you know?

(d) What kind of triangle is *PCQ*? How do you know?

(e) Is *QC* longer, shorter, or the same length as *PC* ? How do you know?

(f) Is *Q* inside, outside, or on the circle? How do you know?

(g) Why can't this happen? *Hint:* What does it mean to say that a line is tangent to a circle?

(h) Since it is impossible for *PC* and *t* **NOT** to form right angles, . . . (Finish this sentence.)

18. When Jake was in school, students did not have calculators.

In order to find the sine of an angle, students had to use tables. Part of such a table is given in Display 3.14 where *θ* is measured in degrees.

θ	*sin θ*	*θ*	*sin θ*	*θ*	*sin θ*	*θ*	*sin θ*	*θ*	*sin θ*
1	.0175	11	.1908	21	.3584	31	.5150	41	.6561
2	.0349	12	.2079	22	.3746	32	.5299	42	.6691
3	.0523	13	.2250	23	.3907	33	.5446	43	.6820
4	.0698	14	.2419	24	.4067	34	.5592	44	.6947
5	.0872	15	.2588	25	.4226	35	.5736	45	.7071
6	.1045	16	.2756	26	.4384	36	.5878	46	.7193
7	.1219	17	.2924	27	.4540	37	.6018	47	.7314
8	.1392	18	.3090	28	.4695	38	.6157	48	.7431
9	.1564	19	.3256	29	.4848	39	.6293	49	.7547
10	.1736	20	.3420	30	.5000	40	.6428	50	.7660

Display 3.14

(a) Are there any ideas you get about the sine from this table that you did not get before, when computing these numbers on your calculator?

(b) You have previously studied the idea of *linear interpolation*. Remember? Use the above table and linear interpolation to estimate sin 27.4°. Now compute sin 27.4° on your calculator. Do you think the two answers are close together?

19. A baseball has a radius of 1.45 inches. The Earth has a radius of (about) 4000 miles.

(a) If a piece of string is put around a great circle on this baseball, how many inches of string are needed?

(b) If a piece of string is put around a great circle on this baseball, but then moved one inch "out" from the surface, how many inches of string must be added to the amount in part (a) to make a complete circle?

(c) How many inches of string are needed to go around the equator of the Earth?

(d) If a string is put around the equator of the Earth, but then moved one inch "out" from the surface, how many inches of string must be added to the amount in part (c) to make a complete circle?

(e) Do the answers to parts (b) and (d) make sense to you? Explain!

20. A new ski lodge is being built in Vermont, and the builder wants to allow for a skylight. Display 3.15 shows a cross-sectional plan for the roof. Calculate the height w, in meters, allowing for the skylight.

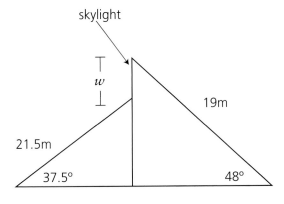

Display 3.15

3.2 The Cosine of an Acute Angle

Learning Outcomes

After studying this section, you will be able to:

Write the definition of the cosine of an acute angle in a right triangle as a ratio;

Use a calculator to find the cosine of an acute angle;

Use the cosine of an acute angle as a problem solving tool;

Explain how to estimate the distance from the Earth to the Moon.

Betty watched and enjoyed the Winter Olympics on TV. She thought that skiing looked easy and seemed to be a lot of fun, so she bought a pair of skis and went up to the mountains in Colorado to a ski jump. She was warned that learning to ski jump took a lot of time and practice, but Betty was sure there would be no problem. Just like the Olympic skiers, she went down, then up, and then down.

Boy, did she go down! Nobody really knows how many bones were broken, but she was in the hospital for several weeks. When Betty was first taken to the hospital, the doctors wanted X rays taken so that they could see where the bones were broken.

One of the problems faced by medical people is that X rays don't usually show exactly where a bone is broken. This happens because the bone is not always parallel to the X ray film. For example, suppose that we look at a side view. The horizontal line segment is supposed to be the film and the darkened line is a bone. The *X* mark on the bone indicates where a break is located (Display 3.16).

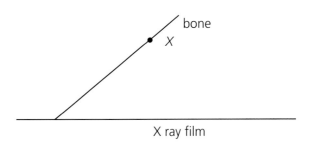

bone

X

X ray film

Display 3.16

Doctors would like to know the location of the break. It would help, for example, to know the distance L from A to X (Display 3.17).

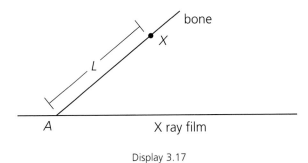

Display 3.17

What doctors can measure from the X ray film, however, is the distance AB indicated in Display 3.18.

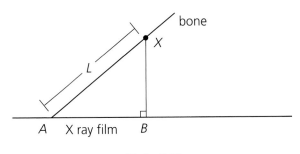

Display 3.18

Doctors frequently know (or can estimate) the angle XAB. They want to use this to find L. Suppose angle XAB is 30° (and the distance AB on the X ray film is 9 inches (Display 3.19).

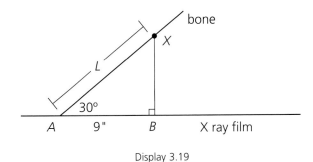

Display 3.19

Using a scale diagram, draw a triangle ABX similar to that in Display 3.19 and estimate the length L.

Look closely at the right triangle *XAB* (Display 3.20).

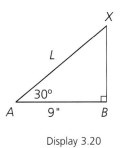

Display 3.20

From our study of similar triangles, we know that all of the right triangles shown in Display 3.21 are similar,

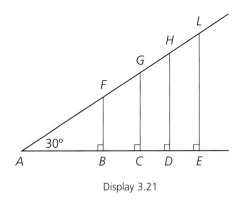

Display 3.21

so the following ratios of lengths are equal.

$$\frac{AB}{AF} = \frac{AC}{AG} = \frac{AD}{AH} = \frac{AE}{AL}$$

Indeed, for any right triangle with an acute angle of 30°, the ratio of lengths

$$\frac{adjacent\ side}{hypotenuse}$$

is going to be the same number (Display 3.22).

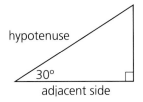

Display 3.22

Mathematicians have found that this ratio, known as *cosine 30°*, is 0.8660 to four decimal places. Show how this ratio can be used to estimate the length L in Display 3.20 without using a scale diagram. Does this estimate agree with (or come close to) that obtained when you used a scale diagram?

a

One can follow the same procedure with any acute angle θ in a right triangle. The **cosine** of an acute angle in a right triangle is the ratio of the length of the adjacent side to the length of the hypotenuse (Display 3.23). That is,

$$\cos \theta = \frac{adjacent\ side}{hypotenuse}$$

Display 3.23

The purpose of this section is to make you aware of how this ratio $\cos \theta$ can be used to solve many measurement problems.

As another example, consider the following situation.

b

1. The distance from the surface of the Earth to the surface of the Moon is about 240,000 miles. Olympic runners have been able to run about 14 miles per hour. What if an Olympic runner were able to keep on running at this speed along a road from the Earth to the Moon. How long would it take?

2. Racing cars have been known to travel more than 170 miles per hour. What if a race car were able to travel at 170 mph on a road 240,000 miles long from the Earth to the Moon. How long would it take?

 How long did it take Apollo 11 to travel from the Earth to the Moon?

How did anyone come up with the estimate that the distance from the surface of the Earth to the surface of the Moon is about 240,000 miles? Remember Hipparchus, the Greek astronomer, who over 2000 years ago estimated the radius of the Earth to be about 4000 miles? Well, he also estimated the distance from the center of the Earth to the center of the Moon. Hipparchus used a diagram similar to that in Display 3.24.

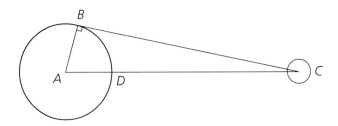

Display 3.24

He knew that the lengths of *AB* and *AD* were each about 4000 miles. He was also able to use instruments to measure angle *BAC* as 89.05°. Let's rotate triangle *ABC* and put it into the position shown in Display 3.25:

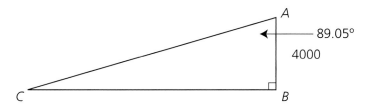

Display 3.25

From this display one observes

$$\cos 89.05° = \frac{4000}{AC}$$

or, using a calculator,

$$0.01658 = \frac{4000}{AC}$$

or

$$AC = \frac{4000}{0.01658} \approx 241{,}255 \text{ miles}$$

What a genius!

You have now seen two important ratios related to acute angles—the *sine* and the *cosine*. There is a useful relation between these ratios which will be needed for later material. The following activities should help you discover this relation.

1. In the table of Display 3.26, we have computed $(\sin 25°)^2 + (\cos 25°)^2$ for the first line. Using measures for angle *A* (other than 25°) copy and complete the table using a calculator.

Angle *A*	$(\sin A)^2 + (\cos A)^2$
25°	1

Display 3.26

2. Look at the right triangle in Display 3.27.

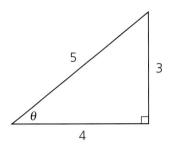

Display 3.27

What is $(\sin \theta)^2 + (\cos \theta)^2$?

3. What conjecture would you make about $(\sin q)^2 + (\cos q)^2$ for any angle? Let's examine additional examples of our conjecture, but let's use the table feature of the TI-82 (TI-83) to save time. Enter in the Y= list: $y_1 = (\sin x)^2$, $y_2 = (\cos x)^2$, and $y_3 = (\sin x)^2 + (\cos x)^2$. Make sure you are in Degree mode. Press 2nd WINDOW (The display shows TABLE SETUP.) and set the TblStart to 1, and $\triangle$ Tbl to 1. Select AUTO for both variable choices. Press 2nd GRAPH (for Table). Use the right arrow key to access the column for y_3. What do you see? Now use your down arrow to scroll through 89 degrees. What results are you seeing in the y_3 column? Do you think the results will change if you work in increments of 0.5 degrees instead of 1 degree? Reset your TABLE SETUP menu and check the table columns.

4. Now look at the triangle in Display 3.28.

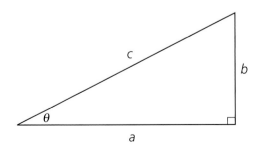

Display 3.28

Write each of the following in terms of *a*, *b*, and *c*.

(a) $\sin \theta =$ (b) $(\sin \theta)^2 =$

(c) $\cos \theta =$ (d) $(\cos \theta)^2 =$

What do you notice about $(\sin \theta)^2 + (\cos \theta)^2$?
It is standard to write
$$(\sin \theta)^2 \text{ as } \sin^2 \theta$$
and
$$(\cos \theta)^2 \text{ as } \cos^2 \theta$$
The relation noted above can now be written as
$$\sin^2 \theta + \cos^2 \theta = ?$$

Problem Set: 3.2

Problems 1–5 will help you become familiar with computing the cosine of an angle, using a calculator. For each figure, find the value of *x* to two decimal places.

1.

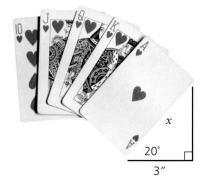

20°
3"

2.

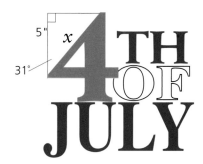

5"
x
31°

3.2 The Cosine of an Acute Angle

3.

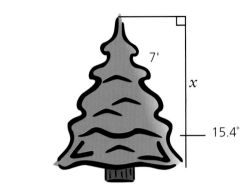

4.

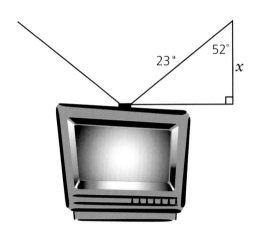

5.

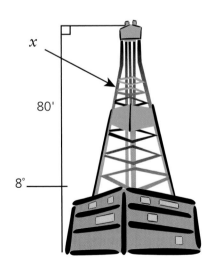

6.   For an acute angle θ in a right triangle (Display 3.29), it is customary to define the **secant of** θ, written sec θ, as the ratio of the length of the hypotenuse to the length of the adjacent side. That is,

$$\sec \theta = \frac{hypotenuse}{adjacent\ side}$$

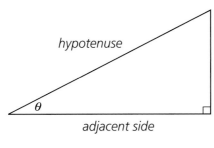

Display 3.29

(a) What is the relation between the sec θ and cos θ?
(b) Why there is no need for a **sec** key on a calculator?
(c) What is sec 31.7°?

7. For an acute angle θ, explain why neither sin θ nor cos θ can be greater than 1.

8. You want to put an antenna on a flat roof. The antenna tower is 17 feet high. A wire making an angle of 35° with the vertical side of the tower is to be used to help support the tower (Display 3.30). How long is the wire?

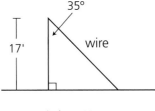

Display 3.30

9. Remember Jake who had to use tables to compute the sine of an angle? Well, believe it or not, he had to use other tables to compute the cosine of an angle. Part of such a table is given in Display 3.31 where θ is measured in degrees.

θ	cos θ	θ	cos θ	θ	cos θ	θ	cos θ	θ	cos θ
1	.9998	11	.9816	21	.9336	31	.8572	41	.7547
2	.9994	12	.9781	22	.9272	32	.8480	42	.7431
3	.9986	13	.9744	23	.9205	33	.8387	43	.7314
4	.9976	14	.9703	24	.9135	34	.8290	44	.7193
5	.9962	15	.9659	25	.9063	35	.8192	45	.7071
6	.9945	16	.9613	26	.8988	36	.8090	46	.6947
7	.9925	17	.9563	27	.8910	37	.7986	47	.6820
8	.9903	18	.9511	28	.8829	38	.7880	48	.6691
9	.9877	19	.9455	29	.8746	39	.7771	49	.6561
10	.9848	20	.9397	30	.8660	40	.7660	50	.6428

Display 3.31

a) Are there any ideas you get about the cos θ from this table that you did not get before, when computing these numbers on your calculator?

b) Use the above table and linear interpolation to estimate cos 27.4°. Now compute cos 27.4° on your calculator. Do you think the two answers are close together?

c) How would you compare the table of sine values in Display 3.14 with the table of cosine values in Display 3.31?

10. If you position yourself at point P in the middle of one end of a board used for table tennis and look at the end of the table tennis net, the angle formed is 33.7°. The distance between a point Q at the end of the net and P is 5.4 feet. Find the length of the table tennis net and the length of the table shown in Display 3.32.

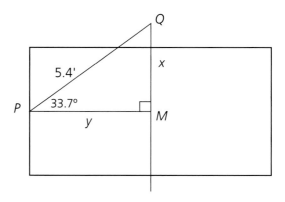

Display 3.32

3.3 The Tangent of an Acute Angle

Airports have used what are called *ceilometers* to find out how high the clouds are in order to see whether or not planes should be allowed to take off or land. A ceilometer consists of three pieces. The first item is a light projector (like a movie or slide projector, but bigger). This projector throws a bright beam of light vertically (straight up) into the clouds (Display 3.33).

Projector

Display 3.33

The light from the projector makes a spot of light on the clouds.

Another instrument, some distance away from the projector, detects the light spot (Display 3.34).

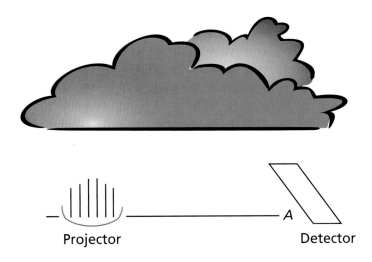

Display 3.34

At the location of the detector there is also an instrument that measures the angle at *A*. The distance from the projector to the detector is known. We now have a right triangle (Display 3.35) where the distance *CA* is known and the measure of angle *A* is known. Suppose *CA* has a length of 1500 feet and angle *A* measures 78° (Display 3.36).

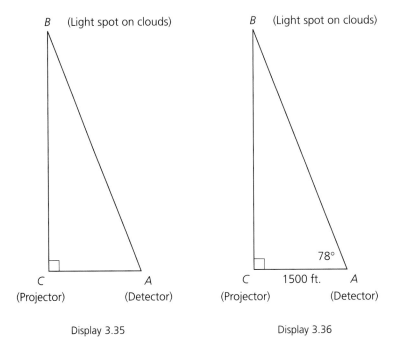

Display 3.35   Display 3.36

1. Using the cosine of an angle, find the length of *AB* in feet.
2. Using the answer from part 1 above and the Pythagorean Theorem, find the distance *CB* in feet. That is, find how high the clouds are.

There is an easier way to solve this problem. From our study of similar triangles, we know that all of the right triangles in Display 3.37 are similar:

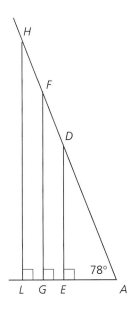

Display 3.37

so that the following ratios of lengths are equal:

$$\frac{HL}{AL} = \frac{FG}{AG} = \frac{DE}{AE}$$

Any one of these equivalent ratios is called the **tangent of 78°**, which is written **tan 78°**. In general, the **tangent** of an angle θ in a right triangle, written **tan** θ, is the ratio of the length of the opposite side to the length of the adjacent side (Display 3.38). That is,

$$\tan \theta = \frac{opposite\ side}{adjacent\ side}$$

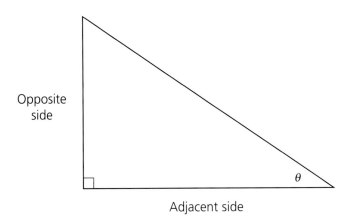

Display 3.38

Let's return to our problem of finding the cloud height (Display 3.39).

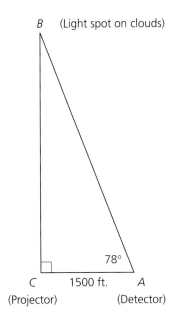

Display 3.39

1. Using a calculator, find tan 78°. (Make sure your calculator is in Degree mode.)
2. Using the result of the first problem, estimate the height of the clouds in Display 3.39. Does this result agree with your previous estimate?

For another example involving the tangent of an angle, consider the following: Wires and metal tubes are part of many different types of instruments and machines, including automobiles, walkmen, cameras, TV sets, etc.

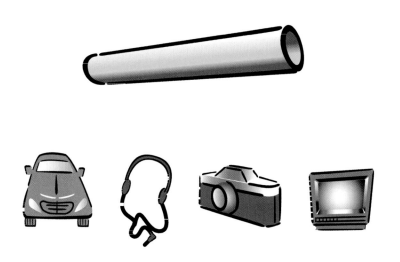

During construction of such items one sometimes needs to know the diameter of the wires or tubes being used. One device that has been used for measuring diameters is the V-gauge. A side view of a V-gauge is given in Display 3.40.

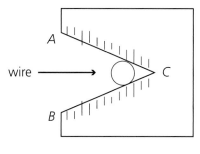

Display 3.40

For this particular V-gauge, the angle *ACB* measures 40°.

1. How do you think a V-gauge is used to measure the diameter of the wire in Display 3.40?

a

2. Other than a V-gauge, do you know of other methods or other tools for measuring the diameter of a wire or a tube?

Let's magnify part of the side view of the V-gauge and insert the radius lines (Display 3.41).

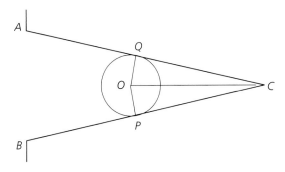

Display 3.41

In this diagram, *O* is the center of the circle representing the wire (or tube), while *P* and *Q* are the points where the wire touches the segments *CB* and *CA*, respectively.

1. What is the measure of angle *OPC*? Explain.

2. What is the measure of angle *OQC*? Explain.

b

3. What is the measure of angle *OCP* and of angle *OCQ*? Explain.

Our job is to find the length of the radius *OP*. By doubling this number we can compute the diameter of the wire.

If you know that the length of *CP* is 7mm, do you have enough information to find the length of *OP*?

c

Return to our V-gauge (Display 3.42).

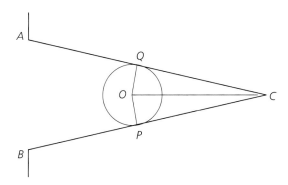

Display 3.42

We know that the measure of angle OCP is 20°. Thus the ratio $\frac{OP}{CP}$ is nothing but the tangent of 20°. That is,

$$\tan 20° = \frac{OP}{CP}$$

The tangent of 20° can be found on your calculator. First make sure you are in the degree mode. Then push the TAN 20 ENTER keys. You will find

$$\tan 20° = .3639702343$$

We now have

$$.3640 = \frac{OP}{CP} \text{ (using four decimal places for tan 20°).}$$

If, for example, we know that CP is 9 millimeters in length, then

$$.3640 = \frac{OP}{9}$$

so $OP = 3.2760$ mm, and it follows that the diameter of the wire is 6.5520 mm.

In this chapter we have been looking at ratios of lengths with names like sine, cosine, tangent, etc. The study of such ratios is known as *trigonometry*.

A Word to Know: **Trigonometry** is a branch of mathematics which deals with the connections between sides and angles of triangles and related geometric figures.

About Words

The word *trigonometry* comes from the Greek words *trigonon*, meaning triangle, and *metron*, meaning to measure.

Problem Set: 3.3

Problems 1–7 will give you practice using your calculator to find the tangent of an angle. In each case, find *x*.

1.

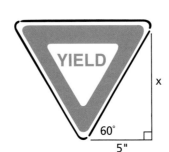

4"

45°

x

2.

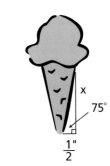

x

75°

$\frac{1}{2}$"

3.

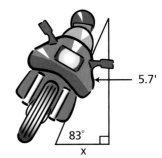

x

30°

35 yards

4.

5.7'

83°

x

5

YIELD

x

60°

5"

6.

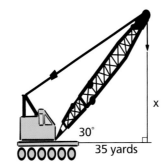

x

6' 3"

15.4°

7.

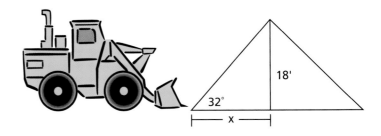

18'

32°

x

8. In the Display 3.43, two tracking stations are located at points A and B. Points A and B are 40 miles apart. At the tracking stations, people are measuring the angles of a weather balloon located at point C.
   The measurements of the angles are given in the diagram. What is the height h of the weather balloon?

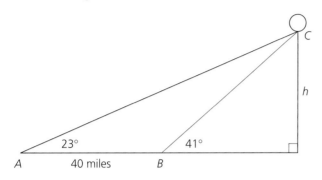

Display 3.43

9. The tangent of an angle can be written in terms of the sin θ and cos θ Explain how

$$\tan \theta = \frac{\sin \theta}{\cos \theta}$$

Recall that $\sin^2 \theta + \cos^2 \theta = 1$. By dividing both sides of this equation by $\cos^2 \theta$, show that

$$\tan^2 \theta + 1 = \sec^2 \theta$$

10. In a right triangle (Display 3.44), with an acute angle it is customary to define the **cotangent of** θ, written cot θ, to be the ratio

$$\cot \theta = \frac{adjacent\ side}{opposite\ side}$$

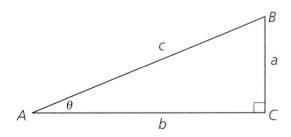

Display 3.44

(a) How is the cotangent of an angle related to the tangent of an angle?

(b) Why is there no need for a **cot** key on a calculator?

(c) What is cot 43.5°?

11. Using Display 3.45, explain the following identities:

$$\sin (90° - \theta) = \cos \theta \qquad \cos (90° - \theta) = \sin \theta$$

$$\tan (90° - \theta) = \cot \theta \qquad \cot (90° - \theta) = \tan \theta$$

$$\sec (90 - \theta) = \csc \theta \qquad \csc (90° - \theta) = \sec \theta$$

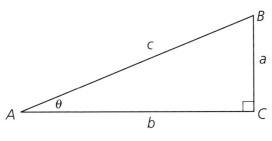

Display 3.45

12. A surveyor wants to find the height of the mountain in Display 3.46. The measurements indicated in the diagram are made. What is the height of the mountain?

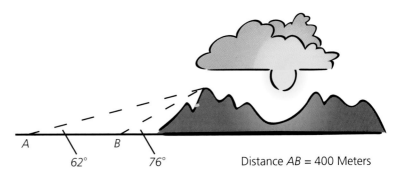

Display 3.46

13. From two tracking stations A and B which are 400 miles apart, the elevation angles of a satellite are determined to be $32°$ and $63°$, as illustrated in Display 3.47:

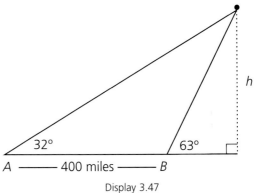

Display 3.47

What is the height h of the satellite?

14. In forestry, trigonometry is sometimes used to determine the height of a tree. How do you think trigonometry is used to determine the height h of a tree (Display 3.48)? What measurements are made? Make up an example to show your ideas.

Display 3.48

15. (a) Using a calculator, compute tan 0°. How would you explain this answer to a friend?

(b) What happens when you try to compute tan 90° on a calculator?

16. Explain why

$$f(\theta) = \tan\,\theta\,,\text{ for } 0° < \theta < 90°$$

can be considered a function.

17. In a coordinate plane, draw a straight line which has a positive slope. Explain how the slope of this line is related to the tangent of an angle.

3.3 The Tangent of an Acute Angle

3.4 What Do These SIN⁻¹, COS⁻¹, and TAN⁻¹ Keys Do?

Learning Outcomes

After studying this section, you will be able to:

Use SIN⁻¹, COS⁻¹, and TAN⁻¹ keys on a calculator to solve inverse problems;

Explain how $\sin^{-1}x$, $\cos^{-1}x$, and $\tan^{-1}x$ can be viewed as inverse functions;

Identify the domains of the functions $\sin^{-1}x$, $\cos^{-1}x$, and $\tan^{-1}x$.

In the previous three sections you have become aware of uses for the SIN, COS, and TAN keys on a calculator. You will notice that there are second level keys marked SIN⁻¹, COS⁻¹, and TAN⁻¹. The purpose of this section is to introduce these keys by having you demonstrate their role in solving measurement problems.

1. Using your ruler and protractor, draw a 3-4-5 right triangle.

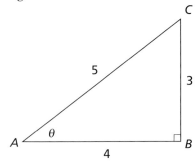

Display 3.49

Your job is to find the angle θ. Using your protractor, measure your angle θ as carefully as possible. What is your answer? Compare your answer with other students in the class.

2. We know from Display 3.49 that

$$\tan \theta = \frac{3}{4} = 0.75$$

$$\sin \theta = \frac{3}{5} = 0.60$$

$$\cos \theta = \frac{4}{5} = 0.80$$

But what is the angle θ? A problem like this is called an *inverse problem*. Take the angle you obtained in problem 1. Using your calculator, compute the tangent of your angle. Is it 0.75 or close to 0.75? Compute the sine of your angle. Is it 0.60 or close to 0.60? Compute the cosine of your angle. Is it 0.80 close to 0.80?

3. In Display 3.50 we see that $\sin \alpha = \frac{5}{7} = 0.7143$ (to four decimal places). Using whatever method you want, try to find or estimate the angle or α (read *alpha*) in Display 3.50.

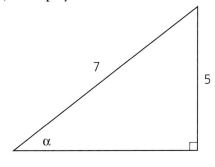

Display 3.50

The problems we are trying to solve, which we have called *inverse problems*, are just the type of problems for which the SIN⁻¹, COS⁻¹, and TAN⁻¹ on a calculator can be used. For example, what if you wanted to find the angle θ in Display 3.51:

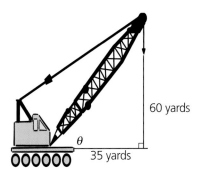

Display 3.51

You can see that

$$\tan \theta = \frac{60}{35} = 1.7143 \text{ (using four decimal places)}$$

We want to find an angle θ such that

$$\tan \theta = 1.7143$$

It is standard to write

$$\theta = \tan^{-1}(1.7143)$$

which is read "θ is an angle whose tangent is 1.7143." You can find such an angle θ on your calculator. Just press 2nd TAN (for TAN⁻¹) followed by 1.7143. You should get

$$\tan^{-1}(1.7143) = 59.74° \text{ (using two decimal places).}$$

1. Using the **SIN**$^{-1}$ (2nd **SIN**) on your TI-83, find the angle β (read *beta*) in Display 3.52:

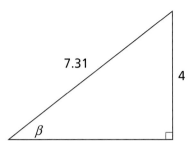

Display 3.52

2. Using the **COS**$^{-1}$ (2nd **COS**) on your TI-83, find the angle α in Display 3.53:

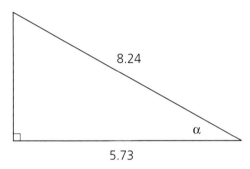

Display 3.53

One may regard sin θ, cos θ, and tan θ as functions with domain $0° < \theta < 90°$. In a similar way, $\sin^{-1}x$, $\cos^{-1}x$, and $\tan^{-1}x$, may be regarded as functions which behave as **inverse functions**. What do we mean by this? In the previous sections we have been entering angle measures, represented by variables θ, x, α or β, into a calculator and computing the sin, cos, or tan of the angle. For example, to compute sin θ, we keyed in the angle measure. (Display 3.54.)

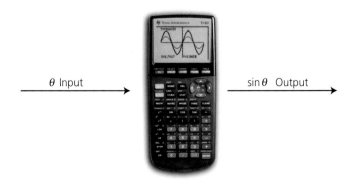

θ Input   sin θ Output

Display 3.54

Now we are reversing the process (Display 3.55).

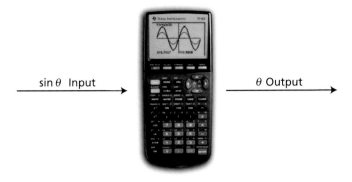

sin θ Input

θ Output

Display 3.55

1. As a numerical example, using your TI-83, find
   sin 24° (Display 3.56).

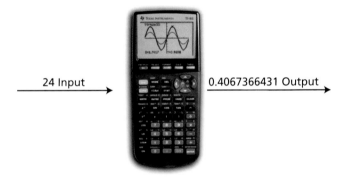

24 Input

0.4067366431 Output

Display 3.56

2. Now, to find the angle measure that has a sin
   value of .4067366431, perform the following
   (Display 3.57).

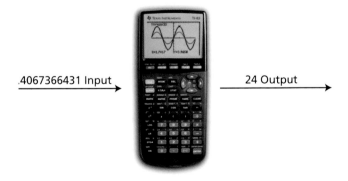

.4067366431 Input

24 Output

Display 3.57

We can read $\sin^{-1}x$ as "the angle between 0 and 90 degrees whose sine is x."

1. Without using your calculator, what is $\tan^{-1}1$?

2. Without using your calculator, what is $\cos^{-1}(\cos 35°)$?

3. Without using your calculator, what is $\sin(\sin^{-1} 0.37542135)$?

4. From the work that we have done so far, what domains would you give to the functions $\sin^{-1}x$, $\cos^{-1}x$, $\tan^{-1}x$ respectively?

As an example of a situation in which these inverse functions can be useful, consider the following: The space station RIM is put in an equatorial orbit 500 miles above the Earth. We wish to locate tracking stations along the equator. Each tracking station has a scanning screen which covers 180° with the horizon as shown in Display 3.58.

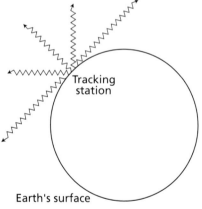

Tracking station

Earth's surface

Display 3.58

The problem is to locate tracking stations close enough to each other so that we do not have gaps where the space station is not being observed by at least one scanner, as in Display 3.59.

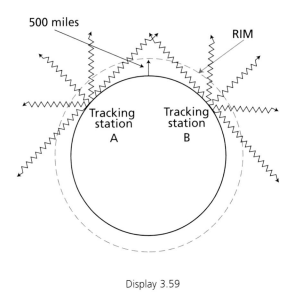

Display 3.59

Now, the furthest apart that stations A and B could be is illustrated in Display 3.60.

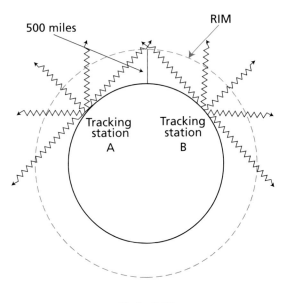

Display 3.60

Using 4000 miles as the radius of the Earth and observing the symmetry in the above figure, you should see that it is necessary to find the length of the arc (part of the circumference) *d* in Display 3.61.

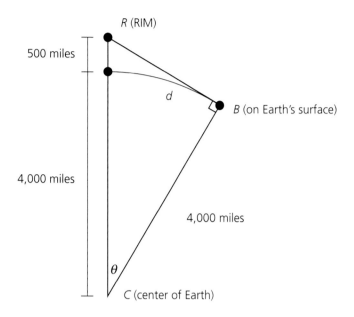

Display 3.61

1. Find the distance *d*. (*Hint*: Find the angle θ. Then use the fact that the length of an arc is proportional to its associated angle.) That is, in Display 3.62,

$$\frac{\theta}{360} = \frac{arc\ length\ d}{circumference}$$

2. How many stations are necessary to be sure there are no gaps along the equator?

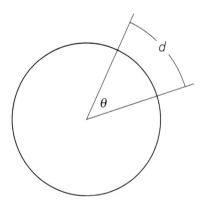

Display 3.62

Problem Set: 3.4

Problems 1–5 will help you become familiar with the "inverse" keys on your calculator. In each problem, find the measure of angle θ .

1.

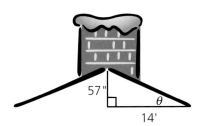

57 "

14'

θ

2.

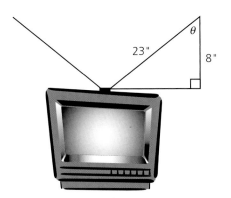

23 "

8 "

θ

3.

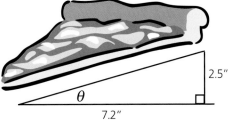

2.5"

7.2"

θ

4.

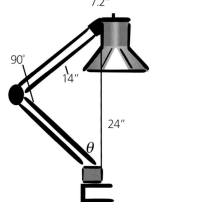

90°

14"

24"

θ

5.

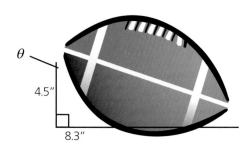

θ

4.5"

8.3"

6. A rectangle is 24 centimeters long and 10 centimeters wide. Find the angles that a diagonal makes with the sides.

7. A 40 foot ladder is used to reach the top of a 30 foot wall. If the ladder extends 4 feet past the top of the wall, what is the angle that the ladder forms with the horizontal ground?

8. A space station is put in an equatorial orbit 200 miles above the Earth. You want to locate tracking stations along the equator. Each tracking station has a scanning screen which covers 180° with the horizon. What is the longest distance allowed between two tracking stations so that there are no gaps?

3.5 The Law of Sines–
The Law of Cosines

There are two laws—one obeyed by sines, the other by cosines. In this section you will see how these laws expand a person's toolbox for solving measurement problems.

In the triangle *ABC* of Display 3.63, where all angles are acute, a perpendicular is dropped from *C* to the segment *AB*.

Learning Outcomes

After studying this section, you will be able to:

Explain the Law of Sines;

Use the Law of Sines in solving measurement problems;

Explain the Law of Cosines;

Use the Law of Cosines in solving measurement problems.

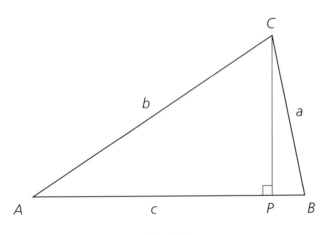

Display 3.63

The letter *P* is used to denote the point of intersection of this perpendicular and the segment *AB*. Observe that

$$\sin A = \frac{CP}{b}$$

and by cross multiplying you have

$$b \sin A = CP$$

1. Show that
$$a \sin B = CP$$

2. Explain why
$$b \sin A = a \sin B$$

3. Explain how one uses the result of problem 2 to obtain
$$\frac{\sin A}{a} = \frac{\sin B}{b}$$

4. Using a process similar to the above, show that

$$\frac{\sin A}{a} = \frac{\sin C}{c}$$

5. Explain why

$$\frac{\sin A}{a} = \frac{\sin C}{c} = \frac{\sin B}{b}$$

The equation in problem 5 above is known as the **Law of Sines.** This law can be a big help in obtaining measurements in triangles where some information is known. The following exercises will help to demonstrate this idea.

1. In the triangle of Display 3.64, find the length of *AC*, the length of *AB*, and the measure of angle *ACB*.

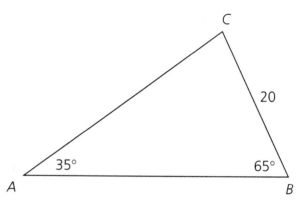

Display 3.64

2. In the triangle of Display 3.65, find the measures of the angles at *C* and at *A*.

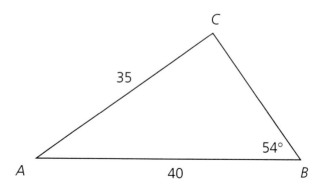

Display 3.65

Problem Set: 3.5

1. Two ships leave the harbor at Boston. The angle between their paths is 43°. One ship is traveling at a rate of 35 miles an hour, the other ship is traveling at a rate of 25 miles per hour. At the end of two hours, what is the distance between the two ships?

2. A Delta Airlines flight from Houston to Cincinnati, a distance of 1029 miles, encounters a violent thunderstorm immediately after takeoff and flies off course by 22.5°. After flying off course for 400 miles, how far is the plane from Cincinnati (Display 3.72)?

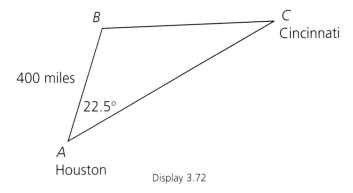

Display 3.72

3. In the triangle of Display 3.73, find the measure of the angle at *B*, the length of *AB*, and the length of *AC*.

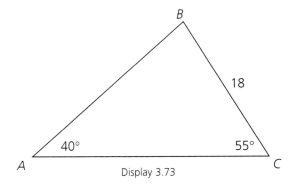

Display 3.73

4. There are three boats off the coast of Long Beach, California. The captain of boat *M* knows that boat *N* is 4.5 miles away and boat *P* is 5.3 miles away. The angle between the two sightings is 40° (Display 3.74).

(a) How far apart are boats *N* and *P*?

(b) The captain realized he made a mistake in calculating the angle between the two sightings. It should have been 32°. Using this angle, how far apart are boats *N* and *P*?

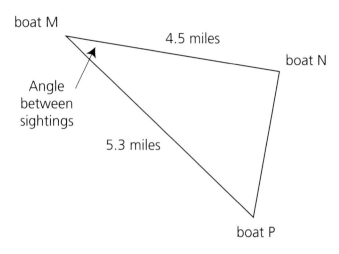

boat M

4.5 miles

boat N

Angle
between
sightings

5.3 miles

boat P

Display 3.74

5. (a) A Major League baseball diamond is a 90 foot square. The pitcher's mound is 60.5 feet from home plate. How far is it from the pitcher's mound to first base?

   (b) A Little League baseball diamond is a 60 foot square. The pitcher's mound is 46 feet from home plate. How far is it from the pitcher's mound to first base?

6. A large building has a roof which is slanted at an angle of 15° from the horizontal. An antenna tower was previously installed in a vertical position on the roof. A person located 100 feet from the base of the tower observes that the roof forms an angle of 24° with the top of the tower (Display 3.75). How high, in feet, is the tower?

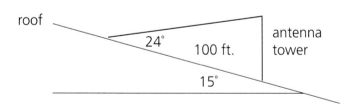

roof

24°

100 ft.

antenna
tower

15°

Display 3.75

7. Roland and Laura are 500 feet apart looking in the sky at a balloon that is between them and in the same vertical plane with them. Roland estimates that the sighting of the balloon makes an angle of 75° with the ground. From her viewpoint Laura estimates that the balloon makes an angle of 50° with the ground. Estimate the height of the balloon.

3.6 Sine and Cosine Curves: Going Around in Circles

On your TI-82 (TI-83), using the MODE key, make sure your calculator is in the Degree mode. Then, using the WINDOW key, insert the following numbers: Xmin = 0, Xmax = 720, Xscl = 10, Ymin = –2, Ymax = 2, and Yscl = 1.

Now, press the Y = key, then key Y_1 = sin X.

Press GRAPH, to obtain a graph of Y_1 = sin X.

1. How would you describe this curve to a friend?

2. Do you have ideas about where or when such a curve would occur in the real world?

   Using the same WINDOW settings as above, use the Y= key to set Y_2 = cos X,

   and using the GRAPH key, obtain a graph of Y_2 = cos X.

3. What ideas do you have about how these graphs are related to the sine and cosine of an acute angle that we have been studying in the previous sections?

   Write a paragraph on how the graph of Y_2 = cos X differs from the graph of Y_1 = sin X.
   Hint: You might want to graph Y_1 = sin X and Y_2 = cos X on the same screen.

Let's begin by looking at some situations where graphs that "look something like these" might occur.

In harbors off the ocean, the height of the water changes with the tides.

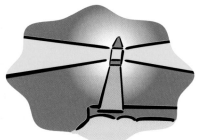

Learning Outcomes

After studying this section, you will be able to:

Identify real world situations where *wavy* or *repeating* curves arise;

Relate the coordinates of points on the circle $x^2 + y^2 = 1$ in the first quadrant to the sine and cosine of acute angles;

Extend the domains of the functions sin x, cos x, and tan x;

Explain how one arrives at the graphs of y = sin x and y = cos x that appear on a calculator screen.

In one harbor, the height of the water was measured as follows, where M denotes midnight on a certain day (Display 3.76).

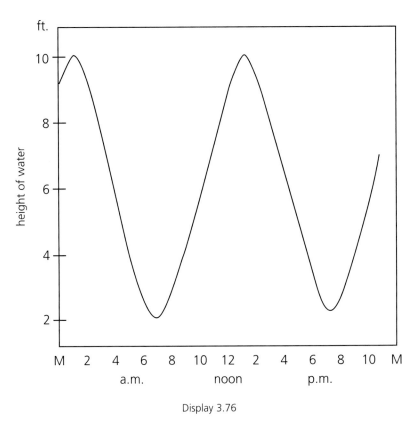

Display 3.76

1. Over what time periods does the water level appear to be getting lower (decreasing)?

2. Over what time periods does the water level appear to be getting higher (increasing)?

A monkey jumped onto a spoke of a windmill. You can see him on the left sides of Display 3.77. The wind is blowing and the windmill is turning clockwise at a steady rate. The monkey holds on tightly and doesn't fall off. As time goes by, the monkey's height above the ground changes.

Display 3.77

At the lowest point the monkey is 10 feet off the ground, and at his highest point he is 30 feet off the ground. What happens if we plot the monkey's height with time? A graph might look something like the following (Display 3.78).

a

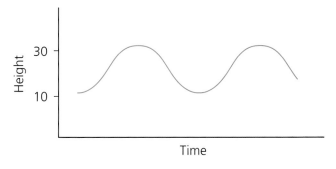

Display 3.78

How would you describe this graph to a friend?

The seasonal changes in the length of daylight may be represented by a graph. Atlanta, Georgia has its longest day with 14 hours of daylight on June 21 and its shortest day with about 9 hours, 20 minutes of daylight on December 21.

On a piece of graph paper, sketch the diagram in Display 3.79. Estimate the position of the two points, the longest day and the shortest day of the year. Estimate some other points and then draw a smooth curve through your points. How would you describe this curve to a friend?

b

Thinking Tip

Try to improve estimates. Any time you make an estimate, try to find some way to make a *better* one.

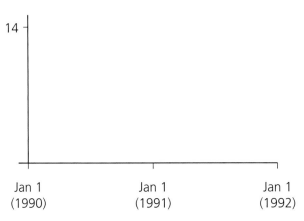

14 –

Jan 1   Jan 1   Jan 1
(1990)   (1991)   (1992)

Hours of daylight in Atlanta, Georgia

Display 3.79

One might call the curves we've been looking at *wavy curves* or *repeating curves*. Such curves occur in many areas. For example, when a string is plucked on a guitar, the string vibrates (Display 3.80(a)), sending waves through the air. Let's look at how this occurs.

Think of the air around the string as consisting of many little balls of air (known as *molecules* of air).

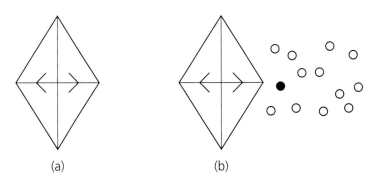

(a)   (b)

Display 3.80

Look at the ball of air that is darkened in Display 3.80(b). As the string vibrates, this ball of air moves back and forth just as the string does (Display 3.81).

Display 3.81

This ball of air hits other balls of air, which, in turn hit other balls of air—all the way to your ear, which you now hear as music. The motion of the ball of air is looked at even closer in Display 3.82.

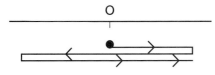

Display 3.82

We assume the ball of air is originally at **O**. The ball then moves back and forth as the string vibrates. Let's put a unit of measurement on the **O** line as follows (Display 3.83).

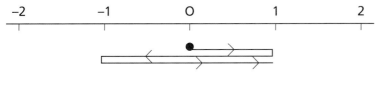

Display 3.83

As time goes by, the coordinate of the ball of air is going to change. On a piece of graph paper, sketch a graph of where the ball is located as time goes by (Display 3.84).

Coordinate of ball of air

Display 3.84

Does this graph look similar to the graph of $Y_1 = \sin X$ that you saw on your calculator? Explain!

We'll now help you see where the graph of $Y_1 = \sin X$ on your calculator comes from and how it is related to the sine of an angle.

To do this, we need points on a circle. Recall that a **circle** is the set of all points a fixed distance (called the *radius*) from a fixed point (called the *center*). When a circle is graphed in a Cartesian plane with center at (0, 0), its equation is surprisingly simple. To derive the equation, all you need to do is use the Pythagorean Theorem.

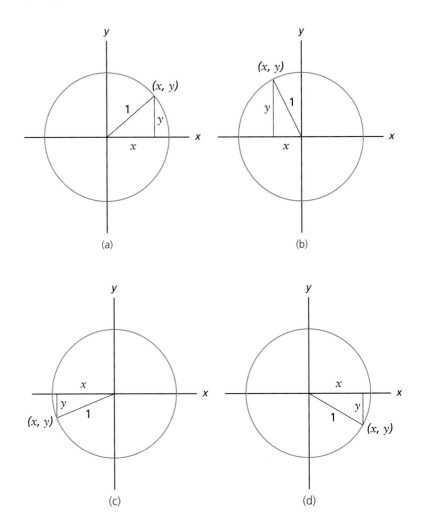

Display 3.85

The circles in Display 3.85 have radius 1, but you could use this procedure for a circle with any radius. Look at the triangles drawn in the circles. If x and y are the coordinates of a point on any one of the circles, applying the Pythagorean Theorem gives

$$x^2 + y^2 = 1$$

In Display 3.85(a), let θ be the angle formed by the positive x axis and the line from the origin to the point (x, y). This information is shown in Display 3.86.

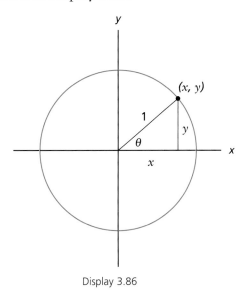

Display 3.86

Observe that

$$\sin \theta = \frac{y}{1} = y \text{ and } \cos \theta = \frac{x}{1} = x$$

That is, *the point (x, y) is the same point as $(\cos \theta , \sin \theta)$.* This fact allows us to extend our ideas about the sine, cosine, and tangent of an angle. Before doing this, however, we look at the point (x, y) above in a more precise way. We think of the angle as starting on the positive x-axis and ending with the line from the origin to the point (x, y), moving in a counterclockwise direction. Suppose we start with the positive x axis and end with the line from the origin to the point (c, d) in Display 3.87. The resulting angle is indicated in the figure.

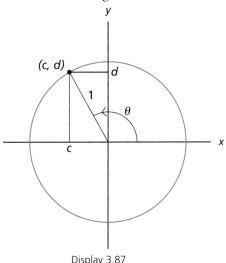

Display 3.87

Now we can see why people define

$$\cos \theta = c$$

and

$$\sin \theta = d$$

In this case, note that the cosine of θ is negative since c is negative. The sine of θ is positive, since d is positive.

Let's try an example! We want to find the coordinates of P in Display 3.88, where $\theta = 45°$.

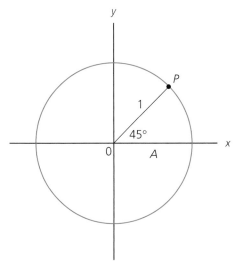

Display 3.88

Drop a perpendicular from P to the x-axis, intersecting the x-axis at point A (Display 3.89).

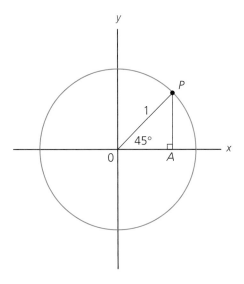

Display 3.89

1. In Display 3.89, why is $OA = AP$?

2. From the diagram and the Pythagorean Theorem, we know that

$$(OA)^2 + (AP)^2 = 1$$

Show how this leads to

$$(OA)^2 = \tfrac{1}{2}$$

3. Using the result of problem 2, find the coordinates of the point P (to two decimal places).

4. Explain how the result of problem 3 shows that $\sin 45° = \cos 45° = 0.71$ (to two decimal places).

REFLECT

In this chapter you have been exposed to the basic ideas of *trigonometry*. This is a subject which is historically a significant and practical one. Historically, trigonometry played a role in the building of the Egyptian pyramids. Today, as well as yesteryear, trigonometry offers practical rules for surveying land, computing mountain heights, etc. The ideas in the final section of this chapter have been very useful in the study of electricity. In particular, alternating current (the kind used in households in the United States) involves back-and-forth surges of current representing a kind of "wavy" motion, similar to the motion depicted in sine and cosine curves. You will see more of this topic in a later book of **MATH** *Connections*.

Problem Set: 3.6

Problems 1–6 will help you become familiar with this new idea of sine and cosine. In each case, find the sine and the cosine of θ.

1.
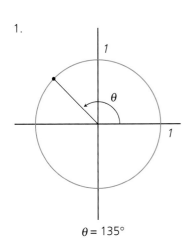

$\theta = 135°$

2.
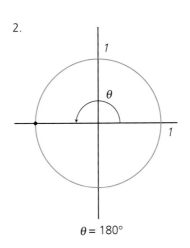

$\theta = 180°$

3.

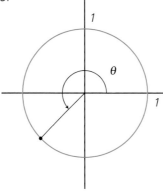

$\theta = 225°$

4.

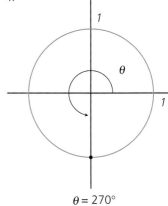

$\theta = 270°$

5.

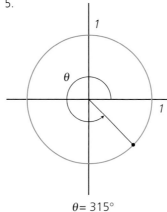

$\theta = 315°$

6.

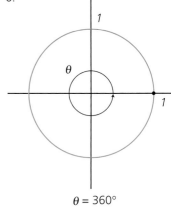

$\theta = 360°$

7. Use a figure similar to the ones in problems 1–6, to determine in what quadrant are the sine and cosine of an angle both negative.

8. Use a figure similar to the ones in problems 1–6, to determine in what quadrant is the sine of an angle positive but the cosine of the angle is negative.

9. Using figures similar to the ones in problems 1–6, answer the following questions:

(a) What is sin 405°?
(b) What is cos 405°?
(c) How are sin 405° and sin 45° related? Explain.

(d) If sin A = 0.7843, where A is an angle measured in degrees, what will sin $(360° + A)$ be? Explain.

(e) If cos B = 0.3449, where B is an angle measured in degrees, what is cos $(720° + B)$? Explain.

Appendix A: Using a TI-82 (TI-83) Graphing Calculator

A graphing calculator is a useful tool for doing many different mathematical things. Once you begin to use it, you'll find that it is powerful, fast, and friendly. In fact, your biggest difficulty may be just getting started for the first time! Because this machine can do a lot, it has lots of complicated looking buttons. But you don't have to know about *all* of them before you start to use *any* of them! The sooner you make friends with your electronic assistant, the more it will be able to help you. Let us introduce you to each other by trying a few simple things.

The Cover

The face of the calculator is protected from dirt and scratches by a cover that slides on and off from the top. When you're using the calculator, this cover slips on the back so that you won't lose it. Always put the cover back over the face of the calculator when you finish using it.

On, Off, [2nd], and Clear

To get the calculator's attention, just press [ON] (at the lower left corner of the calculator). What happens? Do you see a dark block blinking in the upper left corner of the screen? That's the **cursor**, which tells you where you are on the screen. The cursor is always at the spot that will be affected by the next button you push.

Notice that the word OFF is printed in color above the [ON] button, a little to the left of its center. Notice also that there is one key of the same color. It is the key marked [2nd] at the left end of the second row.

When you push [2nd], it makes the next key that you push behave like what is marked above it on the left.

Try it. Push [2nd]. What has happened to the cursor? Do you see an up arrow inside it as it blinks? That's to remind you that [2nd] key has been pushed and will affect the next key you choose. Now push ON . What happens? Did the cursor disappear? You should have a blank screen; the calculator should be off.

It's always a good idea to turn your calculator off when you finish using it. If you forget, the calculator will turn itself off after a few minutes to save its batteries. Sometimes when you are using it, you may put it aside and do something else for a little while. If it is off when you pick it up again, don't worry; just press ON . The screen will show what was there before it shut down.

Pressing CLEAR gives you a blank screen that is ready for new work. But the last thing you did is still stored. Press 2nd then ENTER to bring it back.

Basic Arithmetic

Doing arithmetic on a graphing calculator is no harder than on a simpler calculator. In fact, it's easier. This calculator has a screen that lets you keep track of the problem as you enter it. Let's try a few simple exercises. Turn your calculator on.

- Pick two 3-digit numbers and add them. To do this, just key in the first number, press + and then key in the second number. Your addition problem will appear on the screen. Press ENTER to get the answer.

If you make a mistake when entering a number, you can go back and fix it. The ◁ key lets you move back (left) one space at a time. When you get to your mistake, just key in the correct number over the wrong one. Then move forward (right) to the end of the line by using the ▷ key.

For instance, to add 123 and 456, press 1 2 3 + 4 5 6 ENTER . The screen will show your question on the first line and the answer at the right side of the second line, as in Display A.1.

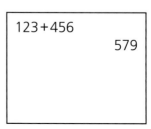

```
123+456
            579
```

Display A.1

- Now let's try the other three basic arithmetic operations. To clear the screen, press CLEAR . Then try subtracting, multiplying, and dividing your two 3-digit numbers. For instance, if your numbers are 123 and 456, press

$$1\ 2\ 3 \boxed{-} 4\ 5\ 6 \boxed{\text{ENTER}}$$

$$1\ 2\ 3 \boxed{\times} 4\ 5\ 6 \boxed{\text{ENTER}}$$

$$1\ 2\ 3 \boxed{\div} 4\ 5\ 6 \boxed{\text{ENTER}}$$

Your screen should look like Display A.2.

Notice that the display uses * for multiplication (so that it is not confused with the letter x) and / for division.

```
123−456
                  -333
123*456
                 56088
123/456
          .2697368421
```

Display A.2

- Here are two, button pushing shortcuts.

If you don't want to redo a problem with just a small change in it, you don't have to reenter the whole thing. 2nd ENTER will bring back the last problem you entered. Just move to the place you want to change, key in the change, and press ENTER . For instance, add 54321 and 12345, as in Display A.3.

```
54321+12345
                 66666
```

Display A.3

Now, to subtract 12345 from 54321, press [2nd] [ENTER]; the next line will show 54321 + 12345. Move your cursor back to the + sign (using [◁]) and press [−]; then press [ENTER]. Did you try it? Your screen should look like Display A.4.

```
54321+12345
              66666
54321−12345
              41976
```

Display A.4

Let's check to see that 41976 is the correct answer by adding 12345 to it and seeing if we get the first number back again. Since you want to do something to the last answer, *you don't have to reenter it*. Press [+]. Does your calculator show Ans+ and the cursor? It should. If you press an operation key right after doing a calculation, the machine assumes that you want to perform this operation on the last answer. It shows that last answer as Ans. Now key in 12345 and press [ENTER]. You should get back the first number, 54321.

1. **Pick two 7-digit numbers and add them. What do you get?**

2. **Now subtract the second number from the first. Can you do it without rekeying the numbers? What do you get?**

3. **Now multiply your two 7-digit numbers. What do you get? What does the E mean?**

4. **Check the last answer by dividing the second of your 7-digit numbers into it. Do it without rekeying the last answer. Do you get your first number back again?**

Multiply 98765432 by 123456. Now check the product in two ways.

a

- Divide by pressing [÷] then entering 123456. Does it check?

- First reenter the product; then divide it by 123456. The product is in scientific notation. To enter it as a regular number, remember that the positive number after the E tells you to move the decimal that many places to the right. Does it check?

1. Divide 97533 by 525 and by 625. One of the answers you get will be exactly right, and the other one will be a very close approximation.

b

   - Which is which?

   - How can you tell?

   - If you hadn't been told that one of the answers is an approximation, how could you know?

2. When an answer is too long to be displayed with ten digits, the calculator shows a ten-digit approximation. Does it do this by just chopping off (truncating) the rest of the digits, or by rounding off? What test would you give your calculator to tell which way it does this?

1. Pick any three-digit number and note it down.

c

2. Repeat its digits in the same order to form a six digit number (like 123123, for example). Key this number into your calculator.

3. Divide your number by 7.

4. Divide your answer by 11. How do you do this without reentering the answer?

5. Divide the last number by 13. What do you notice about the result? Do you think that it is just a coincidence?

6. Pick another three-digit number and repeat steps 2–5.

7. Try to beat the system; see if you can pick a three-digit number that doesn't work this way. What might you try? Why?

8. Can you actually prove that the pattern you see *works every time*? How might you try to do this?

The Two Minus Signs

The calculator has two minus signs. The one on the blue key looks like $\boxed{-}$ and the one on the gray key looks like $\boxed{(-)}$. The blue one, on the right, is for subtraction. It is grouped with the keys for the other arithmetic operations. To subtract 3764 from 8902, for example, you would key in

$$8 \ 9 \ 0 \ 2 \ \boxed{-} \ 3 \ 7 \ 6 \ 4 \ \boxed{\text{ENTER}}$$

Go ahead; do it. Do you get 5138?

The gray minus key, next to the $\boxed{\text{ENTER}}$ key at the bottom, is for making a number negative. It is grouped with the digit keys and the decimal point. To add the numbers -273, 5280, and -2116, for example, you would key in

$$\boxed{(-)} \ 2 \ 7 \ 3 \ \boxed{+} \ 5 \ 2 \ 8 \ 0 \ \boxed{+} \ \boxed{(-)} \ 2 \ 1 \ 1 \ 6 \ \boxed{\text{ENTER}}$$

Try it. Notice that the display shows these negative signs without the parentheses, but they are smaller and raised a little. To see the difference between this negative sign and the subtraction sign, try subtracting the negative number -567 from 1234. Here are the keystrokes.

$$1234 \ \boxed{-} \ \boxed{(-)} \ 567$$

The display should look like this:

$$1234 - {}^-567$$

Raising to a Power

To raise a number to a power, press $\boxed{\wedge}$ just before entering the exponent. Thus, to compute 738^5, press

$$7 \ 3 \ 8 \ \boxed{\wedge} \ 5 \ \boxed{\text{ENTER}}$$

The screen should look like Display A.5.

```
738^5
        2.1891817E14
```

Display A.5

The Menu Keys

Many keys bring a menu to the screen. A menu is a list of functions—things that the calculator is ready to do for you. For instance, press each of the keys across the row that starts with [MATH] . Don't worry about what all those lists say; just pick one out and look at it as you read the rest of this paragraph. Notice that it is actually a double menu. There are two cursors on it, shown as dark blocks. The one in the top left corner can be moved along the top line by using the [◁] and [▷] keys. Each time you move it to a new place on the top line, the menu below changes. The items in each lower menu are reached by using the other cursor, which can be moved up and down along the left side of the screen by using the [△] and [▽] keys.

Once you have put the cursor on the choice you want, you actually make the choice by pressing [ENTER]. This makes the calculator go back to its "home" screen and display your choice. To make the calculator do what you have chosen, press [ENTER] again.

1. How many separate calculator functions can be reached through the menus of the [MATH] key?

2. How many separate calculator functions can be reached through the menus of the [MATRX] key?

Entering Data in a List

The data handling tools are found through the statistics menu.

- Turn your calculator on and press [STAT] . You'll see a menu that looks like Display A.6.

```
EDIT CALC                 EDIT CALC TESTS
1:Edit...                 1:Edit...
2:SortA(                  2:SortA(
3:SortD(                  3:SortD(
4:ClrList                 4:ClrList
                          5:SetUpEditor

     TI-82                      TI-83
```

Display A.6

- To enter data, make sure that the top cursor is on EDIT and the left cursor is on 1: . Then press ENTER . Your screen display should look like Display A.7, with the cursor right under L1.

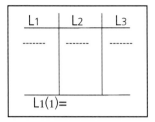

Display A.7

Note that if the display shows numbers in the L1 column, you'll have to clear the data memory. There are two ways to do this.

Get out of this display (by pressing 2nd QUIT) and go back to the STAT menu. Press 4 . When ClrList appears, press 2nd 1 then ENTER ; Done will appear. Now go back to the STAT screen and choose 1:Edit .

or

Without leaving this display, use the △ and ◁ keys to move your cursor to the top of the column and highlight L1. Press CLEAR and then the ▽ key. List L1 should be cleared.

- Now it's time to enter the data. The calculator stores in its memory each data number you enter, along with an L1 label for that entry. The first number is called L1(1), and the second is called L1(2), and so on. We'll ignore the L2 and L3 labels for now. Key in the first data number, then press ENTER . Notice that L1(2) now appears at the bottom of the screen. Key in the second data number and press ENTER ; and so on, until you have put in all the data. If you make a mistake, just use the arrow keys to move the cursor to your error, type over it correctly, then move back to where you were.

At this point, the calculator has all your data stored in a way that is easy to use, and the data will stay stored even after the calculator is turned off.

Summaries of 1-Variable Data

It is easy to get summary information about data that is stored in a single list.

- Bring up the STAT menu.

- Move the top cursor to CALC. The side cursor should be on 1:1-Var Stats. Press [ENTER].

- 1:1-Var Stats will appear on your screen. Enter the list you want the calculator to summarize. For instance, if you want a summary of the data in list L1, press [2nd] [1] ; then press [ENTER].

That's all there is to it! A screenful of information will appear. Sections 1.3–1.7 in Chapter 1 of Year 1 explain how to interpret that information.

Putting Data in Size Order

The TI-82 (TI-83) have built-in programs that will put your data in size order automatically. Do you have any data stored in L1? If not, enter ten or a dozen numbers at random, so that you can see how the following steps work.

1. Turn the calculator on and go to the STAT menu.

2. To see what is stored in L1, [ENTER] 1:Edit . Then move the cursor left to L1, if it's not there already. Make sure you have some data in this list.

3. Go back to the STAT menu and choose 2:Sort A(then press [ENTER]. Tell the calculator to sort the L1 list by pressing [2nd] [1], then [ENTER]. Your calculator screen should now say Done. To see what it has done, reopen List 1 (using [STAT] 1:Edit) . Your data should now be listed in ascending order — that is, from smallest to largest as you read down the list. The A in SortA(stands for ascending order.

Now go back to the STAT menu and choose 2:SortD(then press [ENTER]. Tell the calculator to sort the L1 list again. (Press [2nd] [1] [ENTER].)

1. When the screen says Done, what has your calculator done? Look at L1 again to help you answer this question.

2. What does the D in SortD(stand for?

Once the data are in size order, it is easy to find the median. For example, if you have 21 data items in all, the median is just the 11th one in the sorted list. Scroll through the data (using the [△] key) until you find L1(11). Its value is the median. If you have 20 data items, the median is halfway between the 10th and 11th items in the sorted list. Scroll through the data until you find L1(10) and L1(11). Then calculate the number halfway between them.

Finding the mode is just as easy. Count repeated items in this list. The one that is repeated the most times is the mode.

The Graph Window

This kind of calculator is called a graphing calculator because it can *draw graphs*. The screen on a graphing calculator can show line drawings of mathematical relationships. It does this with two kinds of coordinate systems—*rectangular coordinates* or *polar coordinates*. In this part we shall use only rectangular coordinates; polar coordinates will appear much later. If you are not familiar with the idea of a rectangular coordinate system, you should review the first section of Chapter 3 in Year 1 now.

Your calculator leaves the factory with standard coordinate axes built in. To see what they look like, turn on your calculator and press [GRAPH] (in the upper right corner). You should see a horizontal and a vertical axis crossing the middle of the screen. The horizontal axis is called the *x*-**axis**, and the vertical axis is called the *y*-**axis**. If your screen doesn't show this, press [ZOOM] and choose 6:ZStandard . Examine this display carefully; then answer the following questions.

1. Assuming that the dots along each axis mark the integer points, what is the largest possible value on the *x*-axis? On the *y*-axis?

2. What is the smallest possible value on the *x*-axis? On the *y*-axis?

3. Does it look as if the same unit of measure is being used on both axes?

4. Why do you suppose the spacing between the units is not exactly the same everywhere on an axis? Do you think that this might cause a problem?

The standard coordinate axis setting can be changed in several ways. This is done using the menu that appears when you press WINDOW . Try that now. You should get Display A.8.

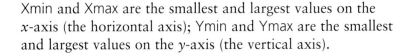

```
WINDOW FORMAT        WINDOW
  Xmin = -10           Xmin = -10
  Xmax = 10            Xmax = 10
  Xscl = 1             Xscl = 1
  Ymin = -10           Ymin = -10
  Ymax = 10            Ymax = 10
  Yscl = 1             Yscl = 1
                       Xres = 1
     TI-82                 TI-83
```

Display A.8

Xmin and Xmax are the smallest and largest values on the *x*-axis (the horizontal axis); Ymin and Ymax are the smallest and largest values on the *y*-axis (the vertical axis).

Xscl and Yscl are the scales for marking off points on the axes. The setting 1 means that each single integer value on the axis is marked. To see how the scale value works, change Xscl to 2. Move the cursor down, using ▽ , then just key in 2 in place of 1.) Now press GRAPH . What change do you notice? Now go back to the WINDOW menu (press WINDOW) and change Yscl to 5. Return to the graph (press GRAPH). What has changed?

You can ignore the Xres = 1 line on the TI-83 for now. If you're really curious, see p. 3–11 of the TI-83 Guidebook.

Change the WINDOW settings so that they look like Display A.9. Then look at the graph and answer these questions.

1. Where on the screen is the origin of the coordinate system?

2. Does it look as if the same unit of measure is being used on both axes?

3. Does it look as if the spacing between the units is the same everywhere on an axis?

4. What happens when you press △ then ▽ ?

WINDOW FORMAT	WINDOW
Xmin = 0	Xmin = 0
Xmax = 9.4	Xmax = 9.4
Xscl = 1	Xscl = 1
Ymin = 0	Ymin = 0
Ymax = 6.2	Ymax = 6.2
Yscl = 1	Yscl = 1
	Xres = 1
TI-82	TI-83

Display A.9

If you have worked through the previous questions, you found that pressing ⟨△⟩, ⟨▽⟩ puts a cross exactly in the middle of your screen and two numbers at the bottom. The cross is the cursor for the graphing screen, and the numbers are the coordinates of the point at its center. In this case, the cursor is at $(4.7, 3.1)$. It can be moved to any point on the graph by using the four arrow keys ⟨△⟩, ⟨▽⟩, ⟨◁⟩, ⟨▷⟩ at the upper right of the keypad.

Move the cursor to the point $(4, 3)$. How far does the cursor move each time you press ⟨◁⟩ or ⟨▷⟩? How far does it move each time you press ⟨△⟩ or ⟨▽⟩? Now move the cursor directly down to the bottom of the screen. What are the coordinates of the lowest point you can reach?

These new WINDOW settings are better than the standard one in some ways, and worse in others. Let's look again at the Standard coordinate system and compare it with the one we just saw. To get back to the standard settings, press ⟨ZOOM⟩, then press ⟨6⟩ to choose ZStandard. The Standard coordinate axes should appear immediately.

These questions refer to the Standard coordinate axes.

1. Where is the cursor to begin with? How do you find it if you can't remember?

2. Try to move the cursor to the point $(4,3)$. How close can you get to it?

3. How far does the cursor move each time you press ⟨◁⟩ or ⟨▷⟩?

4. How far does it move each time you press ⟨△⟩ or ⟨▽⟩?

5. Move the cursor directly down to the bottom of the screen. What are the coordinates of the lowest point you can reach?

6. In what ways is this coordinate system better than the one we set up for the previous set of questions? In what ways is it worse?

7. How might we fix the bad features of this system without losing the good ones?

Another useful WINDOW setting is 8:ZInteger in the ZOOM menu. When you press 8 , coordinate axes appear, but they are still the standard ones. Press ENTER to get the Integer settings.

These questions refer to the Integer coordinate axes.

1. Try to move the cursor to the point (4, 3). How close can you get to it?

2. How far does the cursor move each time you press ◁ or ▷ ?

3. How far does it move each time you press △ or ▽ ?

4. Why is this setting named Integer?

5. In what ways is this coordinate system better than the one we set up for the previous set of questions? In what ways is it worse?

6. How might we fix the bad features of this system without losing the good ones?

To plot a point (mark its location) on the graphing screen, go to the point-drawing part of the DRAW menu, like this.

Press 2nd   PRGM and move the top cursor to POINTS .

Choose 1 to make the ENTER key mark cursor locations. If you want to mark some points and erase others, choose 3. This lets the ENTER key change the state of any point the cursor is on; it will mark one that isn't already marked, and will unmark one that is. *Hint:* If you have plotted too many points and you want to start over, you can go to ZOOM menu and press 6 . This will wipe out everything you have plotted and return to the Standard coordinate settings. If you were using different coordinate settings, you will have to redo them in the WINDOW menu. If you want to erase some points, see Drawing Points on a graph section in the TI Guidebook.

Problem Set: Appendix A

1. What WINDOW settings do you need in order to put the origin at the upper right corner of your screen? What can you say about the coordinates of the points that can be plotted on this screen?

2. What WINDOW settings do you need in order to put the origin at the upper left corner of your screen? What can you say about the coordinates of the points that can be plotted on this screen?

3. Choose the Integer setting for the coordinate axes and plot the points (30, 14), (-5, 20), (-26, -11), and (6, -30). Then write the coordinates of two points that lie within the area of the graph window but cannot be plotted exactly with this setting.

4. Find WINDOW settings to form a coordinate system such that the points (120, 80) and (-60, -40) are within the window frame.

    (a) How far does the cursor move each time you press ◁ or ▷ ?

    (b) How far does it move each time you press △ or ▽ ?

    (c) Can you put the cursor exactly on (120, 80)? If not, how close can you come? Plot this point as closely as you can.

    (d) Can you put the cursor exactly on (-60, -40)? If not, how close can you come? Plot this point as closely as you can.

    (e) Can you put the cursor exactly on (0, 0)? If not, how close can you come?

5. Find WINDOW settings to form a coordinate system such that the cursor can be put exactly on the points (20, 24.5) and (-17.3, -14).

    (a) What is the initial position of the cursor?

    (b) How far does it move each time you press ◁ or ▷ ?

    (c) How far does it move each time you press △ or ▽ ?

    (d) Can you put the cursor exactly on (0, 0)? If not, how close can you come?

Drawing Histograms

Drawing a histogram is very easy. All you have to do is choose a few numbers to tell the calculator how wide and how tall to make the bars, as follows. Turn your calculator on and press [WINDOW]. The screen should look like Display A.10, maybe with different numbers.

```
┌─────────────────────┐    ┌─────────────────────┐
│ WINDOW FORMAT       │    │ WINDOW              │
│   Xmin = -10        │    │   Xmin = -10        │
│   Xmax = 10         │    │   Xmax = 10         │
│   Xscl = 1          │    │   Xscl = 1          │
│   Ymin = -10        │    │   Ymin = -10        │
│   Ymax = 10         │    │   Ymax = 10         │
│   Yscl = 1          │    │   Yscl = 1          │
│                     │    │   Xres = 1          │
└─────────────────────┘    └─────────────────────┘
        TI-82                      TI-83
```

Display A.10

The numbers in this WINDOW list tell the calculator how to set the horizontal (X) and vertical (Y) scales.

- Xmin, an abbreviation of *X minimum*, is the smallest data value the picture will show. You should set it at some convenient value less than or equal to the smallest value in your data set.

- Xmax, an abbreviation of *X maximum*, is the largest data value the picture will show. Set it at some convenient value greater than or equal to the largest value in your data set.

- Xscl, an abbreviation of *X scale*, says how to group the data. It is the size of the base interval at the bottom of each bar of the histogram. For instance, Xscl = 10 will group the data by 10s, starting from the value of Xmin that you chose.

- Ymin is the smallest frequency of any data group. It is never less than 0, which usually is a good choice for it.

- Ymax represents the length of the longest bar. Choose a convenient number that is not less than the largest frequency of any data group, but not much larger.

- Yscl determines the size of the steps to be marked on the vertical (frequency) scale. For small data sets, set it to 1. If your setting for Ymax is much larger than 10, you might want to set Yscl larger than 1. A little experimenting will show you how to choose a helpful setting.

- If you have a TI-83, the last line at the bottom of this display is Xres = 1. It's a pixel resolution setting for graphing functions; ignore it for now.

Now your calculator is ready to draw a histogram.

- Press [STAT PLOT] (actually, [2nd] [Y=]), choose 1 and press [ENTER] .

- Choose these settings from each row by moving the cursor to them with the arrow keys and pressing [ENTER] each time.

  – Highlight On.

  – Highlight the histogram picture.

  – Set Xlist to the list containing your data (L1, L2, etc.).

  – Set Freq:1 .

Now press [GRAPH] — and there it is!

Drawing Boxplots

The TI-82 (TI-83) calculators can draw boxplots. All they need are the data and a few sizing instructions. Here's how to do it.

- Turn the calculator on, press [STAT] and choose 1:Edit... from the EDIT menu. Check which list contains the data you want to use. Let's assume it's in L1.

- Press [WINDOW] and set the horizontal (X) and vertical (Y) scales. If you have forgotten how to set your WINDOW, refer to "The Graph Window" section. Choose convenient numbers for the X range—Xmin less than your smallest data value and Xmax greater than your largest data value, but not too small or too large. You don't want the picture to get squeezed into something you can't see well! Also set Xscl to some convenient size.

- The Y settings don't matter as much. However, for the TI-82, if you set Ymin to –1 (Be sure to use the [(–)] key!) and Ymax to 4, the X scale will appear nicely in a readable location under the boxplot. For the TI-83, Ymin = -2 and Ymax = 2 work a little better.

- Press [STAT PLOT] (actually, [2nd] [Y=]), choose 1: and press [ENTER]. Select these settings from each row by moving the cursor to them with the arrow keys and pressing [ENTER] each time.

    On; the boxplot picture; L1 from the Xlist; 1 from Freq

- Now press [GRAPH]—and there it is!
- To read the five-number summary, press [TRACE] and use the [◁] and [▷] to display the five numbers one at a time.

Graphing and Tracing Lines

If you want the calculator to graph a line or a curve, you must first be able to describe the line or curve by an algebraic equation. Once you have the equation for what you want to draw, you must put it in the form

$$y = [\text{something}]$$

For a straight line, that's not a problem; we often put the equation in this form, anyway. For some other kinds of curves, putting them in this form can be a little messy. In this section we shall deal only with straight lines.

All graphing begins with the [Y=] key. When you press this key for the first time, you get the screen in Display A.11.

$Y_1 =$
$Y_2 =$
$Y_3 =$
$Y_4 =$
$Y_5 =$
$Y_6 =$
$Y_7 =$

TI-82

Plot1	Plot2	Plot3
$\backslash Y_1 =$		
$\backslash Y_2 =$		
$\backslash Y_3 =$		
$\backslash Y_4 =$		
$\backslash Y_5 =$		
$\backslash Y_6 =$		
$\backslash Y_7 =$		

TI-83

Display A.11

These lines allow you to put in as many as ten different algebraic equations for things you want drawn. The subscript number gives you a way to keep track of which equation goes with which picture on the graph. To see how the process works, we'll make the first example simple—two straight lines through the origin.

Key in -.5X on the $Y_1=$ line, *using the* $\boxed{\text{X,T,}\theta}$ *key to make the X*; then press $\boxed{\text{ENTER}}$.

It is important to use $\boxed{\text{X,T,}\theta}$ for X because that's how the calculator knows that you are referring to the horizontal axis.

Key in -.25X on the $Y_2=$ line and $\boxed{\text{ENTER}}$ it.

Be sure to use the $\boxed{(-)}$ key for the negative sign. If you don't, you'll get an error message when you ask for the graph. If you want to wipe out one of these equations and redo it, just move the cursor back to the equation and press $\boxed{\text{CLEAR}}$.

Now your work is done. Press $\boxed{\text{GRAPH}}$ and just watch as the calculator draws the lines. If you forget which line goes with which equation, or if you want to see the coordinates of the points along your lines, press $\boxed{\text{TRACE}}$ and then move the cursor with the $\boxed{\triangleleft}$ and $\boxed{\triangleright}$ keys. When you do this, the coordinates of the cursor's position appear at the bottom of the screen. For the TI-82, a number appears in the upper right corner to tell you which equation you're tracing. For the TI-83, the equation appears in the upper left hand corner. In this example, when you press $\boxed{\text{TRACE}}$ you will be on $Y_1=$ -.5X, the first of the two lines we entered. Try it. Now move back and forth along this line.

To switch from one line to another, use the $\boxed{\triangle}$ and $\boxed{\triangledown}$ keys. Notice that, in this case, either of these keys gets you to the other line. That's because we are only graphing two equations. If we were graphing more than two, these keys would move up and down the *list of equations*, regardless of where the graphs appeared on the screen.

There is a way to remove the graph of an equation from the screen without erasing the equation from your list. For example, let us remove the line $Y_1=$ -.5X from the picture. Go back to the $\boxed{\text{Y=}}$ list. Notice that the $=$ sign of each equation appears in a dark block. This shows that the graph of this equation is turned on. To turn it off, move the cursor to the $=$ sign and press ENTER . The dark block will disappear. To turn it back on, put the cursor back on $=$ and press ENTER again.

Approximating Data by a Line

This section refers to a situation that commonly arises in the analysis of two variable data. Such data can be represented as points on a coordinate plane, and it is often useful to know if the pattern of points can be approximated by a straight line. A common way of doing this is called *least-squares approximation*. An explanation of this process and its use appears in Chapter 4 of Year 1. This calculator section provides a simple example of how to get the TI-82 (TI-83) to give you a least-squares approximation of a set of data.

Let's look at a very small, simple data set. The process is exactly the same for bigger, more complicated data sets. Here are four points of two variable data.

$$(1, 2) \quad (2, 3) \quad (3, 5) \quad (4, 6)$$

If you plot these points on a coordinate plane, you will see that they don't all lie on the same line. Don't just take our word for it; make a sketch! The calculator uses the least-squares method to find automatically the line of "best fit." Section 4.3 (in Chapter 4) describes how this method works and what best fit means. These are the instructions for getting the calculator to do all the tedious work for you.

First of all, you need to have the data entered in two *separate data storage lists. You get to* these lists by pressing STAT and choosing 1:EDIT... from the EDIT menu. When you press ENTER , you should get Display A.12.

Display A.12

If the columns already contain data that you don't want, you can clear them out in either of two ways.

- Press [STAT] and choose 4:ClrList from the menu that appears. When the message ClrList appears, enter the name of the list you want to clear. (Press [2nd] [1] for L1, [2nd] [2] for L2, etc.) Then press [ENTER] ; the screen will say Done. Now press [STAT] to return to the process of entering data.

- Go to the MEM screen (press [2nd] [+]) and choose 2:Delete... (press [2]). Choose 3:List... from the menu that appears. The screen will show the name of each data storage list that contains data. Use the arrow keys to pick the ones that you want to clear out; press [ENTER] for each one. Now press [STAT] to return to the process of entering data.

Enter the first coordinate of each data point into list L1; put its second coordinate in list L2. The four data points of our example should appear as shown in Display A.13.

L1	L2	L3
1	2	-------
2	3	
3	5	
4	6	
-------	-------	
L2(5) =		

Display A.13

Now we are almost done. Press [STAT] and go to the CALC menu. Choose LinReg(ax + b) . When you press [ENTER] , the screen will display an algebraic description of the line of best fit. For our example, it looks like Display A.14.

- The second line, y = ax + b, just tells you that the information is for slope-intercept form. Notice that the TI-82 (TI-83) use a, not m, for the slope here.

- The third line says that the slope is 1.4.

- The fourth line says that the y-intercept is .5.

Note that on the TI-82, the last line shows the **correlation coefficient,** a measure of how good the fit is. The correlation coefficient is not discussed in your textbook. A detailed explanation of how it works will have to wait until you study statistics in more depth. But, in case you are curious about it, here is a little more information. The correlation coefficient is always a number between –1 and 1, inclusive. 1 and –1 stand for a perfect fit, with all points exactly on the line. (1 is for lines with positive slope; –1 is for lines with negative slope.) The closer r is to 0, the worse the fit.

```
LinReg
y = ax + b
a = 1.4
b = .5
r = .9899494937
```
TI-82

```
LinReg
y = ax + b
a = 1.4
b = .5
```
TI-83

Display A.14

Putting together this information about our example, we see that the least-squares line is described by the equation

$$y = 1.4x + .5$$

Graph the line $y = 1.4x + .5$. Are any of the four data points on it? How can you be sure?

Using Formulas to Make Lists

Sometimes it is useful to make a new list of data from an old one by doing the same thing to each data value. For instance, you might want to add a fixed number to each value, square each value, or find the distance of each value from some particular number. Instead of computing the new list one entry at a time, you can do it all at once if you can express your process as a formula.

Here's how the process works.

- Go to the STAT menu. Enter a list of data in L1, and then clear L2 and L3.

- To add 5 to each entry in L1, move the cursor over to the second column, then up to the heading, L2. The bottom line of your display should read L2= (without any number in parentheses).

- The trick here is to let the symbol L1 stand for each element of the list L1. That is, we make L1 *a variable*.
  Key in L1 + 5 ; the bottom of your screen should read L2 = L1 + 5 .

- Now press ENTER and watch the entire column for L2 fill out automatically!

- To list in L2, the square of each entry in L1, put the cursor on L2 (at the top of the column). Then enter L1^2 (or L1 * L1).

- Now let us list in L3 the midpoint between the L1 entry and the L2 entry. Put the cursor back on L3 at the top of the column and press CLEAR . This removes the old formula. Now key in (L1 + L2)/2 and press ENTER .

1. List at least ten data values in L1.

2. Write a formula to list in L2 the distance between 17 and each entry in L1. Remember: Distances are never negative numbers. Then use it.

3. Write a formula to list in L3 the square of the difference (which may be negative) between each entry in L_1 and 17. Then use it.

4. Write a formula to list in L4 the square root of each entry in L3. Then use it.

5. How are columns L2 and L4 related? Explain.

Drawing Circles

To draw circles directly on a graph, use 9:Circle(in the DRAW menu. (The DRAW menu appears when you press 2nd DRAW .) 2:Line(can be used to draw segments, which lets you add radii, diameters, and other segments to your drawings of circles.

Before beginning, make sure that all the functions on your Y= screen are turned off. If they are not, their graphs will appear when you draw circles and segments. Also make sure that all STAT PLOTS are turned off.

Follow these instructions to draw a circle directly on a graph.

1. From the ZOOM menu, choose ZStandard (to clear any unusual WINDOW settings). Then choose ZSquare or ZInteger, which displays the graph window.

2.   From the DRAW menu, choose 9:Circle(.

3.   Choose a point for the center by moving the cursor to this point and pressing [ENTER] .

4.   Choose the radius for your circle by moving the cursor this many units away from the center and pressing [ENTER] .

You can continue to draw circles by repeating the last two steps. To clear the screen before drawing a new circle, use :ClrDraw in the DRAW menu. If you want to stop drawing circles, press [CLEAR] .

Follow the steps above to draw each of these items.

1. a circle with center (0, 10) and radius 5

2. a circle with center (12, −7) and radius 15

3. four circles with center (0, 0)

a

You can also draw a circle from the Home Screen (the calculator's primary display WINDOW) by following these instructions. You can use this same method to draw circles from a program.

1.   From the Home Screen, choose Circle(from the DRAW menu.

2.   Input the coordinates of the center, followed by the radius; then press [ENTER] . For example, if you enter (0, 10, 5), the calculator will draw a circle with center at (0, 10) and radius 5, using whatever ZOOM WINDOW setting is current.

3.   To return to the Home Screen, press [CLEAR] .

1. Draw a circle with center (3, 2) and radius 7 directly from the Home Screen. If your graph does not look like a circle, how can you adjust the graph WINDOW so that it does?

b

2. Draw four concentric circles around (0, 0) directly from the Home Screen. Earlier you were asked to draw this figure directly on a graph. Which method is easier for you? Why?

Appendix B:
Using a Spreadsheet

Computers give us many different tools for doing and using mathematics. One of these tools is called a **spreadsheet**. These days, a spreadsheet is an easy-to-use and very powerful computer program, but the idea of a spreadsheet is really much simpler and older than computers. Originally, a spreadsheet was just an oversized piece of paper, with lines and columns that made it easier for accountants and bookkeepers to keep their work in order.

You can make a spreadsheet on a lined piece of paper:

- Make a narrow border across the top and down the left side of the sheet.

- Divide the rest of the paper into columns from top to bottom. Six columns of about equal width will do for now.

- In the left margin, number the lines, beginning with 1, to the bottom of the page.

- Across the top margin, name each column with a letter from A to F in alphabetical order.

Your paper should look something like Display B.1.

	A	B	C	D	E	F
1						
2						
3						
4						
5						
6						
⋮						

Display B.1

The Cell Names

Each box in this grid has its own address — the letter of its column followed by the number of its row. For instance, C4 refers to the box, third column (column C), on the fourth line (row). The electronic spreadsheets that computers handle look just like this, and each position in them is addressed in just the same way. Electronic spreadsheet manuals often call the boxes **cells**. We'll do the same thing, so that you become used to the term.

Here are a couple of questions to get you comfortable with the way cells are addressed:

- Make a copy of Display B.1 and shade in these cells: A2, B3, C4, D5, E6, A6, B5, D3, E2. What shape do you get?

- If you wanted Display B.1 to be shaded in a checkerboard pattern, with alternating cells filled in, which cells would you shade? Write out all their addresses. There's more than one way to do this.

The advantage of electronic spreadsheets over handmade ones is that the electronic ones do the computations for you, *IF* you ask them properly. If you know how to speak the language of your spreadsheet program, you can get it to do all the hard work very quickly. The main idea to remember is:

A spreadsheet is powerful because it can find and work with numbers that appear anywhere on it by using the cell names.

Therefore,

When working with a spreadsheet, always try to build what you want, step by step, from the first data you enter. The fewer numbers you have to enter, the easier it is for the spreadsheet to do your work.

The rest of this appendix shows you how to get an electronic spreadsheet to work for you. For practice, each new process will be introduced by using it to deal with this problem:

> You are sent to the local supermarket to buy at least 2 pounds of potato chips for a club picnic. The club treasurer tells you to spend as little money as possible.

Now, there are many different brands of potato chips, and each brand comes in several different size bags. How can you compare prices in a useful way? Well, the bag sizes are measured in ounces. If you divide the price of the bag by the number of ounces, you'll get the price per ounce (this approach is called *unit* pricing). We'll set up a spreadsheet to tell you the price per ounce of every kind of potato chip bag your market sells.

> *Don't just read the rest of this appendix*: **DO IT! Work along with the instructions using your own spreadsheet.**

Entering Numbers and Text

There are three different kinds of things you can put in a cell – numbers, text, and formulas. Most spreadsheets distinguish between numbers and text automatically:

1. If you enter numerical symbols only, the entry is treated as a number.

2. If you begin an entry with letters or other symbols not related to numbers (even if numbers are entered along with them), the entry is treated as text.

Note that if you want a number (such as a date or a year) or a number-related symbol (such as $) to be treated as a text entry, you have to tell the machine somehow. Check your user's manual for the way your spreadsheet program does it.

Display B.2 lists the prices of different brands and sizes of potato chips, including the special sale prices for the day. These are actual data from a supermarket. To enter these data in their most useful form, you should use *three* columns—one for the brand, one for the weights (in ounces), and one for the prices. Put the information of Display B.2 into columns A, B, and C now.

Brand of Chip	No. of Ounces	$Cost of Bag
Cape Cod	11 oz.	2.49
Eagle Thins	9.5 oz.	1.99
Humpty Dumpty	6 oz.	1.19
Humpty Dumpty	10 oz.	1.68
Lay's	6 oz.	0.95
Lay's	14 oz.	2.79
O'Boisies	14.5 oz.	2.79
Ruffles	6 oz.	1.39
Ruffles	14 oz.	2.79
Tom's	6 oz.	1.39
Tom's	11 oz.	1.69
Wise	6 oz.	1.39
Wise	10 oz.	1.48

Display B.2

The standard column width of your spreadsheet probably is not big enough to handle some of the brand names. Find the Column Width command and adjust the width of column A to 15 spaces. While you're at it, you might as well adjust the width of column B (the ounces) and column C (the price) each seven spaces wide. This will make the display look a little neater.

Entering Formulas

If you want the spreadsheet to calculate an entry from other data, you have to give it a formula to use. You also have to begin with a special symbol to let it know that a formula is about to be entered. The special symbol depends on the type of spreadsheet you have. Excel uses the symbol = ; Lotus 1-2-3 uses the symbol + ; your software might use something else.

Calculate the price per ounce of Cape Cod chips by entering the formula C1/B1 into cell D1. As soon as you enter it, the number 0.226363 should appear. This is correct, but more accurate than we need. Three decimal places should be enough. Find the spreadsheet command that fixes the number of decimal places and use it to set the column D display to 3 places.

Copying Formulas

To get the price per ounce of Eagle Thins, all you have to do is copy the formula from cell D1 to cell D2. Do that. Check the spreadsheet manual to see how to copy from one cell to another. As soon as you do it, the number 0.209 will appear. Now look at the formula itself. Notice that it says C2/B2; that is, when you copied the formula one cell below where it started, the spreadsheet automatically changed the cell addresses inside it by that amount. This automatic adjustment process is one of the most powerful features of the spreadsheet. Next we'll use it to get the price per ounce of *all* the other kinds of chips at once!

Repeated Copying

You can copy a cell entry over and over again, all at once, along as much of a row or column as you mark out. If the entry is a formula, the spreadsheet will automatically adjust the cell addresses in it at each step. In some spreadsheet programs (such as Excel), this is done by the Fill command. In others (such as Lotus 1-2-3), it is done as part of the Copy command, by highlighting the entire region of cells into which you want the formula copied.

Find out how this works for your spreadsheet. Then copy what's in D2 into cells D3 through D13 and watch all the per ounce prices appear immediately. At this point, your spreadsheet should look something like Display B.3.

	A	B	C	D
1	Cape Cod	11	2.49	0.226
2	Eagle Thins	9.5	1.99	0.209
3	Humpty Dumpty	6	1.19	0.198
4	Humpty Dumpty	10	1.68	0.168
5	Lay's	6	0.95	0.158
6	Lay's	14	2.79	0.199
7	O'Boisies	14.5	2.79	0.192
8	Ruffles	6	1.39	0.232
9	Ruffles	14	2.79	0.199
10	Tom's	6	1.39	0.232
11	Tom's	11	1.69	0.154
12	Wise	6	1.39	0.232
13	Wise	10	1.48	0.148

Display B.3

 What *formula* is being used in cell D3? In D7? In D13?

Inserting Rows and Columns

Now let's put in column headings so that the spreadsheet is easier to understand. Move the cursor to the beginning of row 1 and use the Insert Row command of your spreadsheet to put in two rows at the very top. Cape Cod should now be in cell A3. We'll use the first row for headings and leave the second row blank. Enter Brand in A1, ounce in B1, price in C1 and enter $/oz. in D1. Change the width of column D to 7 spaces.

Because we've moved everything down, the row numbers no longer correspond to the number of brands listed. Make space to renumber the rows that list the brands, like this: Move the cursor to the top of the first column and use the Insert Column command to put two new columns at the far left. Cape Cod should now be in cell C3.

Numbering Rows

Now let's try a little experiment. We'll number the brands in two different ways. Make the two new columns, A and B, only 4 spaces wide. Now put the numbers 1 through 13 down these two columns, starting at the third row, in these two ways:

- In column A, enter each number by hand—the number 1 in A3, the number 2 in A4, and so on, down to the number 13 in A15.

- In column B, enter the formula B2+1 in cell B3. The number 1 will appear because the spreadsheet treats the empty cell B2 as if it had 0 in it. Now copy this formula into all the cells from B3 through B15.

Do columns A and B match? They should. If they don't, ask your teacher to help you find what went wrong. At this point, your display should look like Display B.4.

	A	B	C	D	E	F
1			Brand	oz.	$/bag	$/oz.
2						
3	1	1	Cape Cod	11	2.49	0.226
4	2	2	Eagle Thins	9.5	1.99	0.209
5	3	3	Humpty Dumpty	6	1.19	0.198
6	4	4	Humpty Dumpty	10	1.68	0.168
7	5	5	Lay's	6	0.95	0.158
8	6	6	Lay's	14	2.79	0.199
9	7	7	O'Boisies	14.5	2.79	0.192
10	8	8	Ruffles	6	1.39	0.232
11	9	9	Ruffles	14	2.79	0.199
12	10	10	Tom's	6	1.39	0.232
13	11	11	Tom's	11	1.69	0.154
14	12	12	Wise	6	1.39	0.232
15	13	13	Wise	10	1.48	0.148

Display B.4

Ordering Data

Another handy feature of an electronic spreadsheet is that it can put in order data that is listed in a column. It can put numbers in size order, either increasing or decreasing. Most spreadsheets can also put text entries in alphabetical order. To do this, you need to find the Sort command and tell it what list of data you want to rearrange. In Excel, Sort is in the Data menu; in Lotus 1–2–3, it's in the Select menu. The computer prompts you for a little more information, such as whether you want ascending or descending order, then does the sorting.

Note that some spreadsheets move entire rows when they sort; others can be told just to rearrange the data in a single column. Check your user's manual to see how your spreadsheet works. In this example, we assume that the spreadsheet moves entire rows when it sorts.

Let's rearrange the potato chip list according to the price per ounce, from most expensive to least expensive. Follow your spreadsheet's instructions to sort the per ounce prices in column F in ascending order. Which kind of potato chip is the best buy? Which is the worst buy?

Look at columns A and B.

1. Do they still match? What has happened? Explain.

2. What would have happened if you had entered the number 1 in B3, then entered the formula =B3+1 in B4? Explain.

Now that we have all this information, how do we find out how much it will cost the club for the 2 pounds of potato chips? Here's one plan:

- Compute the number of ounces in 2 pounds.

- Multiply the cost of 1 ounce by the total number of ounces needed.

Warning. There's something wrong with this approach; what is it?

We'll do this on the spreadsheet because it provides an example of a different way to use cell addresses. To find the total number of ounces, we just multiply the number of pounds (2) by 16. Make these entries on the spreadsheet:

- In C17, enter number of lbs.; in D17, enter 2.

- In C18, enter number of oz.; in D18, put the formula that multiplies the entry in D17 by 16. What is that value?

Constant Cell Addresses

To find out how much 2 pounds of each kind of potato chip will cost, first set column G to display in currency format. Then move the cursor to cell G3. This should be the first blank cell at the end of row 3. We want this cell to show the number of ounces to be bought (in D18) multiplied by the price per ounce (in F3). Let's try it.

- Enter the formula D18*F3 in G3. The result should be $4.74.
  Is your first kind the Wise 10-oz. bag?

- So far, so good. Now copy this formula to the next line, in G4. What do you get? $0.00? How come?

- Look at the formula as it appears in G4. Does it say D19*F4? What happened?

Remember that when you shift a formula from one location to another, the spreadsheet automatically shifts every cell address in exactly the same way. We copied this formula to a location one row down from where it was, so the spreadsheet added the number 1 to the row number of each cell address in the formula. Now, we want that to happen to one of these addresses, but not to the other. That is, the cost of the kind of potato chip in row 4 should use the price per ounce in F4, but it should still use the total number of ounces from D18.

To prevent the spreadsheet from automatically adjusting a cell address when a formula is moved, enter the cell address with a $ in front of its column letter and a $ in front of its row number.

This means that you should go back to cell G3 and enter the multiplication formula $D$18*F3. Now copy this to G4. Do you get $4.92? Good. If not, what went wrong? Ask your teacher if you need help figuring it out. Now copy this formula into cells G5 through G15. Column G now should show the cost for 2 pounds of each kind of potato chip in your list.

Go to G1, make this column 7 spaces wide and enter the word cost as the column heading.

1. According to column G, which kind of potato chip is the best buy?

2. Why is that *not* necessarily the best buy for your club?

3. What's wrong with letting this answer tell you what kind to buy? *Hint*: How many *bags* would you have to buy?

The INT Function

As the hint in the box above suggests, using the information in column G to guide your choice may not be a good idea because the supermarket sells potato chips by the bag. In order to know how much it will cost to get at least 2 pounds of chips, you first must know how many bags you'll need.

How do you do that? Easy, right? Just divide 32 oz. (2 lbs.) by the number of ounces in a single bag. If you get a mixed number, add 1 to the whole-number part.

For example, if you want at least 32 oz. in 10 oz. bags, divide 32 by 10. You get 3.2 as an answer, but, since you can't buy 0.2 of a bag of chips, you need 4 bags

There's a spreadsheet function—called INT—that makes this very easy to compute automatically. The INT function gives you the greatest integer less than or equal to the number you put into it. For instance:

$$\text{INT}\left(3\tfrac{1}{3}\right) = 3$$

$$\text{INT}(2.98) = 2$$

$$\text{INT}(5) =$$

Let's use this function to carry out the computation we just did, finding how many 10 oz. bags of Wise potato chips we need in order to have at least 2 pounds. But instead of entering the numbers in separately, we'll get them from other cells on the spreadsheet. Move to cell H3 and enter the formula

$$\text{INT}(\$D\$18/D3) + 1$$

Just to make sure you understand what we're doing, answer these questions before moving on:

1. What does $D$18 stand for?

2. Why are the $ symbols there?

3. What does D3 stand for?

4. What number is $D$18/D3?

5. What number is INT($D$18/D3)?

6. What number is INT($D$18/D3)+1?

7. If you copy this formula to cell H4, how will it read?

a

Now use the Fill command to copy this formula into cells H4 through H15. For each kind, the number you get says how many bags you need in order to have at least two pounds of chips. Put the heading bags at the top of this column H, and make the column 5 spaces wide.

Now we can finish the problem. To find the cost of at least 2 lbs. of each kind of chip, multiply the number of bags you need by the cost of a single bag. Enter a formula in I3 that does this; then copy it into I3 through I15. Finish your spreadsheet display by renaming column G cost 1 and naming column I cost 2 and changing the width of column I to 6 spaces.

1. If you *must* get at least 2 lbs. of chips and you want to spend as little as possible, which kind do you buy?

2. How many bags do you buy?

3. What does it cost you?

b

The next questions show off the power of spreadsheets for testing out different variations of a situation. Each part is exactly the same as above, except that the total number of pounds of chips is different. Answer each one by changing as little as possible on your spreadsheet.

1. If you *must* get at least 3 lbs. of chips and you want to spend as little as possible, which kind do you buy? How many bags do you buy? What does it cost you?

2. If you *must* get at least 4 lbs. of chips and you want to spend as little as possible, which kind do you buy? How many bags do you buy? What does it cost you?

c

3. If you *must* get at least 5 lbs. of chips and you want to spend as little as possible, which kind do you buy? How many bags do you buy? What does it cost you?

Problem Set: Appendix B

1. These two questions refer to the potato chip spreadsheet that you just made.

   (a) Add a column J that shows the total number of ounces of potato chips of each kind that you get when you buy enough bags to get at least two pounds of them. What formula will compute these numbers?

   (b) Add a column K that shows the number of *extra* ounces (more than 2 pounds) that you get when you buy enough bags to get at least two pounds of them. What formula will compute these numbers?

2. Make a spreadsheet like the one for the potato chips to deal with this problem:

   (a) Your favorite aunt runs a shelter for homeless cats. As a present for her birthday, you decide to give her 5 pounds of canned cat food. You want to spend as little money as possible. The brands, sizes, and prices for the canned cat food at the supermarket are shown in Display B.5. What brand and size is the buy, and how many cans of it should you get? What will it cost?

   (b) Your best friend thinks you have a great idea. She decides to buy your aunt 5 pounds of canned cat food, too. If you both chip in and buy a combined present of 10 pounds of canned cat food, what is the best buy of canned cat food for your combined present? Explain your answer?

Brand of Cat Food	No. of Ounces	Cost
Alpo	6 oz.	3 for $1.00
Alpo	13.75 oz.	$ .65
Figaro	5.5 oz.	$ .37
Figaro	12 oz.	$ .66
Friskies	6 oz.	$ .35
Friskies	13 oz.	$ .58
Kal Kan	5.5 oz.	4 for $1.00
Puss 'n Boots	14 oz.	$ .55
9 Lives	5.5 oz.	3 for $ .88
9 Lives	13 oz.	$ .48
Whiskas	5.5 oz.	3 for $1.00
Whiskas	12.3 oz.	$ .55

Display B.5

3. Here's a bonus question.

   (a) Invent a problem about breakfast foods that is like the potato chip and cat food problems.

   (b) Go to your local supermarket and gather the brand, size, and price information that you will need to solve your problem.

   (c) Using the data you gather for part (b), set up a spreadsheet that solves the problem you invented in part (a).

Appendix C: Programming the TI-82 (TI-83)

After you have been using the TI-82 (TI-83) for a while, you may notice that you are repeating certain tasks on your calculator over and over. Often you are repeating the same sequence of keystrokes, which can become very tiresome. Programs give you a way to carry out long sequences of keystrokes all at once, saving you a great deal of time and energy.

In this appendix we will show you some simple TI-82 (TI-83) programs and how to enter and use them. In the textbook, there are some other programs which you will find useful in solving problems.

Correcting Mistakes

When you enter a program you will almost surely make some keying mistakes. You can use the arrow keys to back up and key over any mistakes. To insert something new, rather than keying over what is already there, give the insert command (INS above the [(DEL)] key) by keying

$$\boxed{\text{2nd}} \quad \boxed{\text{(DEL)}}$$

Use the [(DEL)] key to delete the current character.

Entering Programs

To enter a program, give the [NEW] command under the [PRGM] menu by keying

$$\boxed{\text{PRGM}} \quad \boxed{\triangleleft} \quad \boxed{\text{ENTER}}$$

Your calculator should look like Display C.1. You are now in program writing mode. Whatever you key in will be stored in the program you are creating, rather than being executed directly. To get out of program writing mode, give the QUIT command.

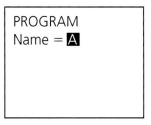

Display C.1

Next you need to name your program so that you can use it. We will start with a very short and not very useful program just to test your ability to enter a program and run it. Give your program the name ADD. Normally, to enter the capital letters that are above and to the right of some of the keys you must press the [ALPHA] key first. When naming a program, however, the calculator goes into **ALPHA** mode automatically. This means you *don't* have to press the [ALPHA] key when entering the letters in the program name. Key in

Your calculator screen should now look like Display C.2

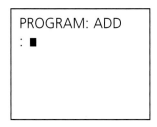

Display C.2

We now need to enter the actual program commands. Our test program will ask for two numbers and then add them. Each line of the program begins with a colon. At the end of each line of the program press [ENTER]. The first line of our program asks for the first of the two numbers it will add. The two numbers that we tell the calculator to add are called the *input* for the program. The Input command is the first item under the I/O section of the **PRGM** menu. We will store the input in memory A. Key in

The TI screen should now look like Display C.3.

```
PROGRAM: ADD
: Input A
: ■
```

Display C.3

The next line in the program asks for another number and stores it in memory location B. Enter the second line now, based on the way you entered the first line. Your screen should now look like Display C.4.

```
PROGRAM: ADD
: Input A
: Input B
```

Display C.4

The third line adds the numbers stored in memories A and B and stores the result in memory C. Key in

[ALPHA] [A] [+] [ALPHA] [B] [STO ▷] [ALPHA] [C] [ENTER]

The new screen is in Display C.5.

```
PROGRAM: ADD
: Input A
: Input B
: A + B→C
: ■
```

Display C.5

We finish our program with a statement which displays the result of adding the two numbers (now stored in memory C). The display command Disp is the third item under the I/O section of the PRGM menu.

Key in

PRGM   ▷   3   ALPHA   C

The resulting screen is in Display C.6

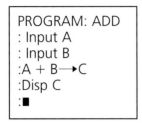

```
PROGRAM: ADD
: Input A
: Input B
:A + B→C
:Disp C
:■
```

Display C.6

We are done writing the program! To quit programming mode use the QUIT key (above the MODE key). The program is automatically saved. Key in

2nd   QUIT

You are now back to the Home Screen, where you started.

Running Programs

To run the program we just keyed in, we go to the EXEC section of the PRGM menu, key in the number of the program we want to run, and then press ENTER . We will assume that the program named ADD that we just entered is program number 1. Key in

PRGM   1   ENTER

If you entered the program correctly, a question mark appears asking for input. If there is an error, look at the next section on editing programs. This question mark is produced by the first line of your program. You are being requested to type in the first of two numbers, which will then be added by the program. Let's suppose that we want to add the numbers 4 and 5. Press 4 then press ENTER . A second question mark appears asking for the second number. Press 5 and press ENTER again. The result, 9, should appear. The screen now looks like Display C.7.

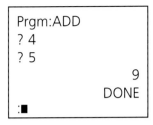

Display C.7

To run the program again, just press the [ENTER] key. You don't have to go through the PRGM menu to run the program the second time, as long as no other calculations have been performed in between. Try adding two other numbers to see how this works.

Quitting Programs

If you are in the middle of running a program and you want to stop the program, press [ON] key. To try this out, run the ADD program again, but this time when the first question mark appears, press [ON] . The screen should look like Display C.8.

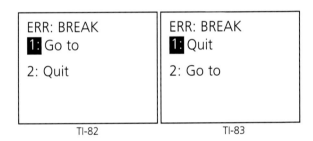

Display C.8

Press [2] to quit the program and return to the Home Screen. Pressing [1] puts you back in program writing mode at the point in the program where you stopped the program.

Editing Programs

If your program doesn't work, or if you just want to make changes to a program, you use the EDIT section of the PRGM menu. Key in

Appendix C: Programming the TI-82 (TI-83)

This should put you back in the ADD program (assuming it is program 1). Your screen should look just as it did when you left the program writing mode (see Display C.6). Use the arrow keys and the insert [INS] and delete [(DEL)] keys as explained in the Correcting Mistakes section.

To open space for a new line, put the cursor at the beginning of a line, give the insert command [INS] and then press [ENTER]. To try this on your ADD program, use the arrow keys to put the cursor at the beginning of the second line of the program and key in

[2nd] [(DEL)] [ENTER]

Your screen should look like Display C.9.

```
PROGRAM: ADD
: Input A
:
: Input B
: A + B—→C
: Disp C
:
```

Display C.9

The blank line we just created will not affect the program, so we can just give the QUIT command to leave the program writing mode.

A Useful Program

Now that you have some practice with writing, editing and running programs, let's take a look at a program that you might really find useful.

Graphing With Parameters

Suppose that we want to graph the equation of a straight line, say $y = ax + 5$, for several values of a. The constant a is called a *parameter*. First we can enter the expression AX + 5 as expression Y₁ under the [Y=] menu. We can then store numbers in memory A and press [GRAPH]. The problem is that we only see the graph for one value of A at a time. The following program allows you to easily produce graphs for many values of A and keep all of the graphs on the screen together.

Enter the program shown in Display C.10, using what you
learned from the **Entering Programs** section. Name the program
PARAMS. Note: DrawF is item 6 under the DRAW menu
(above the [PRGM] key) for the TI-82. Y_1 is item number 1 of
the Function sub menu under the **Y-vars** menu (above the
[DRAW] [VARS] key). For the TI-83, Y_1 is found by keys

[VARS] [▷] [1] [1] [ENTER]

```
PROGRAM: PARAMS
: Input  A
: DrawF  Y₁
: ■
```

Display C.10

The program is simple, but saves quite a few keystrokes. You
put in a value for A, and then the function is graphed using the
DrawF command.

To use this program you must store your function in function
memory Y_1 and then *turn off* Y_1 (put the cursor on the = and
press ENTER). Your Y= WINDOW should look like
Display C.11. Notice that the = is *not* highlighted, indicating
the function is off.

```
Y₁ = AX + 5
Y₂ =
Y₃ =
Y₄ =
Y₅ =
Y₆ =
Y₇ =
Y₈ =
```

Display C.11

To set the graph WINDOW to the Standard setting, press the 6
under the ZOOM menu. Your WINDOW settings should appear
as in Display C.12.

WINDOW FORMAT	WINDOW FORMAT
Xmin = -10	Xmin = -10
Xmax = 10	Xmax = 10
Xscl = 1	Xscl = 1
Ymin = -10	Ymin = -10
Ymax = 10	Ymax = 10
Yscl = 1	Yscl = 1
	Xres = 1
TI-82	TI-83

Display C.12

Now run the program. Try starting with an A value of 1. Press
1 then ENTER in response to the question mark. You
should see a graph of the function $y = 1x + 5$. To run the
program again, first press the CLEAR key (to get back to the
Home Screen) then ENTER . Try an A with a value of -2 this
time. Now both the graphs of Y = AX + B for A = 1 and for
A = -2 should be on the screen, as shown in Display C.13.

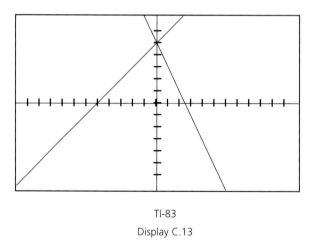

TI-83

Display C.13

If you want to clear the graph screen, use ClrDraw, which is
item 1 under the DRAW menu.

You only need to change the function stored in Y₁ to graph any
other function with one parameter. For instance, try graphing
the function $y = a^x$ for various a values.

Appendix D: Linear Programming With Excel

The graphical method of solving Linear Programming problems is explained in the text. The limitation of this method is that it is applicable only to problems with two variables.

Linear Programming is one of the most used mathematical methods in real-world problem solving. Only rarely are two variables present in a realistic problem. Mathematicians have developed methods to solve Linear Programming problems with any number of variables; a computer program is then needed to carry out the computations. One commonly used computer program which solves Linear Programming problems is called **LINDO™**.

Several spreadsheet programs can solve Linear Programming problems. Microsoft Excel, Lotus 1-2-3, and Quattro Pro are such spreadsheet programs. We will look at how Excel 5.0 solves linear programming problems, but we will not explain the method Excel uses. This is known as treating the program as something mysterious—we can follow the instructions for using the program, but we don't know how the program gives a solution to the problem. Knowing how to solve simple problems graphically helps us to understand the output from the program, even if we don't understand the exact method the computer is using. Just imagine that Excel is using a method similar to the one you learned for two variable problems.

Our first example will be a very simple problem with only two variables. Then we can solve the problem graphically as in the textbook and check our answer against the answer from the computer. We will then extend the problem to three variables; here a graphical solution is not possible.

Problem

A new housing development is being built near Bart's house. Bart has noticed that the construction workers often leave the site to get lunch. Always on the lookout to earn money, Bart figures that he can make lunches for the workers and sell them at a profit. We will assume there are enough workers and Bart can sell all of the sandwiches that he can make.

Bart decides to make two types of lunches. The first lunch will have two sodas and one sandwich (the Thirsty Worker Lunch) and the second type of lunch will have two sandwiches and one soda (the Hungry Worker Lunch). Bart plans to buy the sandwiches and sodas from a local deli for $3.00 per sandwich and $0.50 per can of soda. He will sell the Thirsty Worker Lunches for $5.00 and the Hungry Worker Lunches for $8.00. This means that Bart's profit for each Thirsty Worker Lunch is $1.00 and his profit on each Hungry Worker Lunch is $1.50.

Bart has one problem. The deli doesn't open until 11:30 a.m., which is too late to make lunches and have them ready for the workers. He figures he needs to buy his supplies the night before, but that means he needs to keep the (24 cans) of soda in the family refrigerator. Bart finds a cooler in the basement that will hold 20 sandwiches.

How many Hungry Worker Lunches and how many Thirsty Worker Lunches should Bart prepare in order to make the most money? His constraints are that he can use only 20 sandwiches and 24 sodas as explained above.

Solution

SETUP

First we need to formulate the problem as a linear programming problem. Let x represent the number of Thirsty Worker Lunches and y the number of Hungry Worker Lunches that Bart prepares. Then Bart's profit P is

$$P = 1.00x + 1.50y$$

The soda constraint would be

$$2x + y \leq 24$$

and the sandwich constraint would be

$$x + 2y \leq 20$$

The other two constraints which we don't want to forget are

$$x \geq 0 \text{ and } y \geq 0$$

Computer Solution

Our goal is to set up the spreadsheet as shown in Displays D.1 and D.2 and to show the formulas that you actually key into each cell. Display D.2 shows what the result should look like on your spreadsheet. To get this result, follow the steps below.

1. Key in a title for the spreadsheet in cell A1; we used "Bart's Lunch Business." Don't key in any quotation marks. We dressed up the title a bit by making the font larger (12 point) and using the Outline style; just select cell A1 and choose Font from the Format menu.

2. Key in x in cell A3, y in cell B3 and P = 1.00x + 1.50y in cell C3.

3. Cells A4 and B4 will represent the initial guess for x and y. These guesses don't have to be good; they just have to make sense. The easiest guesses are 0 for both x and y, since they satisfy all the constraints. Therefore, key in 0 in A4 and 0 in B4.

4. Key in = 1.00 * A4 + 150 * B4 in cell C4. This represents the profit for the x and y you chose. You should see 0 appear since x and y are now 0.

5. Key in the word constraints in cell A6. We will use row 7 to label the constraints, and row 8 to put in the constraints as formulas.

6. Key in $x + 2y$ < = 20 into cell A7 and $2x + y$ < = 24 into cell B7 as labels for the sandwich and soda constraints.

7. Key in the **left side only** of the sandwich constraint into cell A8. Therefore you key in = A4 + 2 * B4 into cell B7. Similarly key in = 2 * A4 + B4 into cell B8. At this point zeros should appear in these cells since x and y are both 0.

	A	B	C
1	Bart's Lunch Business		
2			
3	x	y	P=1.00x+1.50y
4	0	0	=1*A4+1.5*B4
5			
6	constraints		
7	x+2y<=20	2x+y<=24	
8	=A4+2*B4	=2*A4+B4	

Display D.1

8. Select cells A3 through C8 and choose CELLS: Alignment from the Format menu. Choose center for horizontal alignment. Then choose CELLS: Number from the Format menu and select 0.00. Your spreadsheet should now look like Display D.2

	A	B	C
1	Bart's Lunch Business		
2			
3	x	y	P=1.00x+1.50y
4	0.00	0.00	0.00
5			
6	constraints		
7	x+2y<=20	2x+y<=24	
8	0.00	0.00	

Display D.2

We are now ready to tell the computer to find the solution to our linear programming problem. We use a capability of Excel called the Solver to get the solution. You may have noticed that we have not actually specified all of the information for the constraints. In particular, we need to tell Excel that cells A4 and B4 need to be positive (x and y should be positive), that cell A8 should be less than 20 and cell B8 should be less than 24 (the sandwich and soda constraints). We do this as shown below.

9. Choose Solver from the Tools menu. The goal is to get the Solver dialogue box to look like Display D.3.

10. Type C4 in the Set Target Cell box. You don't need to type the $s; they will be added by Excel automatically. This box tells the computer which cell to maximize; in our problem C4 is the cell that represents Bart's profit.

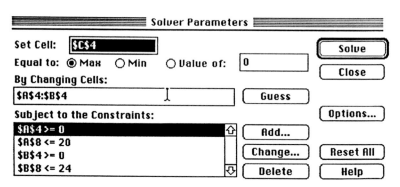

Display D.3

11. Type A4:B4 in the By Changing Cells box. This instructs the computer to adjust the cells in this range (the number of

Thirsty Worker and Hungry Worker Lunches in our problem) until cell C4 is at a maximum.

12. Put the constraints into the Subject to the Constraints box. For each you must click the Add button, which brings up another dialogue box as shown in Display D.4. Key in the Cell Reference and the Constraint value (the right-hand side of the constraint inequality). Click on the $<=$ drop-down menu to choose $<=$ or $>=$ (you can also choose $=$ or int for integer).

Cell Reference:	Constraint:
$A$8	<= ⬇ =20

OK	Cancel	Help

Display D.4

13. Click the Max button in the Equal To line to indicate that this is a maximization problem (it is probably already chosen).

14. Click the Solve button, and Excel will attempt to solve the problem. Excel will then report whether it found a solution or not. If a solution was found, just click OK in the dialogue box that pops up, and the values of the variables which provide the solution will have replaced the initial guesses that you gave in step 3.

Bart's Lunch Business

x	y	P=1.00x+1.50y
9.33	5.33	17.33

Constraints:

x+2y<=20	2x+y<=24
20.00	24.00

Display D.5

15. Summarize your findings and explain the spreadsheet for someone who might not be familiar with the problem. Display D.5 shows the solution to our problem, as well as a short verbal description of the results. We also dressed up

our report with a little formatting (using Borders from the Format menu and turning off the gridlines with Display from the Option menu). Note that, in this problem, we needed to round our results since fractional parts of a lunch do not make sense.

Summary of Findings

Bart is going to sell two types of lunches. We let x represent the number of Thirsty Worker Lunches, which contain two sodas and one sandwich. We let y represent the number of Hungry Worker Lunches, which contain one soda and two sandwiches. Bart's constraints are that he can use at most twenty sandwiches and twenty-four sodas. His profit P is $1.00 on each Thirsty Worker Lunch and $1.50 on each Hungry Worker Lunch.

The tables in Display D.5 resulted from performing a linear programming analysis of the problem. What they show is that Bart should make 9 Thirsty Worker Lunches and 5 Hungry Worker Lunches. The values in the table need to be rounded since Bart can't make a fraction of a lunch. His profit will be less than the $17.33 shown in the table; his actual profit will be

$$1(9) + 1.5(5) = \$16.50$$

Extension to Three Variables

Suppose that Bart decided to make a third type of lunch with 2 sandwiches and 2 sodas (Super Lunches). Let z represent the number of Super Lunches. Bart will sell Super Lunches for $9.00; his profit on these lunches would be $2.00. Then the new profit formula would be

$$P = 1.00x + 1.50y + 2.00z$$

The new constraints would be

$$2x + y + 2z \leq 24 \text{ and } x + 2y + 2z \leq 20$$

for soda and sandwiches. Display D.6 shows what formulas you would type into the cells. Display D.7 shows how the spreadsheet would look before solving.

	A	B	C	D
1	Bart's Lunch Business			
2				
3	x	y	z	P=1.00x+1.50y+2.00z
4	0	0	0	=1*A4+1.5*B4+2*C4
5				
6	constraints			
7	x+2y+2z<=20	2x+y+2z<=24		
8	=A4+2*B4+2*C4	=2*A4+B4+2*C4		

Display D.6

	A	B	C	D	E
1	Bart's Lunch Business				
2					
3	x	y	z	P=1.00x+1.50y+2.00z	
4	0.00	0.00	0.00	0.00	
5					
6	constraints				
7	x+2y+2z<=20	2x+y+2z<=24			
8	0.00	0.00			

Display D.7

When you now invoke the Solver, there are several changes you must make in the Solver dialogue box. You need to add the constraint C4 > = 0 ($z \geq 0$ in the problem) into the Subject to Constraints box, change the By Changing Cells box to A4:C4, and change the Set Target Cell box to D4. After these changes, click Solve; the spreadsheet displays the solution to the new problem as shown in Display D.8.

	A	B	C	D	E
1	Bart's Lunch Business				
2					
3	x	y	z	P=1.00x+1.50y+2.00z	
4	4.00	0.00	8.00	20.00	
5					
6	constraints				
7	x+2y+2z<=20	2x+y+2z<=24			
8	20.00	24.00			

Display D.8

We see by looking at Display D.8 that the addition of a new type of lunch has a significant effect on the solution to Bart's problem. Now Bart should make 4 Thirsty Worker Lunches and 8 Super Lunches and no Hungry Worker Lunches. His profit goes up from $16.50 to $20. We don't need to round this time since the values of the variables come out as whole numbers.

A big advantage to using the computer solution for this type of problem (besides being able to solve problems with more than two variables) is that we can easily change any part of the problem and get instant feedback on how the answer changes. For example, if Bart increases the amount he charges for the Hungry Worker Lunches, common sense tells us that at some number it would become profitable to make some of these lunches. What is that number?

To answer the previous question, you could try increasing the selling price of Hungry Worker Lunches to $8.60 to see if this changes the solution. This changes the profit on these lunches to $2.10. The only change in the problem is that the new profit formula is

$$P = 1.00x + 2.10y + 2.00z$$

Just change cells D3 and D4 to reflect the new information and run the Solver again. We find that, indeed, it is now profitable to provide some Hungry Worker Lunches (the result is interesting—check it out). With more guess and check we could pin down exactly the point where the y variable enters the problem.

Follow up Exercise

Carry out the process that was started. Keeping all other quantities in the problem constant, try different values for the price for the Hungry Worker Lunches until you find the number at which it just becomes profitable to make some of these lunches. Thus, it should be the case that if you lower the price of these lunches by any small amount, the solution to the Linear Programming problem has $y = 0$ in it, but if you increase the price by any small amount the solution for y is greater than 0. Discuss what happens to all variables and the total profit as you make these changes.

acute angle   An angle of measure less than 90° (but more than 0°).

alternate interior angles   Two nonadjacent interior angles on opposite sides of a transversal that intersect two lines.

altitude (of a triangle)   A line segment drawn from one vertex to the opposite side, that is perpendicular to the side.

angle   A figure formed by two line segments or rays with a common endpoint.

angle bisector   A line or ray that divides an angle in half.

axis of symmetry   A line that divides a figure in half so that each half is a mirror image of the other.

base unit   In a system of measurement, a unit which is chosen (for convenience) and by which other units of measure are defined.

complementary angles   Two angles whose measures have a sum of 90°.

congruent angles   Two angles that have the same measure.

congruent figures   Figures that have the same shape and size.

constant   A number or symbol representing a value that doesn't change.

constant of proportionality   The number that one variable is multiplied by in a direct proportion, or the number that is divided by one variable in an inverse proportion.

converse (of a universal statement)   A statement which interchanges the subject and the predicate of the given universal statement.

convex polygon   A polygon in which the measure of each angle is less than 180°.

corresponding angles   The angles, one interior and one exterior, on the same side of the transversal that intersects two lines.

cosine (of an acute angle)   In a right triangle, the cosine of an acute angle is the ratio of the length of the adjacent leg to the length of the hypotenuse.

counterexample   An example that proves a universal statement to be false.

cubic inch A cube with each edge one inch long.

cubic meter A cube with each edge one meter long.

direct variation A relationship between two variables such that one is a positive constant times the other.

directly proportional (variables) Two variables such that one is a positive constant times the other.

discrete Separate, distinct.

discrete mathematics The branch of mathematics that deals with processes related to counting separate, distinct objects.

domain (of an equation) The set of all numbers for which an equation makes sense (is either true or false).

equilateral polygon A polygon in which all sides have the same length.

exterior angle (of a polygon) An angle formed by one side of a polygon and the extension of an adjacent side.

geometric construction A procedure for creating a geometric object with a compass and an unmarked straightedge.

gnomon The upright, triangular component of a sundial.

hypotenuse The longest side of a right triangle; the side opposite the right angle.

identity (equation) An equation that is true for *all* numbers in its domain.

interior angles (of a polygon) The angles that open toward the inside of the polygon.

inverse cosine An acute angle whose cosine is a specified number between 0 and 1.

inverse sine An acute angle whose sine is a specified number between 0 and 1.

inverse tangent An acute angle whose tangent is a specified positive number.

inverse variation A relationship between two variables such that one is a positive constant divided by the other.

inversely proportional (variables) Two variables such that one is a positive constant divided by the other.

isosceles triangle A triangle with two sides of equal length.

leg (of a right triangle) One of the sides of a right triangle that is not the hypotenuse.

line segment A set of points on a line consisting of two endpoints and all the points between them.

Mercator map A flat map of the world that represents directions accurately.

model A representation of something physical or mathematical considered important for a particular purpose.

obtuse angle An angle of measure greater than 90° and less than 180°.

parallel lines Straight lines in a plane that never intersect, no matter how far they are extended.

parallelogram A quadrilateral with both pairs of opposite sides congruent; equivalently, a quadrilateral with both pairs of opposite sides parallel.

perimeter The distance around (the boundary of) a figure; its length as a path.

perpendicular bisector A line that intersects a given segment at right angles and divides it into two equal parts.

perpendicular lines Two lines that intersect at right angles; i.e., two lines that form congruent adjacent angles.

polygon A polygonal path that starts and ends at the same place and doesn't intersect itself anywhere in between.

polygonal path A sequence of line segments each connected to the next by a common endpoint.

proportion An equality between two ratios.

Pythagorean triple Three positive numbers a, b, and c such that $a^2 + b^2 = c^2$.

ratio One number divided by another; a common fraction.

ray Part of a line that starts at a particular point and extends infinitely far in one direction.

reflex angle An angle of measure greater than 180°, and less than 360°.

regular polygon A polygon with all sides the same length and all angles equal in measure.

rhombus A quadrilateral with all its sides congruent (the same length).

right angle An angle of measure 90°.

right triangle A triangle that has a right angle as one of its three angles.

scaling factor The constant that describes the size relationship between two similar objects.

side (of a polygon) Any one of the line segments that determines the polygon.

similar objects Two objects such that the distance between any two points of one object is a particular constant times the distance between the corresponding points of the other object. Objects that have the same shape.

sine (of an acute angle) In a right triangle, the sine of an acute angle is the ratio of the length of the side opposite the angle to the length of the hypotenuse.

slope measure (of an angle) The perpendicular distance from any chosen point on one ray of the angle to the other ray divided by the distance from the vertex to the foot of the perpendicular of the other ray.

straight angle An angle of measure 180°.

supplementary angles Two angles whose measures have a sum of 180°.

tangent (of an acute angle) In a right triangle, the tangent of an acute angle is the ratio of the length of the side opposite the angle to the length of the adjacent leg.

transversal A straight line that intersects two or more other coplanar straight lines at distinct points.

triangulation The process of dividing a polygon into nonoverlapping triangles.

unit cube A cube that measures one unit of length along each edge.

universal statement A statement of the form: "All [SOMETHING] are [SOMETHING ELSE]."

vertex A common endpoint of two sides of a polygon or an angle.

vertical angles Two angles such that the angles formed by two intersecting lines do not have a common side.

volume (of a three dimensional object) The number of unit cubes (of some unit length) needed to fill up the space it occupies.

Index

A

α (alpha), 255, 256
AAA (angle-angle-angle),
   183, 201, 206
AAS (angle-angle-side),
   182, 186
About Words
   acute, 139
   altitude, 69
   angle, 133
   bi-, 28
   bisect, 28
   flat (plano), 7
   geometry, 4
   gnomon, 155
   Mercator, Gerhardus, 5
   obtuse, 139
   percent, 110
   perimeter, 19
   periscope, 19
   plano, 7
   polygonal path, 15
   ratio, 110
   reflex, 141
   super-, 134
   superimpose, 134
   transversal, 157
   trigonometry, 180, 249
Acute angle, 139, 143
Adjacent side, 234
Aldebaran, 176, 177
Alpha (α) 255, 256
Algebraic proof, 73
Algebraic symbols, 216
Algorithm, 76
Alice in Wonderland, 107-109
Alternate exterior angles,
   159
Alternate interior angles, 159
Altitude of a triangle, 69, 168
Angle(s), 20, 133
   acute, 139, 143
   alternate exterior, 159
   alternate interior, 159

base, 186
bisector, 185
complementary, 161
concave, 198
congruent, 33, 34
corresponding, 158, 206
exterior, 194, 195
interior, 194
obtuse, 139, 143
reflex, 141, 143
right, 28, 35, 143
straight, 143
sum of polygon, 195-197
sum of triangle, 160
supplementary, 151
vertical, 151
Area, 43, 203
   of a rectangle, 59, 62
   of a right triangle, 48
   of a triangle, 72, 102
   tiling, 43-46, 49
Axes of symmetry, 34-37
Axis of symmetry, 24-26,
   34-37, 39

B

β (beta), 256
Babylonians, 138
$b(n) = 3 + 10.99n$, 6
Base
   angles, 186
   of a triangle, 69, 184
   units, 8
Bisector, 28, 185
   perpendicular, 28
Box, George, 7

C

Cable, 9
Carroll, Lewis, 107-109
Ceilometers, 243
Chain, 9
Circle, 276
   arc length, 260
   $x^2 + y^2 = 1$, 271
Classify, 18

Clockwise, 141
Complement, 161, 166
Complementary angles, 161
Concave angle, 198
Concave polygon, 198
Congruent, 26, 33-35, 47,
   48, 133, 167
   determined up to, 167
   angles, 33, 34, 133
   segments, 26
   triangles, 133, 167
   AAA, 201, 206
   AAS, 182, 186
   ASA, 180, 182, 186
   SAS, 173, 186
   SSS, 169, 183, 186
Constant, 113
   of proportionality (k),
     91-94
   scaling factor, 91, 114
Construction, geometric, 27
Continuous mathematics, 8
Converse, 38
   of the Pythagorean
     Theorem, 83
Convex, 190, 195
Coordinate system, 86
Corresponding
   angles, 158, 159, 201, 206
   points, 113
   vertices, 123
Cosecant, 228
Cosine, 235, 237
   $\cos^{-1}$, 254, 255
   domain of, 256
   inverse of, 256
   Law of, 267
Cotangent, 251
Counterclockwise, 141, 277
Counterexample, 38
Cross multiplication, 112,
   222
Cubic inch, 99
Cubic meter, 99

Cubic units, 211

D

Decagon, 18

Degree, 138, 140

Degree scale, 140

Determined figures, 167
   up to congruence, 167, 172

Diagonal, 74

Digit, 9

Direct variation, 91, 93
   varies directly, 91
   varies directly as the square, 93
   varies inversely, 93

Directly proportional, 91

Discrete mathematics, 7

Distance between points, 86

Distributive Law, 55, 57, 59, 61, 63
   geometric illustration, 58-62
   multiplication over addition, 57

Domain, 56, 256

E

English system, 8

Equal fractions, 112

Equations, 6
   domain, 56
   identity, 56

Equiangular, 41

Equilateral
   polygon, 19
   triangle, 26, 186

Equivalent statements, 160

Estimate, 46
   inner, 46
   outer, 46

Euclid, 14

Euler, Leonhard, 5

Exploration
   volume related to area, 100

Exterior angle, 194, 195, 197

F

Facts to Know
   AAA (angle-angle-angle similarity), 201
   AAS (angle-angle-side congruence), 182
   angle sum of exterior angles, 195
   angle sum of polygon, 193
   angle sum of triangle, 160
   area scaling factor, 205
   area of triangle, 72
   ASA (angle-side-angle congruence), 180
   corresponding angles of similar polygons, 201
   if and only if, 158
   N-sided polygon, 193
   Pythagorean Theorem, 82
   SAS (side-angle-side congruence), 173
   SSS (side-side-side congruence), 167
   volume scaling factor, 212

Fathom, 9

Foot, 8

Fractions (equal), 112

Function
   inverse, 256-260
   of cosine, 256
   of sine, 256
   of tangent, 148, 149, 256

Furlong, 9

G

Geometric construction, 27

Geometry, 3, 5
   continuous mathematics, 8
   plane, 7, 102

Gnomon, 155

Grade, 138

Gravity, Law of, 97

Gusset, 147

H

Hand, 9

Heptagon, 18

Hexagon, 18

Hexagram, 30

Hipparchus, 224, 229, 236

HO scale, 111-114

Hypotenuse, 48, 49
   right triangle, 49

I

Identity, 56

If and only if, 158

Inner estimate, 46

Interior angles, 194, 196, 197

Interpolation, linear, 230

Inverse
   function, 256
   of cosine, 256
   of sine, 256
   of tangent, 149, 256
   problem, 254
   variations, 93, 94

Isosceles, 81, 184

Isosceles right triangle, 81

K

k, 91-94, 114
   constant of proportionality, 91- 94 114, 212
   scaling factor, 91, 114, 205

Kite, 208, 209

L

Labeling, 49

Latitude, 154

Law, 57
   algebraic, 55
   Distributive, 55, 57, 59, 61, 63
   of Cosines, 267
   of Gravity, 97
   of Sines, 264

Legs of a right triangle, 48, 49

Length,
   digit, 9
   foot, 9
   palm, 9

span, 9
Length of an arc, 260
Light law, 94
Light-year, 188
Line
   of symmetry, 24
   parallel, 157
   perpendicular, 28
   segment, 11, 27
Linear interpolation, 230

M
Mathematical model, 6
Mathematics
   continuous, 8
   discrete, 7
Measurement, 3, 7
   cubic inch, 99
   foot, 8, 9
   line segment, 11
   meter, 8
   palm, 9
   slope, 136
   span, 9
   unit cube, 99
   unit of, 138
Mercator, Gerhardus, 5
Mercator map, 5
Metric System, 8, 138
Midpoint, 26
   of a segment, 26, 27
Models, 6
   mathematical, 6

N
n-gon, 193-196
n-sided polygon, 193-196
Newton's Law of Gravity, 97
Nonagon, 18, 40
Non-convex polygon, 194

O
Obtuse angle, 139, 143
Octagon, 18, 40
Operation (add, multiply), 61
Opposite side, 36, 80, 223
O scale, 110-114
Outer estimate, 46

P
Palm, 9

Parallel, 157
Parallelogram, 36, 37, 167-170
   axes of symmetry for, 37
Pentagon, 18
Pentagram, 29
Percent, 110
Perimeter, 19, 43
Periscope, 19
Perpendicular, 28
   bisector, 28
   drop a, 28, 37
Phrase(s) to Know,
   acute angles, 139
   alternate interior angles, 159
   constant of proportionality, 91-94
   corresponding angles, 158
   directly proportional, 91
   if and only if, 158
   inversely proportional, 94
   obtuse angles, 139
   reflex angles, 141
   supplementary angles, 151
   varies directly, 91
   varies directly as the square, 93
   varies inversely, 93
   varies inversely as the square, 94
   vertical angles, 151
Planar region, 204
Plane geometry, 7, 102
Polygon, 16, 18, 190-197
   angle sum, 195-197
   area of, 59, 62
   concave, 198
   convex, 190, 195
   decagon, 18
   equilateral, 19
   exterior angles, 194, 195
   heptagon, 18
   hexagon, 18
   hexagram, 30
   interior angles, 194, 196
   n-sided, 196
   nonagon, 18, 40

   non-convex, 194
   octagon, 18, 40
   parallelogram, 36, 37, 167-170
   pentagon, 18
   pentagram, 29
   perimeter, 19
   quadrilateral, 18
   rectangle, 35
   regular, 32
   rhombus, 34
   sides, 18
   squares, 44
   triangle, 18
   triangulation of, 74-76, 180, 190, 204
Polygonal path, 15-19
Proportion, 111-115
   constant of, 91-94
Protractor, 140
Pythagoras, 80
Pythagorean Theorem, 80-83 86, 87, 102
   $a^2 + b^2 = c^2$, 82
   algebraic version, 82
   converse of, 83
   geometric version, 82
Pythagorean triple, 85
Pythagoreans, 80

Q
Quadrilateral, 18, 32, 35-39
   number of sides, 78
   number of triangles, 78
   parallelogram, 36, 37,167-170
   rectangle, 35, 37, 125
   rhombus, 34-37
   square, 36

R
Radian, 138
Radius, 223, 224, 276-278
Ratio, 110-113, 126
Ray, 133
Rectangle, 35-37, 125
Reflex angle, 141, 143
Regular polygon, 28, 32, 195
Rhombus, 34-37
   axes of symmetry for, 34

Right angle, 28, 143
Right triangle, 47, 48, 49
   adjacent side, 234
   area of, 49
   hypotenuse, 48
   isosceles, 81, 184
   labeling, 49
   opposite side, 223
   Pythagorean Theorem,
    80-83, 86, 87, 102, 276
   side lengths, 48
   similar, 124, 125
   Rotations, 141

S
SAS (side-angle-side), 173,
   186
Scaling factor, 92, 114,
   125-127, 205, 206
   constant of
    proportionality, 114
Secant, 241
Segment
   bisector, 28, 185
   line, 9
   midpoint of, 26, 27
Shrinking, 109, 125
Side of triangle
   adjacent, 234
   opposite, 223
Similar, 108, 109, 113, 121
Similar figures, 109, 121
Similarity, 108
Sine, 222, 223, 237
   inverse of, 256
   Law of, 264
   SIN^{-1}, 254, 255
Slope, 135-140
Slope measure, 136
Span, 9,
Square, 36
   centimeter, 44
   inch, 44
   unit, 44
   wobbit, 44
SSS (side-side-side), 167,
   169, 183, 186
Star of David, 30

Straightness, 11
Straight angle, 143
Stretching, 125, 200
Sun, 188
Sundials, 154-156
Superimpose, 134
Supplementary angles, 151
Symbols
   α (alpha), 255, 256
   β (beta), 256
   k (constant), 91, 113
   $θ$ (theta), 223, 256
Symmetry, 24, 32, 33
   axis of, 24-26, 34-37, 39
   line of, 24

T
TAN^{-1}, 149, 254, 255
Tangent, 245-249
   function of, 148, 149
   inverse of, 149, 254-258
Theta ($θ$), 223, 256
Tiling, 43, 49
Time quotations, 154
Transversal, 157-159
Triangle, 18, 66-72
   AAA, 183, 201, 206
   AAS, 182, 186
   adjacent side, 234
   altitude of, 69, 168
   angle sum, 160
   area of, 72, 102
   ASA, 180, 182, 188
   base of, 69, 184
   congruent, 133, 167
   construct, 66, 68
   isosceles, 81, 184
   opposite side, 36, 80,
    223
   right, 47-49
   SAS, 173, 186
   similar, 108, 109, 113, 121
   SSS, 167, 169, 183, 186
   vertices, 20, 122, 123, 133
Triangulation, 76-77, 180,
   190, 204
Trigonometry, 180, 214, 249
Truss, 147

Turnout, 134
U
Unit of measure, 138
   cube, 99
   inch, 99
   length, 11, 66, 67
   meter, 99
Unit square, 44
Universal statement, 38
V
V-gauge, 247
Varies (variation)
   directly, 91-93
   inversely, 93, 94
Verne, Jules, 225
Vertex, 20, 122, 123, 133
Vertical angles, 151
Vertices, 20, 122, 123, 133
Volume, 99, 100, 211, 212
   three dimensional
    object, 99, 100, 212
W
Wobbit, 12, 66
Words to Know
   altitude, 69
   base, 69
   complement, 161
   complementary angles,
    161
   corresponding points,
    113
   similar, 113
   trigonometry, 249
X
x-axis, 135, 277
x-coordinate, 276
Y
y-axis, 135, 276
y-coordinate, 277
Yard, 9
Z
Zapf Dingbats, 31
Zoom, 126, 127
Zuben Eljanubi, 176-177